The Bartender's Pantry

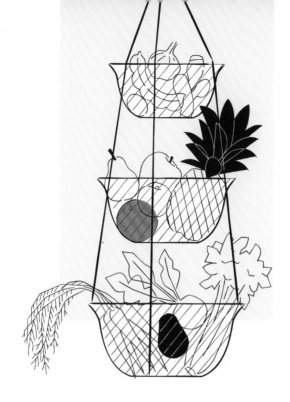

The Bartender's Pantry

A Beverage Handbook for the Universal Bar

Jim Meehan with Emma Janzen
Illustrations & Design by Bart Sasso
Photographs by AJ Meeker

TEN SPEED PRESS
California | New York

Contents

Introduction 1

Recipe Index 10

The Pantry

Sugars 16

Spices 46

Dairy 78

Grains & Nuts 110

Fruits 142

Vegetables, Flowers
& Herbs 180

Coffee 212

Tea 242

Soda & Mineral Water 272

Ferments 304

The Prep Kitchen

Bar Staples 336

Specialty Cordials 341

Spirit Infusions 345

Sugar-Free Solutions 351

Afterword 358

Acknowledgments 360

Bibliography 366

Index 370

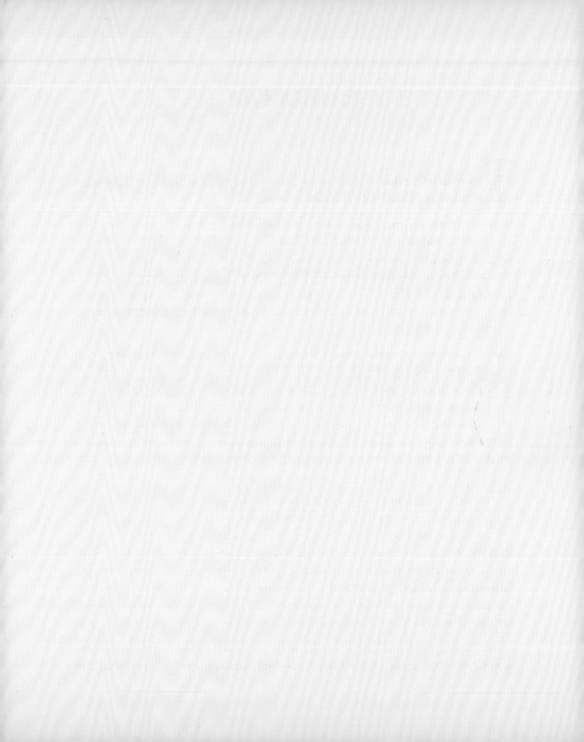

Introduction

The food and drink rituals I grew up with in the suburbs of Chicago were humble and practical for a family of six.

Every morning, my mom steeped bags of Lipton's tea in a stainless-steel pot to sip piping hot with a teaspoon of granulated sugar and a splash of 2% milk. While her Quaker Oats warmed, she scooped ground coffee from the plaid Stewart's tin for my dad's morning cup into a drip coffee maker. He drank it with a splash of half-and-half in a ceramic mug while toggling between smoking a Marlboro Red and maneuvering a Datsun 210's stick shift to transport us to school in the morning.

I vividly remember summer trips to Michigan, where we stayed with my maternal grandmother, who kept a huge stack of old *Gourmet* magazines and cooked fresh vegetables from her garden in a kitchen with a collection of copper pans that rivaled Julia Child's. But my parents didn't cook like my grandmother. They made pragmatic decisions about food and cooking because they worked double shifts throughout much of my childhood and had four boys to feed. We're all grown and out of the house now, but they still take their tea and coffee the same way.

My eating and drinking experiences changed once I began working in bars and restaurants. I visited the incredible farmer's markets around the state capitol in Madison, Wisconsin. I worked alongside some of the most celebrated chefs in America in New York City. I moved to Portland, Oregon, where the food scene is so earnest it was lampooned on the TV sitcom *Portlandia*. I've had so many *pinch-me* moments in these places, and more when I was initiated into a deeper understanding and appreciation of food and beverage thanks to the time, attention, and care of bakers, chefs, sommeliers, farmers, brewers, distillers, baristas, and my fellow cooks, bartenders, and servers.

I didn't know much about tea, for example, until I worked at Gramercy Tavern, which procured some of the best loose-leaf teas in America from Sebastian

Beckwith of In Pursuit of Tea. From smoky lapsang souchong to verdant lemon verbena, I was surprised to find these new-to-me teas and tisanes tasted perfectly balanced and vibrant without sugar, honey, lemon, or milk. Working with Sebastian made me realize the world of tea was so much more vast, varied, and delicious than I had previously encountered.

Later, I expanded my palate with travel. For instance, in San Francisco, a pilgrimage to Elizabeth Prueitt and Chad Robertson's Tartine Bakery made me rethink every loaf of bread I've ever eaten. Their now-famous sourdough is a taste experience that engages all the senses; the texture goes from an airy crumb to an armored crust, and when I cut through its shell, the aromas of fruit, grass, and grain stop me in my tracks. Discovering new flavors and culinary practices, and revisiting old favorites like the ones championed at Tartine, is a joyful practice that guides my eating and drinking rituals.

My life experiences inform the way I perceive ingredients as a bartender. Every time I taste a coffee or fruit or spice, I wonder if it's really the best version I can find, or if I need to search further to source something more appropriate for the application at hand.

Today, the practice of continuously evaluating the quality of ingredients and understanding their origins drives my work as a bartender. I am not alone in this; the sentiment, I believe, is driving today's cocktail zeitgeist. We've moved beyond rejiggering recipes from the "Golden Age" of the late nineteenth and early twentieth centuries. Now, bartenders are blazing new paths by prioritizing transparent sourcing, environmentally sustainable farming, and worker rights alongside the way ingredients taste or function in a recipe. Bartenders are increasingly caretaking the narratives of these ingredients—past, present, and future—in addition to coaxing out their best qualities in the glass.

The axis for this new era of bartending isn't just centered around the base spirits, bitters, and liqueurs; it has expanded to include the mixers, too. I've identified sugars, spices, dairy, nuts, grains, vegetables, flowers, herbs, fruits, coffee, tea, sodas, mineral waters, and ferments as the "universal" ingredients that comprise the components of the bartender's pantry.

I've written two books that feature spirits and subordinate these zero-proof mixers. I stand by them as works of their time, but today, the pantry ingredients are ushering mixology into the twenty-first century. That's why instead of glancing past these ingredients and their preparations, I've made them the focal point of this handbook.

In the following pages, you will find primers on ten different families of ingredients. Each one can be used to make cocktails and many may be served unmixed. Each family gets its own chapter, with a contemporary overview and tips for sourcing, storing, and preparing them as components of the mixers used in classic and modern cocktail recipes. I want to draw attention to how these ingredients are grown, processed at origin, and shipped. I want you to meet some of the people who bring them to us, and learn how proper tools, functional serviceware, and reliable recipes become critical building blocks of a dynamic bar program or home bar.

Each one of these ingredients has a complex history, with thorny ethical considerations and quality benchmarks. I hope you're ready to dig into policy and politics, because we can't talk about sugars, spices, tea, and coffee without examining the role colonialism and capitalism play in bringing these ingredients to the bar. And we can't survey these subjects without interest in the welfare of the land, the people who farmed it, and those who profit from that work today. Reconciling this history in our mixing practices should matter to both bartenders and our guests.

This book is a celebration of the ingredients in the bartender's pantry along with the people who help stock it. Every one of the world's best bars is powered by a team of the world's best prep people (many of whom tend bar, too), who check in the produce orders, make the syrups, extract juice from fruits and vegetables, monitor infusions, pick and prep all the herbs, neatly organize the storage areas, and much more before opening the bar for service. Here, we focus on their work, and in following their lead, you will not only improve your drinks mixing, but also enrich your social circle with a whole community of growers, wholesalers, and experts to help you navigate your way.

The Precepts of the Pantry

Unlike in *Meehan's Bartender Manual* and *The PDT Cocktail Book*, I am the narrator rather than the subject of this story. What I've gathered here stands on the shoulders (and quotes liberally) from food scientists like Harold McGee, food historians like Anne Mendelson, food policy advocates like Alice Waters, and category authorities like Sandor Katz. I've highlighted their findings, positioning their ideas with a drink maker's aspirations front and center.

Before we begin, I want to acknowledge a few fundamental precepts I kept close to heart while writing this book. These are the principles that serve as the foundation of my drink-making practice:

Bartending is an interdisciplinary craft, which means there is value in knowing a little bit of information about a lot of different ingredients. As drinks makers, we don't need an encyclopedia's worth of knowledge about every ingredient we work with in order to make delicious cocktails. I aim to eschew our culture's current fetishization of specialization and place more cache on the virtues of being a generalist: so this is a handbook, not an exhaustive manual. My hope is that you establish a baseline of knowledge about each ingredient and best practices for working with it, and then pursue further knowledge at your own pace.

The journey of learning about these ingredients is just as important as the destination of delicious drinks. Many forces in our capitalistic culture want you to believe that every drink should take one minute to assemble, or require two ingredients, or already come preassembled. This is not the approach you'll find here. I believe there is both pleasure and growth to be found in avoiding the quick fix; and the more you learn, the more you practice, the more your relationship with these ingredients and their purveyors strengthens and deepens. I have experienced this metamorphosis myself as I researched, interviewed, sourced, and tested recipes for this book, so I am confident when I say the investment—of time, energy, and resources—is well worth it.

Making cocktails is an act of play. Yes, some people might think it's blasphemous to mix with the best versions of the most delicious ingredients in the world. But the point of mixing drinks is that we measure ingredients into a shaker to make something new and cool and fun—like a magician with a rabbit and a hat. That's the alchemy, the sleight of hand, the delicious distraction we perform, and it requires us to practice this work with intentionality, joy, and playfulness. I will make Jacques Selosse Champagne Bellinis with perfectly ripe white peaches and I won't lose sleep over it, and neither should you.

These ingredients are not only components used to make drinks; working with them also opens networks to cultivate and support communities. Growing, harvesting, and preparing food and drinks into something delicious is a vital community-building act—one that we should preserve and celebrate as much as we are capable of in our daily lives. To get the most out of this work, you'll need to navigate perspectives outside your expertise and create relationships with purveyors outside your social circles. You'll have to listen to others and learn from them; these are good things! Approach the work with optimism, an open mind, and humility and watch as your world opens up.

Housekeeping Items

While this book attempts the broadest possible survey of the subject matter, because of its modest ambition—handbook, not an encyclopedia—some parameters needed to be drawn logistically. I've chosen the recipes to serve this function. With some exceptions, if an ingredient hasn't been called for in the recipe section it won't get much coverage, if any, in the chapter prologues.

To collect the recipes, I asked some of the best bartenders on the planet for recipes featuring these ingredients in thoughtful and innovative applications to capture the fullest spectrum of their usage. Where it felt appropriate, I supplemented them with creations of my own featuring preparations like Türk Kahvesi, or Turkish coffee, to show how many traditional beverages typically served unmixed perform brilliantly in cocktails as well.

I meticulously tested each contributor's recipe in my home kitchen. For those shared by professionals who develop but do not write recipes for a living, I made minute adjustments to proportions and procedures to yield a more faithful estimation of the drink. All the contributors gave me permission for these adjustments, but the changes were done at my discretion—so any criticism of a recipe's quality or complexity should be directed toward me.

I recommend following the mixing directions as closely as resources permit to gain an understanding of what's been published before making your own changes. Some of these recipes are straightforward, and others may require multiple preparations for you to feel comfortable adapting them.

You'll notice some recipes are credited as "from" a creator, while others are "by"; this is an attempt to distinguish ownership from improvisation, an imprecise classification. Recipes are mutable instructions, like jazz tunes, that morph over time based on who is arranging the material and how they want to play it. So "from" means the attributed contributor is presenting their of-the-moment interpretation of what might otherwise be considered a classic or elemental beverage. "By" indicates it is an original recipe by the named contributor, and not an interpretation of a well-known preparation.

And finally, while most of the recipes were once served at a restaurant, café, or bar, these places come and go, so I've linked the attribution to the originator(s) and added establishment names only when it felt necessary to contextualize the biographies of these contributors. While you certainly don't need to ask for permission to prepare these recipes at home, bartenders should consider asking the authors of drinks for permission and include attribution on menus, taking extra care to not obscure any cultural connections in the process.

Sourcing Suggestions

I've included purchasing considerations for each ingredient in its respective chapter, but here are ten universal tips for sourcing the best-quality ingredients.

1. **Shop Small and Local.** Supporting small and independent local businesses (farmers, producers, stores) will put you in closer conversation with those who are producing and selecting your food. It also puts money into the local economy and reduces the carbon footprint of transporting food long distances in planes, trains, and automobiles. "You can get peaches at the grocery store, but I can tell you exactly how mine are tasting and know that everyone who worked to get them to you was paid a fair wage," says Abby Schilling—a third-generation fruit farmer at Mick Klug Farms in St. Joseph, Michigan—in an interview with Abra Berens for her book *Pulp*. "I could grow

everything cheaper if I didn't pay people right or treat the land right. If people value those things, they have to show up and support them."

2. **Be Prepared to Pay More.** High-quality ingredients are going to cost more money because it takes time, labor, and resources to grow them, plus additional resources to properly process, source, and retail them. Every person along the food chain deserves to make a wage that provides quality of life, and you're paying for that on the consumer end, too. As author Dan Saladino puts it in *Eating to Extinction,* "we get the food system we pay for." For the vast majority of us with limited resources, investing in this means certain ingredients will go from seasonal staples to items we splurge on for special occasions. Shifting our evaluation of this change from having a misguided right to eat cheaply to embracing the righteous privilege of eating equitably is crucial.

3. **Packaging is Paramount.** Most producers who are serious about maintaining the integrity of what's inside the package typically pay attention to keeping oxygen, light, moisture, and bacteria out—and giving you a way to see inside to verify the food's quality rather than distracting you with gaudy graphic design or merchandising gimmicks. Coffee, tea, grain, nuts, sugar, and spice packages should be sold in resealable, vacuum-sealed or airtight packs. (For coffee, it's the type of package with one-way valves to release post-roasting gas without letting air in.) If the ingredient comes in an unnecessarily heavy bottle, wrapped in gratuitous card stock, or priced unreasonably high, chances are you are being sold on a brand rather than an ingredient. Look for recyclable or reusable packaging to minimize waste.

4. **Do Your Homework.** Most of the ingredients we buy come from companies with websites, social media pages, and reviews revealing their standards and ethics. The more information provided—and the more specific the information—the easier it will be for you to determine whether the ingredient was brought to market by people who share *your* values. This is especially important for imported goods like tea, coffee, sugar, and spices, which tend to be sold internationally through many middlemen who intentionally muddy the water for muckrakers. Look for a farm or cooperative of origin, plus information about how the ingredient was grown, harvested, and processed.

5. **Make It Personal.** There's a sign over the cash register at Tommy's Mexican Restaurant, which has been in business for over 50 years in San Francisco, with a quote from Patricia Fripp (an award-winning public speaker and entrepreneur) that says: "To build a long-term, successful enterprise, when you don't close a sale, open a relationship." Whether it's at a farmer's market, a big-box grocery store, or an online retailer, make an effort to connect with food workers. When you return, share positive feedback when you have it and strive to make conversations more than transactional.

6. **Organic Matters.** In *What to Eat,* Marion Nestle is unequivocal about the verifiable virtues of organic agriculture: "The organic seal tells you that the producers of the foods followed a long list of rules: they did not use any synthetic pesticides, herbicides, or fertilizers; they did not plant genetically modified seeds, use fertilizer derived from sewage sludge, or treat the seeds or foods with irradiation; and they kept records of everything they did and showed the paperwork and everything on their farms to inspectors from a USDA-accredited state or private certification agency any time they were asked to, announced in advance or not." The cost of organic certification can be a barrier for many farmers who otherwise follow good organic standards, but I still buy organic whenever I can for the assurance of the aforementioned practices.

7. **Seek Out Heirlooms.** Most of the ingredients highlighted in this book come from industries that have been highly consolidated over time, which results in more uniform and less flavorful options for consumers. Heirloom varieties—the historical breeds of plants and animals that fell by the wayside when large-scale agriculture took hold of our primary food systems in the 1950s—are more diverse, sustainable, flavorful, and interesting than popular commercial varieties. Plus, more support for seed-saving organizations and farms that sell heirlooms will help guarantee biodiversity and crops grown for flavor in the future, which is important for food security and environmental sustainability.

8. **Use Your Senses.** Not sure if an ingredient is of good quality? At the conclusion of *The Way We Eat Now,* Bee Wilson urges readers to "try to know your food with your ears, nose, and hands as well as your mouth. Smell it, touch

it, and look at it before you taste it." Cultivating this level of intimacy—really knowing what you're looking for because you've experienced it before—instills confidence when you're shopping. Darrell Corti, who has sourced delicious ingredients from all over the world for the last 60 years at Corti Brothers grocery store in Sacramento, told me in an interview, "if a product in question smells like it's supposed to smell, and it tastes like it's supposed to taste, it's a good product."

9. **Check the Dates.** Many ingredients like dairy, fruits, vegetables, flowers, and herbs undergo dramatic freshness changes over time. Signs of deterioration include wilting, browning, molding, rotting, or fermenting. Other ingredients, like coffee, tea, grains, nuts, and spices, are also perishable, but their freshness is more difficult to discern. For these, harvest date, processing date (roast date for coffee), and packaging date are preferable to a sell-by or expiration date.

10. **Source with Curiosity.** There are so many delicious ingredients from beyond the borders of this country that could be used to diversify our mixed drinks. Look no further than Mexico, where savory sangritas accompany shots of agave spirits, or to India, where yogurt brings piquancy beyond the bowl in refreshing fruit and spice-flavored lassis. Think about the possibilities that come into play when you look at tea through the lens of Chinese history, or harness the earthy qualities of taro root, traditionally found in Taiwanese zhēnzhū nǎichá (bubble tea). That said, it's crucial to approach ingredients and traditional drinks from outside one's own culture with reverence and respect for their origins, instead of appropriating them solely for commercial gain. Following Fripp's advice, open relationships with the people who import these ingredients, pay homage with attribution, be transparent about aspirations and intentions, listen closely to feedback, and adjust with humility when asked.

Recipe Index

Sugars

Oleo Saccharum and Sherbet 28
from David Wondrich

Pineapple Cordial 30
from Paul Calvert

Baja Grenadine 32
by Osvaldo Vázquez

Cucumber-Mint Cordial 34
from Mony Bunni

Pomme and Circumstance 36
by A-K Hada

Gota de Sandía 38
by Danielle Tatarin

Ipswich Old Fashioned 40
by Bob McCoy

Penicillin 42
by Sam Ross

What Cheer 44
by Paul Calvert

Spices

Champurrado 58
from Noah Small

B-Marion Spice Blend 60
by Lior Lev Sercarz

Malabar Infusion 62
by Tyler Cowan

Sangrita Roja 64
from Osvaldo Vázquez

Sangrita Verde 66
from Osvaldo Vázquez

Bandera 68
from Osvaldo Vázquez

Bloody Marion 70
by Jim Meehan

Children of the Corn 72
by Noah Small

Malabar Silver Corn Fizz 74
by Jim Meehan

Choked Up 76
by Leo Robitschek

Dairy

Kadak Spicy Chai 91
from Sana Javeri Kadri

Bartender's Ice Cream 94
from Dana Cree

Yogurt 98
from Mony Bunni

Cultural Consumption 100
by Mony Bunni

Masala Milky Tea Punch 102
by Jim Meehan

Buttered Martini 104
by Monica Berg

Wondermint Malted 106
by Christopher Marty

Coquito 108
from Pablo Moix

Grains & Nuts

Orgeat 118
from Sean Hoard and Daniel Shoemaker

Borodinsky Rye Kvass 121
from Bonnie Morales

Oat Milk 124
from Lydia Parsley

Cashew Horchata 126
from Yana Volfson

Chicha Morada 128
from Erik Ramirez

Castle on a Cloud 130
by Maria Davidoff

Llama del Rey 132
by Lynnette Marrero and Jessica Gonzalez

Arroz con Rum 134
by Yana Volfson

Dragonfly 136
by Jim Meehan

Thunderbird 138
by Masahiro Urushido

Riot Act 140
by Jillian Vose

Fruits

Preserved Cherries 155
from Miles Macquarrie

Grilled Pineapple 158
from Gregory Buda

Cream of Coconut 160
from Jennifer Colliau

"Enhanced" Ruby Red Grapefruit Juice 162
from Chad Solomon

Peach Purée 164
from Sean Hoard and Daniel Shoemaker

Blackberry Consommé 166
from Gabriella Mlynarczyk

"Pimm's" Cup 168
from Gabriella Mlynarczyk

Paloma 170
from Chad Solomon

Windowsill Spritz 172
by Sean Hoard

Lava Lamp 174
by Sam Anderson

Kind of Blueberry 176
by Jim Meehan

Banana Stand 178
by Kevin Diedrich

Vegetables, Flowers & Herbs

Mint Conditioning 190
from Lydia McLuen

Sorrel 192
from Fortuna Anthony

Beet-Raspberry Syrup 194
from Martin Hudák

Corn Water 196
by Wylie Dufresne

Mint Spruce Syrup 198
by Katie Rose

Sorrel Rum Punch 200
from Fortuna Anthony

Light as a Feather 202
by Katie Rose

Celery and Nori 204
by Don Lee

Gin Basil Smash 206
by Joerg Meyer

L'Alligator C'est Vert 208
by Nico de Soto

Salad Bar 210
by Kristina Magro

Coffee

Flash-Brewed Iced Coffee 224
from Michael Yung

Türk Kahvesi 226
from Ria Neri

Espresso 228
from Martin Hudák

London Bridge 232
by Tyler Kleinow

Kahvesi Corretto 234
by Jim Meehan

Penny 236
by Chanel Adams

Back to the Roots 238
by Martin Hudák

Falling Water 240
by Jim Meehan

Tea

Usucha Matcha 252
from Zach Mangan

Gong Fu Shu Pu-Erh 254
from Sebastian Beckwith

Teapot-Brewed Jasmine Tea 256
from Ravi Kroesen

Mizudashi Cold-Brewed Oolong Tea 258
from Rodrick Markus

Longball 260
by Jim Meehan

Dragon Pearl Punch 262
by Julie Reiner

Earl Grey MarTEAni 264
by Audrey Saunders

Comfort's Toddy 266
by Julia Momosé

Speak Low 268
by Shingo Gokan

Q.P. Warmer 270
by Jim Meehan

Soda & Mineral Water

Forced Carbonation 282
from Jim Meehan

Szechuan Ginger Beer 284
by Katie Rose

Cola 286
from Martin Lambert

Grapefruit Soda 288
from Jim Meehan

Lemon-Lime Soda 290
from Nick Bennett

7 & 7 292
from Nick Bennett

Angostura Phosphate 294
from Darcy S. O'Neil

Southern Cola 296
by Greg Best

Gin & Tonic (Classic and Modern) 298
from Camper English

Japanese Whisky Highball 300
from Bobby Heugel

Grail Ale 302
by Jim Meehan

Ferments

Ginger Burns 313
by Cortney Burns

Hōjicha Kombucha 316
from Arielle Johnson

Raspberry Shrub 318
from Neal Bodenheimer

Tepache 320
from Rosio Sánchez

Roffignac 322
from Neal Bodenheimer

Lemon-Ginger Rebujito 324
by Cortney Burns

Gut Punch 326
by Jim Meehan

Slow West 328
by Claire Sprouse

Welcome Mother 330
by Paul Calvert

Peeking Duck 332
by Jim Meehan

Bar Staples

Agave Syrup 337

Cane Syrup 337

Demerara Syrup 337

Honey Syrup 338

Molasses Syrup 338

Simple Syrup 339

Rich Simple Syrup 339

Sorghum Syrup 340

Mineral Saline 340
from Chad Solomon

Specialty Cordials

Genmaicha Syrup 342
from Jillian Vose

Ginger-Agave Syrup 342
from Danielle Tatarin

Grapefruit-Lime Sherbet 342
from Julie Reiner

Enhanced Grapefruit Sherbet 343
from Jim Meehan

Celery Syrup 343
from Don Lee

Malabar Honey Syrup 344
by Jim Meehan

Pandan Syrup 344
from Nico de Soto

Oolong Tea Syrup 344
from Jim Meehan

Spirit Infusions

Blueberry-Infused Gin 346
by Jim Meehan

Chile-and-Grapefruit-Peel-Infused Mezcal 346
by Danielle Tatarin

Coconut-Banana-Infused Bourbon 346
by Kevin Diedrich

Earl Grey Tea–Infused Gin 347
by Audrey Saunders

Butter-Washed Gin 347
by Monica Berg

Grilled-Pineapple-Infused Genever 348
by Gregory Buda

Nori-Infused Apple Brandy 348
by Don Lee

Krambambulya 349
from Israel Morales

P.C.H. Orange Bitters 349
from Kevin Diedrich

Pink Peppercorn Tincture 350
from Jessica Gonzalez and Lynnette Marrero

Sobacha-Infused Apple Brandy 350
by Masahiro Urushido

Sugar-Free Solutions

Boricha Cold Brew 352
from A-K Hada

Brewed English Breakfast Tea 352
from Nick Bennett

Brewed Hōjicha 353
by Julia Momosé

Brewed Lao Cang Xiao Shu Tuo Pu-Erh 353
from Jim Meehan

Cascara Infusion 354
from Tyler Kleinow

Coquito "Tea" Infusion 354
from Pablo Moix

Flash-Brewed Jasmine Tea 355
from Ravi Kroesen

Hibiscus Infusion 355
from Danielle Tatarin

Lemon-Infused Olive Oil 356
from Kristina Magro

Licorice-Root Water 356
from Tyler Kleinow

Radicchio "Juice" 357
from Kristina Magro

Lime Ice Cubes 357
from Greg Best

The Pantry

Ingredient Primers and Featured Recipes

Sugars

In the nineteenth century, cocktail and punch recipes called for chipping pieces of sugar off a large, dense block of "loaf sugar," but its use in mixed drinks has been supplemented over time as new sweeteners have been embraced behind the bar. Occasionally making an appearance outside the glass—like on the rim of a Sidecar or the minty foliage of a Julep—most sweeteners are incorporated into drinks via liqueurs, bitters, and fortified wines, or they are dissolved into syrups. For the latter, we have access to a wide variety of options, from neutral white sugar to less processed options like raw monofloral honey. Most bartenders choose a sugar that best matches the flavor or origins of the other ingredients in a recipe (like agave nectar with mezcal) or as a neutral medium (like simple syrup) to balance the sharp edges of the other ingredients.

While preferences for salty, sour, bitter, and umami flavors must be cultivated, humans are born with a preference for sweetness. The first thing we're fed as infants is lactose-rich milk containing similar properties—a remarkable life source signaling how sugar is vital to our development as a species. Before reedy sugarcane plants were discovered and enterprising people realized their juices could be boiled down into a sticky sweetener, other sugar sources like honey, fruits, and vegetables satisfied our collective sweet tooth.

Scientifically speaking, sugar is a kind of carbohydrate—a source of energy for the body. Glucose and fructose are two of the most common sugars, which combine to form sucrose (table sugar). Fructose, glucose, and sucrose occur naturally in plants of all kinds—including fruits and vegetables—with sugarcane and beets containing the highest percentages of sucrose, and agave nectar being primarily fructose. Generally speaking, sugars do vary in their perceived sweetness, with glucose being least sweet, fructose being most sweet, and sucrose residing between the two.

The sugar we incorporate into food and drink comes from many different sources, and almost every country around the world has its own distinctive types. For practical purposes, this chapter focuses on the sweeteners abundant in North America.

Honey

Before sugarcane became the most widely used sugar in the world in the sixteenth century, honey was most prevalent. The ambrosial sweetener is the work product of bees, who transform flower nectars into viscous honey with natural enzymes in their digestive tracts. It's "the most concentrated natural source of sweetness," writes Harold McGee in *On Food and Cooking*.

The flavor of honey depends on the nectar sources bees visit. Most honey comes from bees that feed from a mixture of different flowers, but "monofloral" honeys—produced by bees that have access to only a single type of flower, like citrus, sunflower, or chestnut, to name a few—have characteristics that echo their aromas. Orange blossom honey, for example, typically bears a subtle citrus note (try it in the Welcome Mother cocktail on page 330), while lavender honey has a velvety herbaceous quality.

The characteristics of honey depend on several other variables too, writes Bi-Rite owner Sam Mogannam in his book *Bi-Rite Market's Eat Good Food,* written with Dabney Gough. "Depending on what plants are available to the bees, the climate, and the time of year, honey can be viscous or runny, mildly flavored or intense. Even honey from the same hive might taste light and floral in the spring, and robust and almost spicy in the fall."

The quality of your honey, and how it is processed (or not) should factor into decisions about which type to use for your drinks. Following are some of the most common forms; generally speaking, the more processed the honey, the easier it will be to mix with, but there will also be less character and flavor.

Raw honey To make raw honey, unfiltered and unpasteurized honey is extracted from the honeycomb by spinning the honeycomb frames in a centrifuge or by relying on gravity to drain it from a honeycomb-filled frame in a box-style beehive. Raw honey is sometimes strained to remove pieces of the comb, but it still contains natural pollen from the blossoms and some trace minerals. It typically has more flavor than processed generic "honey" and has a paste-like viscosity. Raw honey often also comes in monofloral options. In my experience, clover honey, which is the most widely found, works well in all honey-syrup applications. On the other end of the spectrum, varietal honeys like manuka and buckwheat (used in the Thunderbird, page 138) are so distinctive they do not work interchangeably in all honey-syrup recipes. With these honeys, you have to select one to use similar to the way you'd choose between a tequila and a mezcal or vodka and gin, which is remarkable, because the drink can be focused on the honey instead of the spirit.

Regular honey What purveyors generically label as "honey" is often extracted from the hive in the same process as done for raw honey but it is then filtered and pasteurized before packaging. The texture is thinner and the flavor is less vibrant than raw honey. With a nondescript personality, this type of honey could come in handy if you want honey flavor in cocktails, but you don't want its character to steal the show, as a bold raw monofloral honey is apt to do.

Creamed honey Also called whipped honey or churned honey, creamed honey is crystallized honey blended smooth so it's easily spreadable at room temperature. The texture is richer than liquid honey, and it won't crystallize again over time. In cocktails, it works a lot like raw honey.

Comb honey True to its name, comb honey includes the edible wax comb excreted by bees. Visually appealing in its natural state, it is an intuitive option to garnish honey-based cocktails.

SOURCING

Buy organic, raw, or unfiltered local honey from area farmer's markets, co-ops, and natural food stores because they typically provide "a unique taste of the landscape that surrounds you," writes Sam Mogannam. Look for the specific varietal listed to identify what nectars and pollens the bees consumed with an organic certification ensuring they are pesticide-free, as "many commercial producers treat the hives themselves with pesticides to protect the bees from mites that can threaten the colony. This disrupts the bees' reproductive cycles and general health," Mogannam notes.

STORING

Raw honey should be stored sealed in the fridge if used infrequently to prevent it from browning, which can have an adverse effect on the color of a cocktail. When stored uncovered or at room temperature, honey naturally crystallizes, becoming thick, grainy, and cloudy. When honey crystallizes, it is still safe to consume, but it is difficult to integrate into cocktails, owing to its dense viscosity. If this happens, place the jar of honey in a hot-water bath until it liquefies.

Maple Syrup

Maple syrup is produced throughout Eastern Canada and in the American Northeast. Large-scale commercial producers use plastic taps and hoses to transport sap from multiple trees to a central holding tank. The sap is then boiled to concentrate its flavor and sweetness. The longer and hotter the syrup is boiled, the darker the color and the fuller the taste. It takes around 40 parts of sap to make 1 part syrup.

Maple syrup is evaluated for color, clarity, sweetness, and flavor and used to be given an A, B, or C grade in North America, but now each type comes with taste descriptions instead. Here are the most common, listed from lightest to darkest. Each grade of syrup works well in cocktails; choose which one to use based on how the flavor complements or contrasts with the other ingredients in the recipe.

Golden Color with Delicate Taste (formerly "fancy") Usually made at the beginning of the new maple season in late February, the flavor is light and subtle. When paired with strong flavors in a cocktail, this type of maple syrup can add earthy sweetness that doesn't immediately register as "maple" flavor.

Amber Color with Rich Taste (formerly Grade A Medium or Dark Amber) Usually made about mid-season, this is the most popular for all-around use. In cocktails, its closest approximation is demerara or turbinado sugar.

Dark Color with Robust Taste (formerly Grade A Dark Amber or Grade B) As the maple season progresses, the syrup darkens in color and develops a more robust flavor. It's a great choice for recipes in which you want a more prevalent maple flavor to come through.

Very Dark Color with Strong Taste (formerly Grade C) Produced at the end of the season, this type is analogous to the molasses of maple syrup in texture and flavor. Use it in cocktails that call for the most prominent maple flavor.

SOURCING

Look for 100 percent maple syrup, and organic is always best. Because true maple syrup is labor intensive and expensive to produce, many supermarkets stock brands that are artificially colored and sweetened with flavored corn and fructose syrups, so remember to check ingredients lists before purchasing. On a related note, beware of bottles labeled "pancake syrup," Sam Mogannam warns, because it is typically made with artificial flavors.

STORING

Store maple syrup covered in the fridge to prevent it from molding. It can be frozen without diminishing its character to preserve freshness and deter crystallization.

Cane Sugar

Cane sugar is made by chopping and grinding, pounding, or pressing cane stalks to extract juices, which are then processed to varying degrees. Commercial cane sugar typically comes from two sources: mills, which produce unrefined and raw sugars like demerara and turbinado; and refineries, which further process unrefined sugar from mills using industrial techniques that yield white cane sugar.

Generally speaking, the more refining a sugar product undergoes, the less personality it will have. Molasses, brown sugar, and muscovado are good for imparting an earthy sweetness to drinks, while jaggery, demerara, and turbinado have a slight fruity quality that works well in many recipes. Refined white granulated sugars, on the other hand, are primarily used to balance the acidity of citrus—like kosher salt, they don't add flavor (beyond pure sweetness).

Note: Many of the sugars listed below are sometimes made from other sources of sugar. If a sugar's label does not say 100 percent cane sugar, it might be made from sugar beets, palm sap, sorghum, or other plant material.

UNREFINED SUGAR

When sugarcane juice is boiled to the point of crystallization, then cooled and solidified at a sugar mill, it is considered an unrefined sugar. Because this sugar is not put through a centrifuge to separate the crystals from the molasses, it typically retains up to 14 percent natural molasses. Depending on the place of origin and what techniques were used to process the sugar, the visual appearance, intensity of sweetness, and size of granules will differ. "Modern sugarcane mills produce an off-white raw sugar—sometimes called turbinado, muscovado, demerara, or rapadura sugar—while more rudimentary techniques result in a wider range of colors because they are less efficient at removing molasses and impurities," explains Darra Goldstein in *The Oxford Companion to Sugar and Sweets*.

Molasses Once massecuite, a mixture of the sugar crystals and the concentrated syrup resulting from pan boiling the cane juice, is separated by centrifuge, what results is sugar crystals and molasses. Crystals are formed in the massecuite during several rounds of boiling, each of which yields a different grade of molasses and crystal: light molasses (Grade A) comes from the first boiling, dark (Grade B) comes from the second, and blackstrap is the thickest and darkest by-product of the third boiling. The lighter the molasses, the more expressive the cane flavor. Molasses can also be treated with sulfur dioxide as a preservative agent, which imparts a chemical flavor, so look for unsulfured molasses for the purest expression of the sugarcane. If you want a reference point for mixing with molasses in cocktails, the sweetener is featured in the Ginger Burns (page 313), and molasses syrup (page 338) is used to make the Ipswich Old Fashioned (page 40).

Muscovado Muscovado bears much of the cane's minerality and has a texture that resembles wet sand. See the wonderful attributes it brings to the Tepache recipe on page 320.

Jaggery Also called "gur," this Southeast Asian sweetener is made from cane or the sap of coconuts or date palms, which are shaped into cone or brick form. A little jaggery brings earthy depth to the Kadak Spicy Chai (page 91).

Panela Hailing from Latin American countries, panela is similar to jaggery but made using only sugarcane. It comes in light and dark versions, and it goes by different names depending on where it is produced. In Mexico, for example, the sugar is called piloncillo, whereas "panela" is used to identify a sort of fresh cheese. (Piloncillo is used in Noah Small's Champurrado recipe on page 58.)

Sucanat With a brand name derived from the French term for natural sugar *sucre de canne naturel,* sucanat is an unrefined sugar that appeals to vegetarians and vegans because no bone charcoal is used in the processing. The kind Cortney Burns calls for to make the Ginger Burns on page 313 has large granules—almost the size of bee pollen—and a fair amount of molasses.

RAW SUGAR

While the term "raw" might suggest otherwise, this type of sugar is processed at a sugar mill. Like unrefined sugar, the cane juice is extracted and crystallized. Then—in contrast to unrefined sugars—raw sugar is typically spun through a centrifuge to separate most of the molasses (up to 98 percent) from the crystals. The size of the crystals and percentage of natural molasses retained in the sugar vary.

Turbinado A light brown color, with coarse crystals, turbinado is usually labeled "sugar in the raw." Try it in Katie Rose's Szechuan Ginger Beer (page 284).

Demerara Named after the region in Guyana, but not necessarily from there because the term is unprotected, demerara sugar has large, yellow-gold crystals and is incidentally also a cultivar of sugarcane. It is often used interchangeably with turbinado. Use it in the Masala Milky Tea Punch (page 102), Cola (page 286), and Castle on a Cloud (page 130) to taste what it contributes to mixed drinks.

Evaporated cane juice In an NPR piece called "Evaporated Cane Juice: Sugar In Disguise?" Judy Sanchez, a spokesperson for the U.S. Sugar Corporation, confirms: "All sugar is evaporated cane juice. . . . They just use that for a natural-sounding name for a product."

REFINED SUGAR

Refined sugars are made from partially processed raw sugars from sugar mills. These sugars must be further refined—via filtering, evaporation, or with a centrifuge—to be fully processed. In many cases, the sugar must be put through a series of cycles to reach this point, which is why these sugars typically look white (in other words, they contain almost zero percent molasses). Unlike unrefined and raw sugar, refined sugar cannot be certified organic because unauthorized chemical agents are used during the refining process.

Brown sugar Containing a significant amount of moisture, brown sugar is refined white sugar crystals coated with molasses or molasses-like syrup. Brown sugar comes in both light and dark brown versions, depending on the volume of molasses included. Dark brown sugar has a richer flavor than light brown sugar—the latter brings a soft bittersweetness to Rosio Sánchez's Tepache recipe (page 320), which also features muscovado. Traditional real-boiled brown sugar, which is a less refined style, is still available from a few producers, such as Tate & Lyle.

White sugar Bright white table sugar is also sometimes labeled regular "sugar," and it comes in many different granulated sizes, with coarse sugar representing the largest granules and superfine the smallest. Superfine sugar dissolves easily into room-temperature liquids, so it is good for making syrups and sherbets with fruit juice, like Julie Reiner's Grapefruit-Lime Sherbet (page 342) or my Enhanced Grapefruit Sherbet (page 343).

Powdered sugar Also known as "confectioners' sugar," powdered sugar consists of white sugar granules that have been ground into a fine powder, commonly used to make icing and sweetened whipped cream. Powdered sugar usually contains starch to absorb moisture and prevent caking. You can use it to decorate garnishes (like mint sprigs).

SOURCING

Mount Gay Rum estate manager Maggie Campbell, who has a wealth of experience with sugar from working in the rum business since 2012, suggests researching eco-friendly suppliers like Sugar for Good or Bonsucro-certified sugar, and "when it comes to brown sugar, ask if it is colored brown or real-boiled. Ideally, look for organic sugar when available, as conventional sugarcane is often sprayed with pesticides and herbicides."

If you don't want to work with granulated sugar, packaged syrups are also an option. Cane syrup is produced directly from cane juice at sugar mills or from raw sugar at refineries. The crystals are not removed during this process. Syrups are typically golden to medium brown in color and have a mild grassy flavor. Sugar syrups are frequently bottled with preservatives like citric acid to prevent them from molding, and other stabilizers that keep them from crystallizing; these affect both the flavor and the texture of bottled syrups, so if you buy a bottled sugar syrup, look for bottlings free of additives.

STORING

Sugar absorbs moisture and odors, so store it in an airtight container at room temperature and it will keep indefinitely.

Agave Nectar

A sweetener made from agave plants grown in Mexico, agave nectar comes from many different species of the agave, including the Blue Weber, which is used to make tequila. In the late 1980s and early '90s, commercial agave nectars started to be marketed as healthy substitutions for other sugars, but scientists have since disproved this.

Agave nectar and agave syrup are often thought of interchangeably, but syrup is additionally modified by dilution with water, and may include additives like high-fructose corn syrup. Nectar tastes much sweeter than cane sugar when cool, which allows you to use less in cocktails served chilled.

Unlike the maple syrup industry, agave syrup producers have not banded together to establish transparency in regard to nectar production methods that facilitate reliable industry-wide classification of their products. The nectars are typically graded from lightest to heaviest, each representing a different level of color concentration. Some sources say light, amber, and dark versions are heated to 165°F degrees during processing, whereas raw agave nectar is cooked low and slow—below 117°F—to preserve more of its natural character.

Light As the name suggests, light agave nectar has the lightest color and tastes somewhat neutral in character. This style is rather analogous to simple syrup, though thicker in viscosity.

Raw Compared to the other forms of nectar, raw agave nectar showcases more of the natural flavor of the plant, with less heavy caramel qualities. Most bartenders pair raw and light agave nectar with unaged agave spirits like blanco tequila and mezcal to amplify the agave notes without overpowering the subtleties of the spirits.

Amber With a medium hue, amber agave nectar has a flavor akin to honey or light caramel. Use amber agave nectar to make Agave Syrup (page 337).

Dark The richest form, dark agave nectar has the most intense concentration of flavor. Amber and dark agave nectars have enough robust caramel quality to bolster aged agave spirits like añejo and extra añejo tequila.

SOURCING

The words "100 percent agave," or "100 percent agave nectar" listed as the sole item on the ingredient list indicates you've got the pure stuff. If the bottle says "syrup" or "sweetener," it likely contains additives. Organic agave products are preferable.

STORING

Store agave nectar covered in the fridge when not in use.

Sorghum Syrup

A by-product of the sorghum plant—a grass and cereal grain native to Africa that came to America during the transatlantic slave trade—sorghum syrup is made from pressing the stalks of sorghum plants to extract juice, which is cooked down into a sweetener. Sorghum syrup is mainly sucrose and has a distinctive earthy flavor akin to molasses and maple syrup.

SOURCING

Sorghum grows in twenty-one states, from South Dakota to Texas, but most commercial crops are used to make livestock feed and ethanol, so sorghum syrup can be challenging to source. I was directed to seek out Hughes Farm in Georgia, where Paul Calvert of Ticonderoga Club sources sorghum syrup for the What Cheer (page 44). Look for 100 percent sorghum with no additives to prepare your own syrup (see page 340).

STORING

Store your jug of sorghum syrup in a cool, dry place if unopened, and in the refrigerator once opened. It can crystallize—so warm it gently in hot water to reconstitute.

The modern economies of Europe and the Americas have been fueled by the domestication and industrialization of sugarcane (and later beet sugar in France). This was all facilitated by the establishment of a transatlantic slave trade, which profited from the ingredient at a staggering human cost. Still today, the sugar industry grapples with issues of worker safety and equitable wages, plus environmental concerns.

Due to the commodification of sugar, most of the options we have access to now have also been "blended to a level that can become generic," says Maggie Campbell. "Small community mills are not common today in many countries—but they do exist," she says. If you can find single-origin sugars or sugars from small and independent estates in regions where cane flourishes (some are emerging in the Southern U.S.), you will quickly see the difference between industrial sugar and traditionally produced single-estate sugar, which is often made with heirloom cane varieties and expresses the provenance we celebrate in other sweeteners like monofloral honey and maple syrup.

Another less sweet headline to take into consideration: the introduction of sweeteners like corn syrup made from government-subsidized dent corn (a substantially less delicious source than cane) has driven down the price of sweet treats and soda, which has contributed to increased obesity and diabetes rates all over the world. On the coattails of this trend, food industrialists have introduced a rash of new alternative sweeteners (like stevia and monk fruit), as if they're the antidote to the harmful effects of overconsumption.

Since cocktails are freed from the well-funded gravitational pull of wellness trends, most do not feature alternative sweeteners. The one outlier is agave nectar, thanks to the enduring popularity of Julio Bermejo's Tommy's Margarita. Agave nectar has speciously been touted as a low-glycemic sugar for diabetics, but the drink was never intended to be a skinny margarita; Julio only substituted agave for triple sec at his family's restaurant because he wanted to amplify the agave character of the drink.

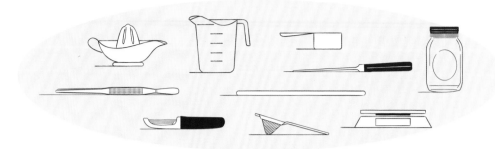

OLEO SACCHARUM AND SHERBET

from David Wondrich

Oleo saccharum—a mixture of citrus peel oils and sugar—was used to sweeten punches in the seventeenth century and has since been revisited by many bartenders during the modern cocktail renaissance. David Wondrich's recipe is one such example that builds on Jeffrey Morgenthaler's vacuum-seal approach. "I discovered you could prepare it in plastic quart takeout containers, but when the *New York Times* wanted to shoot me making a punch for a Melissa Clark video, they balked at the takeout containers, so we compromised on mason jars," Wondrich explained to me. "I found that worked better: you could add the juice to the oleo and make a shrub (or sherbet, a synonymous derivation of the Arabic word *sharāb*) by shaking it in the same container."

Use this method of making sherbet to create the grapefruit sherbet used in the Dragon Pearl Punch (page 262). Lemon sherbet also happens to be the perfect base for lemonade: just add filtered water to taste. YIELDS 10 OUNCES

☐ 4 lemons

☐ 145g (¾ cup) superfine sugar

PREPARE THE "OLEO SACCHARUM"

Pare the rind off the lemons, each in one long spiral. (Reserve the peeled lemons to juice for the sherbet.) Add the lemon peels to a 1-quart mason jar.

Add the superfine sugar to the jar. Seal the jar and shake vigorously to thoroughly coat the peels with the sugar.

Macerate for at least 4 hours, or preferably overnight.

PREPARE THE "SHERBET"

Ream and finely strain 6 ounces of juice from the peeled lemons.

Add the lemon juice to the oleo saccharum.

Seal the jar and shake vigorously until all the sugar dissolves.

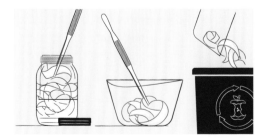

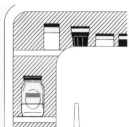

Remove the lemon peels with a pair of tongs and compost them.

Store the sherbet in an airtight container in the fridge for up to 1 WEEK.

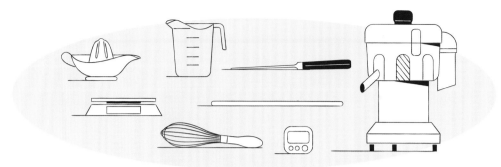

PINEAPPLE CORDIAL

from Paul Calvert

Known for its role in the Pisco Punch, pineapple gum syrup is an enduring and versatile sweetener. Paul Calvert omits gum arabic in his recipe for Ticonderoga Club in Atlanta, which features the cordial in their eponymous house cocktail the Ticonderoga Cup, made with rum, Cognac, oloroso sherry, and lemon juice. "We choose the pineapple as the base fruit because ripe pineapple has a wonderful blend of acid, sugar, and aromatic funk; and because the pineapple, as an emblem, signifies hospitality," Paul recalls. "Our pineapple cordial can stretch the juice and fruit of half a dozen pineapples across a month or more, and it's as good in a Daiquiri as it is drizzled over vanilla ice cream."

Use in the What Cheer (page 44), or in a classic Pisco Punch. YIELDS 14 OUNCES (1¾ CUPS)

- ☐ ½ small (500g) pineapple
- ☐ 4½ ounces filtered water
- ☐ 150g (¾ cup) superfine sugar
- ☐ 150g (¾ cup) evaporated cane juice sugar

Peel and core the pineapple, reserve half for another use, then cut the flesh of the other half into spears.

Run the pineapple spears through the extractor.

Add the extracted juice (about 9 ounces), the water, superfine sugar, and cane juice sugar into a saucepan.

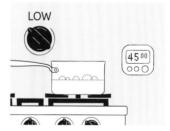

HIGH

Over high heat, bring the mixture to a boil, whisking frequently, about 4 minutes.

LOW

Reduce the heat to low and simmer for about 45 minutes.

Whisk the simmering mixture every 15 minutes.

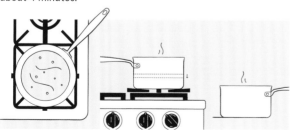

Once the mixture turns golden and is reduced by about 20 percent, remove it from the heat.

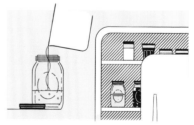

Transfer the syrup to a nonreactive container once it cools. Store, covered, in the fridge for up to 3 WEEKS.

Sugars

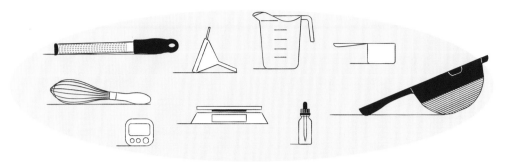

BAJA GRENADINE

by Osvaldo Vázquez

Osvaldo Vázquez, the founder of Bitter & Barrel cocktail bitters, created this preparation for his bar program at Hotel Los Cabos Pedregal in Baja California. Inspired by the cactus fruits that grow in the Santuario de los Cactus, a few hours away in El Trifuno, Vázquez substitutes prickly pear and hibiscus for the bright, tart pomegranate in traditional grenadine. "When we decided to add Prohibition cocktails for adults and healthy options for kids at the resort, I realized we didn't have a good grenadine," he explains, adding that he sources local prickly pear when it's available and commercial purée in the off-season. This is a great example of how bartenders can make a version of a traditional ingredient that better speaks to their locavore ethos.

Use in the Sangrita Roja (page 64), or mix with savory spirits like mezcal and tequila, which both have an earthy quality that pairs well with prickly pears.

YIELDS 18 OUNCES

- ☐ 275g (8 ounces) Perfect Purée of Napa Valley prickly pear purée
- ☐ 5 ounces filtered water
- ☐ 425g (2 cups) superfine sugar
- ☐ 50g (1½ cups) dried hibiscus flowers
- ☐ 2.5g (½ teaspoon) grated fresh lime zest (from 1 lime)
- ☐ 5 drops orange flower water

Add the prickly pear purée, water, and sugar to a medium saucepan and stir over medium-high heat.

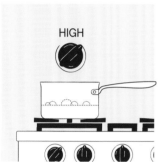

Bring to a boil over high heat, then turn off the heat.

Add the hibiscus flowers. Cover and let sit for 30 minutes.

Add the lime zest and let sit for 10 minutes more.

Fine-strain the mixture into a nonreactive container.

Add the orange flower water and stir to integrate it.

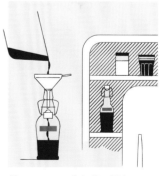

Store, covered, in the fridge for up to **1 MONTH**.

CUCUMBER-MINT CORDIAL

from Mony Bunni

Mony Bunni, who worked with me at Prairie School in Chicago, recommends leaving the skin on the cucumber extracted for this cordial, "as that's where most of the flavor and all of the color comes from." Mony dehydrates her mint by air-drying it on a paper towel until it is crispy and easily crumbles into powder. For the cucumber juice to retain its bright, fresh flavor, don't heat the syrup to expedite the dissolving process, as that will compromise the delicate aromatics of the cordial.

Use this cordial to make her Cultural Consumption (page 100), or mix with spirits like gin, aquavit, or an alcohol-free distilled spirit like Seedlip Garden, which has botanicals that pair nicely with cucumber and mint. YIELDS 12 OUNCES

- ☐ 1 (350g) English cucumber
- ☐ ¾ ounce lime juice (from 1 lime)
- ☐ 2g (¼ teaspoon) kosher salt
- ☐ 2.5g (1½ tablespoons) dried mint
- ☐ 200g (scant 1 cup) white cane sugar

Run the cucumber with the skin on through an extractor to get 6¾ ounces juice.

Pour the cucumber juice into a pitcher. Ream and fine strain the lime juice. Add it to the cucumber juice along with the salt and mint. Let the mint infuse for 6 minutes.

Strain the mixture through a fine-mesh strainer.

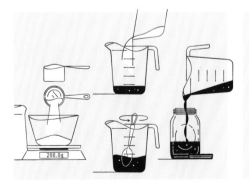

Add the sugar, and stir until it dissolves, about 1 minute. Pour into a nonreactive container.

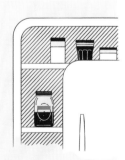

Store, covered, in the fridge for up to 3 DAYS.

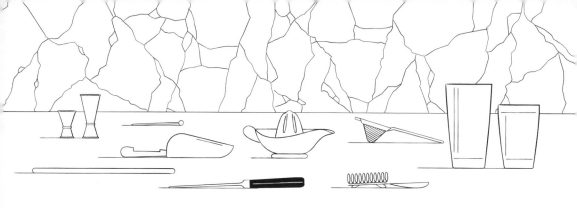

POMME AND CIRCUMSTANCE

by A-K Hada

A-K developed this recipe when she was general manager for Existing Conditions in New York City. Her inspiration was a dessert called "Grandpa's Grapefruit," offered at Russ & Daughters Café on the Lower East Side. "It was a halved and charred grapefruit, covered in maple syrup and sprinkled with wheat germ—the nuttiness and acidity married perfectly," she says. With a classic Collins recipe template in mind, she thinned the maple syrup with the barley infusion, which stands in for the wheat germ conceptually. The maple syrup contributes cooked notes akin to molasses to balance the acidity of the cider. **YIELDS 1 SERVING**

- ☐ 1½ ounces Weller Special Reserve bourbon
- ☐ ¾ ounce Boricha Cold Brew (page 352)
- ☐ ½ ounce Ruby Red grapefruit juice
- ☐ ½ ounce pure maple syrup
- ☐ Ice cubes
- ☐ 1½ ounces Domaine Dupont Cidre Bouché, chilled
- ☐ 3 apple slices, for garnish

Add the bourbon, cold brew, grapefruit juice, and maple syrup to a Boston shaker. Add a scoop of ice cubes. Shake, then add the cider. Double-strain through a Hawthorne and fine-mesh strainer into a chilled Collins glass filled with ice cubes. Garnish with an apple fan affixed by a cocktail pick.

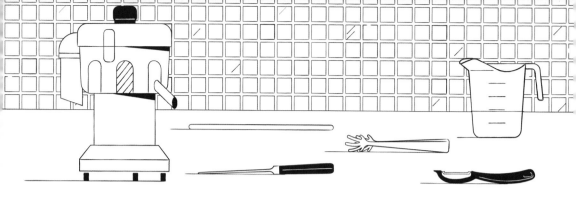

GOTA DE SANDÍA

by Danielle Tatarin

Danielle Tatarin, a Canadian expat whom Osvaldo Vázquez introduced me to on a visit to Baja California, created this cocktail with her own mezcal—Gota Gorda—at her bar in Zipolite, a tiny beach town in southern Oaxaca. Eating watermelon is "a great way to cool down after a trip to the market buying chiles, so it seemed like the perfect combination," she explains, adding how raw agave nectar yields a round mouthfeel on the finish. She usually cuts the agave nectar with equal parts water, tea, or another flavorful ingredient to bring down the sweetness, as she does with ginger for her Ginger-Agave Syrup in this recipe.

YIELDS EIGHT 4-OUNCE SERVINGS

☐ 12 ounces Chile-and-Grapefruit-Peel-Infused Mezcal (page 346)

☐ 11 ounces Hibiscus Infusion (page 355)

☐ 6 ounces Ginger-Agave Syrup (page 342)

☐ 4 ounces watermelon juice

☐ 8 large (2-inch) ice cubes, tempered for 1 to 2 minutes

☐ 8 grapefruit peels, for garnish

Add the mezcal, hibiscus infusion, ginger-agave syrup, and watermelon juice to a nonreactive container. Cover and chill the mixture in the fridge for 1 day to allow the ginger sediment to sink.

Carefully rack the mixture into a service pitcher or punch bowl, and compost the ginger sediment. Ladle or pour the mixture into 8 chilled old fashioned glasses, each filled with a large, tempered ice cube. Garnish each serving with a grapefruit twist.

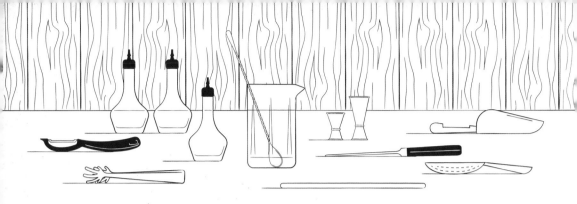

IPSWICH OLD FASHIONED

by Bob McCoy

This riff on an Old Fashioned cocktail invented by Privateer Rum's director of sales Bob McCoy is a case study in how to showcase terroir in a cocktail. The single-origin molasses—which former distiller Maggie Campbell sourced to produce rums during her tenure at the Privateer distillery in Ipswich, Massachusetts—comes from Madre Tierra sugar mill in the village of Santa Lucia, Guatemala. This molasses is fermented and distilled to produce the rum and diluted into a syrup to sweeten the cocktail. Bob says the complexity of the rum's terroir is an added bonus: "We don't talk about terroir in spirits enough, and for us, Ipswich's maritime climate—including the salt marsh directly behind the distillery—adds nuance to our rums, which is highlighted in this cocktail." YIELDS 1 SERVING

- ☐ 2 ounces Privateer Navy Yard rum
- ☐ ½ ounce Molasses Syrup (page 338)
- ☐ 2 dashes Angostura bitters
- ☐ 2 dashes Regan's No. 6 orange bitters
- ☐ 2 dashes Mineral Saline (page 340)
- ☐ Ice cubes, plus 1 large (2-inch) ice cube, tempered for 1 to 2 minutes
- ☐ 1 lemon peel, for garnish

Add the rum, syrup, both bitters, and the mineral saline to a chilled mixing glass. Add a scoop of ice cubes. Stir and strain into a chilled old fashioned glass filled with a large, tempered ice cube. Garnish with a lemon twist.

PENICILLIN

by Sam Ross

Sam Ross, co-owner of Attaboy in New York City, ushered in the use of ginger juice—Sam mixes it into a syrup using 4 parts ginger juice to 3 parts white sugar by weight—in mixed drinks worldwide with this contemporary classic from 2005. He created it at Milk & Honey after Compass Box Scotch founder John Glaser dropped off samples of his whiskies for the bar team to try. Sam named the recipe, which I've adapted using unsweetened ginger juice, as a reference to chicken noodle soup. His family called it, "Jewish penicillin—a dish you have if you're sick with a cold. It's a drink filled with ingredients that have restorative qualities: ginger, lemon, honey, and Scotch leaves everyone feeling rosy." He recommends one if you're feeling under the weather. "You don't need to wait until that point to order one, though," he adds. "It's good anytime." YIELDS 1 SERVING

- ☐ 2 ounces Compass Box Asyla blended Scotch whisky
- ☐ ¾ ounce lemon juice
- ☐ ¾ ounce Honey Syrup (page 338)
- ☐ ½ ounce ginger juice (extracted from 50g fresh ginger root)
- ☐ ¼ ounce Compass Box Peat Monster blended malt Scotch whisky
- ☐ Ice cubes, plus 1 large (2-inch) ice cube, tempered for 1 to 2 minutes
- ☐ 1 piece candied ginger, for garnish

Add the Asyla Scotch, lemon juice, honey syrup, and ginger juice to a Boston shaker. Add a scoop of ice cubes, then shake the mixture. Double-strain through a Hawthorne and a fine-mesh strainer into a chilled old fashioned glass filled with a large, tempered ice cube. Float the Peat Monster Scotch over the surface of the drink with a bar spoon. Garnish with the candied ginger on a cocktail pick.

The Bartender's Pantry

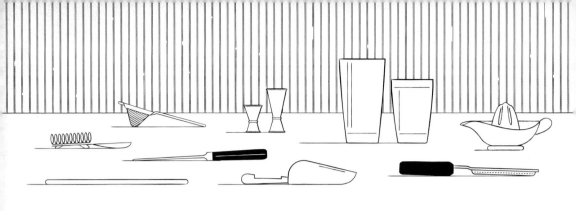

WHAT CHEER

by Paul Calvert

On paper, the pineapple cordial is the star sweetener in this low-ABV Collins invented by Paul Calvert, who co-owns Ticonderoga Club in Atlanta. What drew me to the recipe was the way the sorghum syrup bolsters the sweetness, while adding an earthy element. For Paul, the Southern staple reminds him of the cane sugar in root beer: "It hits a flavor note that simple syrup, honey, or maple syrup just can't swing. Even a bar spoon can elevate a drink the way a pinch of salt or a drop of vinegar does to our food." YIELDS 1 SERVING

- ☐ 2 ounces Scar of the Sea Co-Ferment Cider, chilled
- ☐ 1½ ounces Vieira de Sousa Fine White Port wine
- ☐ ¾ ounce lime juice
- ☐ ½ ounce Pineapple Cordial (page 30)
- ☐ ¼ ounce Sorghum Syrup (page 340)
- ☐ Ice cubes
- ☐ 1 lime, zested, for garnish

Add the cider, wine, lime juice, cordial, and syrup to a Boston shaker. Add a scoop of ice cubes and then roll the mixture between the 2 tins. Double-strain through a Hawthorne and fine-mesh strainer into a chilled Collins glass filled with ice cubes. Garnish with the lime zest.

Spices

Spices commonly appear in cocktails via spirits like gin or aquavit, and in alcohol-based mixers such as vermouth and aromatic bitters, which collectively comprise a bar's liquid "spice rack." As standalone ingredients, though, spices are used sparingly in most recipes—a scraping of nutmeg grated over punch, a burning cinnamon quill in a tropical drink, the savory spice blends of a Bloody Mary, or the cloves pricked into a lemon garnish in a toddy are some of the only sightings. As bartenders look beyond the classic cocktail canon, aromatic seeds, barks, and other dried plant materials are being creatively employed in more drinks. Spices can be used to add a subtle background note, as an aromatic garnish, or championed as the central element of a recipe itself.

n *The Nutmeg Trail,* Eleanor Ford posits that the word *spice* is derived from the Latin word *species*, which means goods of special value. "A sense of their extraordinariness is embedded in their name," she writes. I also find "extraordinary" an apropos term to describe spices; thanks to their artful processing, these ingredients—roots and rhizomes like turmeric and licorice; leaves like bay laurel; flower buds like clove; barks like cassia; pods like cardamom, star anise, and vanilla; fruits like pepper, allspice, and caraway; and seeds like nutmeg, coriander, and cacao—have the durability to be transported as precious cargo from all around the globe.

As our world becomes ever more connected, the broad swath of ingredients we have to mix with is something to marvel upon. "We now mention cardamom in the same breath with vanilla, and ghee is a common staple on the shelves of many grocery stores," writes author Nik Sharma in his book *Season.* "Our interconnected world has transformed how we think about food, and changed the way we eat."

Spices are used to add aroma and bring heat, earthiness, sweetness, or sourness to dishes—and to cocktails. "Although pure ingredients are tasty on their own, they still need a touch of spice to reveal their layers of flavor and really bring them to life," writes Lior Lev Sercarz in *The Spice Companion.* "The sensation you get after eating certain spices creates the perception of sweetness or saltiness without actually adding those elements to a dish—take Sichuan pepper or celery seed, for example."

HARVESTING AND PROCESSING

Generally speaking, harvesting and processing spices is done without much complex machinery. "Nearly every peppercorn you buy has been hand-picked; every true cinnamon quill has been hand-stripped and rolled by traditional cinnamon peelers in Sri Lanka; every vanilla orchid has been hand-pollinated, and every vanilla pod has been handled dozens of times during the arduous curing process," Ian Hemphill explains in *Spice Notes and Recipes.*

This constant interaction with humans means sometimes spices can carry high levels of bacteria. In most cases, spices are sanitized (irradiated) in their countries of origin before getting shipped to their final destinations, and here in the United States the government requires proof of this before spices can be imported. Regardless, this is a primary reason why it's important to know where your spices come from.

The plants we procure spices from bloom seasonally, but spices are typically dried before sale, either by farmers themselves or by a third-party processor. The drying process makes spices easy to ship, trade, and store. Spices may have slightly different flavors depending on their growing conditions; so smell your spices before using them, and adjust proportions as needed.

Seeds and Pods

Aniseed Also called anise, dried aniseeds have a licorice-like flavor thanks to the trans anethole chemical (also found in fennel and star anise). "A great range of licorice-flavored alcoholic drinks throughout the Mediterranean also rely on aniseed for their flavor, such as Greek ouzo, French pastis, Pernod and Ricard, and Turkish raki," writes Jane Lawson in *The Spice Bible*.

Cacao beans The fruit of the *Theobroma cacao* tree produces football-sized fruit pods, each containing a number of seeds, or "beans," which are surrounded by pulp. The flavor attributes change depending on the botanical group, whether Criollo, Forastero, or Trinitario—this is due to the higher ratio of (pale-colored) seeds to flesh. Beans are most commonly fermented and roasted to make chocolate, and crumbled into cacao nibs, which appear in Martin Lambert's Cola recipe (page 286).

Caraway seeds The seeds of *Carum carvi* herbs are native to Central Europe and used in Scandinavian aquavit. "The distinctive flavor of caraway comes from the terpene D-carvone (which it shares with dill), with citrusy limonene being the only other major volatile," writes Harold McGee in *On Food and Cooking*.

Cardamom A warming spice, cardamom comes in two varieties: Malabar—marked by small pods with floral notes—and Mysore, which have a woody, eucalyptus-like freshness. Green cardamom brings an earthy note to the Türk Kahvesi recipe from Ria Neri (page 226).

Cayenne pepper The ground spice we know as cayenne is a blend of a variety of dried hot chiles. Lawson explains: "Cayenne pepper has little discernible aroma, but its potency can be determined by its color. In general, the less red the powder is, the hotter it will be." Cayenne brings a kick to the B-Marion Spice Blend (page 60) and the Welcome Mother (page 330).

Celery seeds Often used in Bloody Mary spice blends, celery seeds are "essentially a concentrated, dried version of the same aromas found in fresh celery (*Apium graveolens*), though of course it lacks the fresh green notes," writes McGee.

Coriander The dried seeds of the cilantro plant, coriander is featured in many cuisines globally. "The small spherical seeds are generally available in two varieties, the most common being light brown in color, which is warm and aromatic in flavor with undertones of citrus and sage," writes Lawson. "The other is Indian, or green, which is much greener in color and fresher in taste."

Fennel seeds From the flowers of the perennial fennel plant (in the carrot family), fennel seeds are most often harvested from sweet varieties that impart a concentrated version of the licorice and anise notes found in the fresh bulb.

Nutmeg Sold as a whole round seed or as a ground spice, nutmeg comes from the *Myristica fragrans* tree. Most common in eggnog and as a grated garnish over tropical drinks and winter warmers, it shines in Lydia Parsley's Oat Milk recipe (page 124), and Krambambulya (page 349) from Israel Morales. The golden membrane of the nutmeg seed, which is called mace, can also be used to infuse the pod's flavor into spirits or syrups.

Paprika Sourced from dried sweet peppers native to tropical climates, paprika has deep red hues and a warm pungency. Note how processing traditions differ by region; for example, the peppers are smoked to make Spanish pimentón, but are sun-dried for Hungarian paprika. Consider these flavor attributes when sourcing, and know each type also has varying degrees of sweetness and pungency. The spice's savory qualities pair well with cayenne and black peppercorn in the B-Marion Spice Blend (page 60).

Star anise Though star anise has a similar flavor to aniseed, the two spices come from totally different plants. Star anise has a sweeter, milder flavor and aroma, as well as a distinctive star shape, so reserve the intact pods for aromatic garnishes. It contributes a resinous note to traditional drinks like Tepache (page 320) and Krambambulya (page 349).

Vanilla With a warm richness thanks to an abundance of vanillin compounds, vanilla is one of the most popular spices used in baking. "True vanilla comes from the pod fruit, often called the 'bean,' of a climbing orchid native to Central and northern South America," Harold McGee explains. There are many varieties, each with somewhat distinct flavors. Most vanilla is processed into an extract—made by soaking it in an alcohol-based solution—because real vanilla pods are the second most costly spice to harvest (after saffron), and demand outweighs supply. Artificial extract does not have the same expressive depth of flavor, so seek out real extracts (and pods when feasible) and use them to aromatize preparations like Champurrado (page 58).

Berries and Flowers

Allspice Primarily grown in Jamaica (which is why it's called the "Jamaica pepper"), allspice is the berry of *Pimenta dioica* trees, native to Central America. Bartenders know its flavor well from rum-based "pimento dram" liqueur, which is a staple ingredient in tropical cocktails.

Cloves The reddish dried flower buds from the *Syzygium aromaticum* tree, cloves are native to Indonesia. According to McGee, the spice has "the highest concentration of aroma molecules of any spice." The buds can be found in many global spice mixes, including Chinese five-spice, garam masala, and the uniquely American "pumpkin spice." Cloves also help deepen the flavor profile of Coquito (page 108), Tepache (page 320), and Cola (page 286).

Cubeb berries Cubeb berries are the unripe fruits—similar in flavor to allspice, eucalyptus, and black peppercorns—of the *Piper cubeba* plant, which is native to Indonesia and is part of the pepper family. The little berries have tiny stems that resemble tails and are typically used as a medicinal spice for a variety of ailments, or as a component of spice blends like the French quatre épices, a mix of nutmeg, clove, ginger, and cubeb berries.

Peppercorns Peppercorns bring a sense of "heat" to food and drink, thanks to a chemical called piperine. They start out as unripe berries on a pepper vine, which are then "harvested at different stages of development and undergo treatments to produce the peppercorns we buy, which vary in color, heat, and aroma," writes Nik Sharma in *The Flavor Equation*. Many varieties of black peppercorn are available; take the Aranya black peppercorn in Kadak Spicy Chai (page 91), for example. The peppercorns we colloquially call pink peppercorns—used in the Llama del Rey (page 132)—come from Peruvian and Brazilian trees from the cashew family; while the Szechuan peppercorns and their Japanese relative sansho peppercorns come from the prickly ash tree. Make Szechuan Ginger Beer (page 284) to experience the zip they add to a drink.

Roots and Barks

Chicory Chicory is the root of a perennial relative of the dandelion, originally cultivated in ancient Egypt. Not commonly used to season food and drinks, it is more famously known as a flavoring agent in coffee. Originally substituted in times of scarcity; chicory is now a staple of New Orleans coffee culture. It is also a key component in St. George's modern coffee liqueur.

Cinnamon Perhaps the most ubiquitous spice used in mixed drinks, cinnamon is the bark of trees in the *Cinnamomum* genus and comes in several varieties. Ceylon cinnamon, also known as Sri Lankan cinnamon or canela, is mild and sweet, while cassia cinnamon is harder, and more pungent in aromatics and flavor. Cinnamon aromatizes the Chicha Morada (page 128), Kadak Spicy Chai (page 91), Oat Milk (page 124), Cashew Horchata (page 126), Sorrel (page 192), Tepache (page 320), and many other mixed drinks featured in this book.

Ginger Employed in both fresh and dried forms, ginger is the fibrous, knobby rhizome (swollen root) of the flowering ginger plant (called *Zingiber officianale*), which grows year-round. Young ginger is soft and tastes mild, while older rhizomes are more fibrous and intensely flavored. The flesh can be crystallized or candied as a garnish. Ground dried ginger is frequently called for in infusions, such as the Malabar Infusion (page 62), Kadak Spicy Chai (page 91), and Sorrel (page 192). Peppery fresh ginger is called for in one of the most ginger-forward drinks on the planet, the Penicillin (page 42).

Licorice root Licorice is the bittersweet root of the flowering plant *Glycyrrhiza glabra*. Its extract is used to make candies and syrups. The chopped and sifted root is preferable to the powder for making Licorice-Root Water (page 356).

SOURCING

Freshness is crucial with spices because even when dried, their quality deteriorates over time. Ori Zohar, co-founder of the spice company Burlap & Barrel, offers a valuable recommendation: "The 'best by' date on the jar will tell you when the spice was packaged, but it won't tell you when it was harvested (often years prior to being packaged), so look for companies committed to sourcing the freshest harvest and that tell you when the ingredients were picked."

If there is no date on the package, trust your senses. "Spices should also have the most vibrant, intense color possible. If they look grayish or faded, that might be a tell that they have been sitting on the store's shelf for way too long," Lior Sercarz suggests. "Also, if you notice a lot of powder on the bottom of a package of whole spices, this can mean they are old and have started breaking down. This is especially true with dried herbs."

Whole vs. ground While many claim whole spices offer more vibrant flavors and aromas than ground ones, that is not a hard-and-fast rule. Sometimes, there is no option between the two. Lior Sercarz notes that dried spices like paprika and ginger can rarely be found whole because "these require heavy-duty hammer mill grinders and are usually ground in their respective countries of origin."

If you prefer ground spices, which infuse into liquid more quickly than whole ones, there is a sense of ritual and tactile enjoyment in grinding them yourself, especially with tools like the mortar and pestle, which have been used for thousands of years. Or use a blade grinder—it gives you quick, consistent results. "The option to do quick pulses or run it longer helps to achieve varying degrees of grind to give you the layers, textures, and appearance you want," Sercarz writes, adding a note to grind each spice separately to "help avoid mistakes and make sure each one gets the proper attention."

Blends Packaged spice blends are easy to find at the store and online—from za'atar and masala to pumpkin spice and adobo—but experts like Sercarz recommend buying single spices and blending them yourself. "For those of us who would rather have control of the ingredients and an outlet for our creative ideas, there really is nothing better than doing it yourself. It also provides the opportunity to fully discover and appreciate each individual spice that goes into a blend, smell its unique aroma, choose how coarsely you want to grind it, and decide what each one brings to the table," he adds.

Blending spices is an art, like perfuming, for which you should consider top notes, middle notes, and base notes to create a well-balanced mix. Try blending spices that inspire you and experiment with them across a range of applications. For an ornery perfectionist like me, spice blending proved to be a humbling experience because it doesn't follow mixology's logic; but if you have the inclination to tinker, blending spices is an alchemy unto itself.

STORAGE

For me, the difference between fresh spices and old jars of spices is like wearing glasses versus staggering around without my contacts. If stored properly in resealable zippered packs or airtight jars and kept away from light, heat, and moisture, ground spices will remain fresh for about a year. Whole spices will retain character for about a year and a half.

Try to buy only what you need so nothing stays on your shelf for too long, and label each spice container with the purchase date so you know how quickly it needs to be used. When buying single-origin spices from different regions, Sercarz suggests labeling and storing by place of origin. For example, if you have nutmeg from Grenada and nutmeg from Tanzania, store them separately because each version has different characteristics.

PREPARATION

Most recipes call for toasting spices before use because heat helps release aromatic oils and brings out more umami notes in their flavor. Lior Sercarz says toasting also helps sanitize spices, which is important because "they travel in bags or boxes all over the world, and it doesn't hurt to make them safer." Some spices will burn quickly, and black and white pepper don't get better when toasted, so consider each ingredient individually for best results.

To toast your spices (either whole or ground), heat a pan on the top of the stove until it is too hot to touch, add the spices, and stir or turn them in the pan until their aroma begins to emanate and the color darkens. To dry-roast your spices, preheat the oven to 325°F and spread the spices evenly on a baking sheet, then place it in the oven. Monitor roast level every couple minutes. The flavor of roasted or toasted spices deteriorates quickly, so only prep what you need.

Salt

Salt is technically a mineral, but I have always used it like a spice. In the drinks world, salt has long been relegated to the rim of a Margarita or as the accompaniment to tequila shots, but in recent years, bartenders have begun salting their drinks the way cooks season their food. As Naomi Duguid points out in *The Miracle of Salt,* "with rare exceptions, the role of salt is not to be tasted on its own as the star of the show but to amplify flavor and in some applications, texture." Author Samin Nosrat expands on the idea in *Salt, Fat, Acid, Heat,* describing salt's relationship to flavor as multidimensional: "Used properly, salt minimizes bitterness, balances out sweetness, and enhances aromas."

All salt originates from the ocean; some are the product of evaporation, while others are mined from lands previously covered by ocean waters. The texture is determined by the way the salt is processed, from solar evaporated fleur du sel and hand-harvested mineral salts that come in distinctive shapes to more utilitarian salts evaporated using industrial methods to yield evenly sized fine, medium, or coarse crystals. "These varying shapes and sizes can make a big difference in your cooking," Nosrat adds. "A tablespoon of fine salt will pack more tightly, and can be two or three times 'saltier' than a tablespoon of coarser salt. This is why it makes sense to measure salts by weight."

Table salt Refined fine-grained salt that may include anti-caking agents and iodine is colloquially known as table salt. Iodine was added as a public health measure almost a century ago—it helps control thyroid function and related activities—but recently, many chefs and bartenders have noted that the mineral adds an unpleasant aroma and taste to food and drinks, and advise opting for other salts for seasoning.

Kosher salt Kosher salt is refined to remove trace minerals, so it lacks some of the depth that other less refined salts offer, but its uniform particles and solubility make it ideal for Mineral Saline (page 340) and rimming glasses for recipes like Choked Up (page 76). Some kosher salts contain anti-caking ingredients, so look for a purveyor like Diamond Crystal that doesn't add them.

Sea salt Sea salt is harvested from seawater either by solar evaporation or by boiling the water over a heat source. It may be further refined to eliminate trace minerals such as calcium, magnesium, and potassium, or left unrefined. Refined sea salt works well diluted with water into a saline, whereas unrefined sea salt is better left as a crunchy finishing salt on garnishes. Sea salt flakes vary in texture, size, and crystal structure, depending on their geographic origin and the process used to collect them.

Pink salt Pink salts whose hue occurs naturally (like Himalayan pink salt, whose color is attributed to its iron content) or as the result of a secondary infusion (like Japanese ume or French wine) are ideal for garnishing or rimming a glass. Some bartenders also like to use pink salts in their drinks to impart minerality. Avoid pink curing salts, sometimes called Prague Powder #1, which are potentially toxic.

SOURCING

"The three basic decisions involving salt are: When? How much? In what form?" writes Nosrat about salt's use in cooking. The same approach applies to beverages. The three primary ways salt is used in cocktails are in the drink, either as solids or diluted into saline that is dashed in from a bitters decanter; on the rim, sometimes combined with other spices; and as garnishes in what cooks call finishing salt. When choosing salt, consider the size and shape of the granules and whether they will dissolve quickly into liquids or look pleasing as a crunchy garnish. Also consider whether the salt has been smoked or blended with other ingredients. Mexican sal de gusano, for example, is often mixed with dried chiles and toasted agave worms—a great option for the rim of drinks made with agave spirits.

STORAGE

"Salt lasts forever," Joshua McFadden writes in his book *Six Seasons,* noting how he keeps salt in jars and saltcellars stored nearby a pepper mill, since he uses both so often during cooking. "Those little shakers on the table are of no help when you cook; you need to feel the salt with your fingers as you add it, so you'll begin to understand how much does what." We all have different-sized hands and fingers—as well as different counter spaces and aesthetics—so readers should choose a visually appealing bowl that offers easy access to fingers and measuring spoons.

TOOLS

Most beverage recipes call for only small quantities of salt, so precise measuring with a gram scale or teaspoon and frequent tasting to see if more is needed are advisable.

Today, the spice industry is consolidated into a handful of large companies that reward growers for prioritizing quantity, speed, and cost rather than flavor, quality, and sustainable farming practices. "The conventional spice supply chain is dumping every variety of pepper together regardless of flavor profile, oil content, or harvest year in the name of large-scale logistics, and losing an incredible opportunity to bring nuanced, unique flavors sourced from thoughtful farms to consumers," says Sana Javeri Kadri, founder and CEO of Diaspora Co. "When a seed has been bred for yield and storability versus aroma and flavor, you're getting a less delicious spice no matter how fresh it is."

Big-box grocery stores typically stock only commodity spices sourced anonymously, so there's little to no information about where the spices were grown, whether sustainable practices were employed, when they were harvested, the conditions of the processing facilities, how well the field workers are treated and paid, and if the farm owners are being fairly compensated. In the absence of this vital background information, looking for a fair trade or organic certification (on a package that is designed to allow you to verify the spice's condition) is all you can do to assess its provenance without help from an informed salesperson.

To challenge the status quo, companies like Diaspora Co. and Burlap & Barrel are focusing on quality, freshness, and integrity by working with small, family-owned, sustainably minded producers that cultivate single-origin heirloom seeds. It is state-of-the-art work; tasting a superlative, really fresh spice can be a transformative experience. And as Javeri Kadri told me, as more consumers push for transparent sourcing and quality over quantity, this small movement grows the potential to transform the industry at large. "I started working with one farmer, and a quiet thought of how the spice industry might do things differently, and four years later, we're still just scratching the surface on this whole new world of flavor that awaits, and we're doing it alongside thousands of folks who are so energized, exciting, and happy to support."

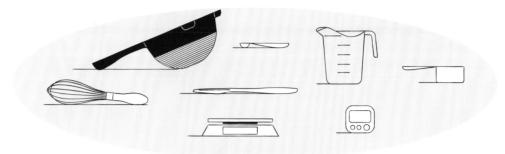

CHAMPURRADO

from Noah Small

Champurrado is a traditional masa-based hot chocolate from Mexico. Empellón corporate beverage director Noah Small developed his version of the recipe for a pairing dinner with guest chef Rick Bayless. "Down in Mexico, everyone makes champurrado a little differently," he says of the spice profile and exact ratio of milk to sugar to chocolate to masa. "I had to tinker with it to find what sat right on my palate." The key ended up being masa nixtamalized in-house from an organic, non-GMO corn variety from Oaxaca called Olatillo Blanco, plus canela. "Cassia cinnamon has more of a hot burn, while canela is warmer and a little more floral—it's a gentler version of the same flavor," he says.

Enjoy on its own (typically warm) or mix into the Children of the Corn (page 72). YIELDS 32 OUNCES

- ☐ 8 ounces filtered water
- ☐ 33g (six 4-inch quills) Ceylon (canela) cinnamon
- ☐ 1 whole (4.5g) vanilla bean
- ☐ 55g piloncillo, broken into small chunks (see page 22)
- ☐ 138g (½ cup) fresh corn masa
- ☐ 24 ounces whole milk
- ☐ 110g (¾ cup) 74% dark chocolate baking wafers
- ☐ 3g (½ teaspoon) kosher salt, or to taste

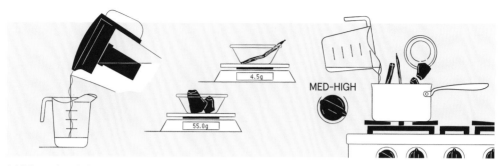

Add the water, 1 cinnamon quill, vanilla bean, and piloncillo to a medium saucepan over medium-high heat.

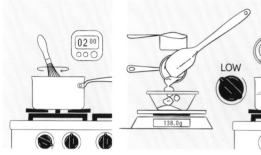

Whisk until the piloncillo is dissolved, about 2 minutes.

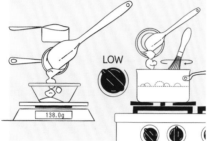

Add the masa and whisk until the mixture reaches a gentle boil, then lower to a simmer.

Add the milk 1 cup at a time, whisking between each addition.

Add the chocolate baking wafers and whisk until melted, about 2 minutes more.

Add salt to taste and whisk to integrate. Fine-strain the mixture into a nonreactive container.

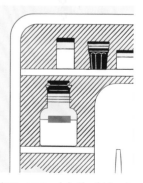

Store, covered, in the fridge for up to 5 DAYS. To serve, reheat over medium heat until it reaches a simmer, then pour into a drinking vessel. Garnish each serving with a cinnamon quill.

Spices

59

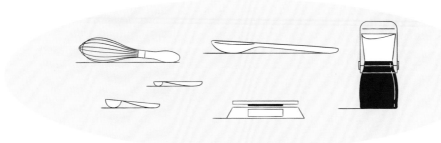

B-MARION SPICE BLEND

by Lior Lev Sercarz

In 2013, chef, author, and spice blender Lior Lev Sercarz created a collection of spice blends individually tailored for the Bloody Mary recipes I developed with four different base spirits: vodka, gin, tequila, and aquavit. Unlike most cocktails, which incorporate a single spice such as nutmeg grated as garnish, or salt on the rim of the glass, this recipe features a complex blend of spices integrated within the mixture. Lior likes to highlight certain flavors and aromas in the dish he's spicing by reinforcing them in the blend, so for this aquavit-inspired version, he added orange, caraway, and anise to the collection's base blend of paprika, celery seed, black pepper, salt, and pimentón.

Use in the Bloody Marion (page 70). YIELDS 127G (SCANT 1¼ CUPS)

GROUND SPICES
- ☐ 20g (1 tablespoon) Spanish smoked paprika
- ☐ 20g (1 tablespoon) Hungarian sweet paprika
- ☐ 5g (2½ teaspoons) granulated orange peel
- ☐ 2g (1 teaspoon) ground ginger
- ☐ 2g (¾ teaspoon) cayenne

WHOLE SPICES
- ☐ 15g (2 tablespoons) black peppercorns
- ☐ 15g (2 tablespoons) cubeb berries
- ☐ 10g (4 teaspoons) anise seeds
- ☐ 10g (1 tablespoon) caraway seeds
- ☐ 5g (1 tablespoon) coriander seeds
- ☐ 5g (1 teaspoon) kosher salt
- ☐ 3g (1½ teaspoons) allspice berries
- ☐ 2g (½ teaspoon) celery seeds

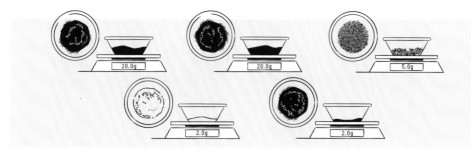

Measure out all the ground spices.

Combine the ground spices in a medium bowl and stir until well-integrated.

Place the whole spices in a grinder and grind to a powder.

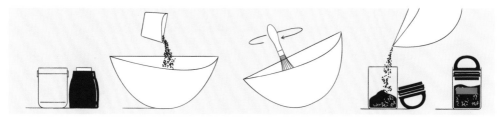

Add the powder from the grinder to the bowl with the ground spices. Whisk until well combined. Store in a nonreactive airtight container for up to 6 MONTHS.

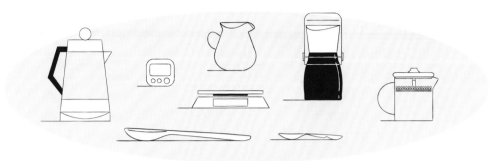

MALABAR INFUSION

by Taylor Cowan

For Spirit Tea co-founder Taylor Cowan, the consistent sourcing of spices and botanicals from regions with ideal growing conditions is paramount for the quality of their herbal tonics. This is especially true for the company's Malabar herbal tonic, which offers a complex blend of Chinese ginger, Malabar black peppercorn, American licorice root, Thai lemongrass, and turmeric. Cowan reinforces the importance of using fresh spices because "once you mill something, its surface area is greatly increased and staleness creeps in rapidly. This is why we coordinate the sourcing time for our herbals to include a fresh milling window to fulfill our partners' weekly needs."

I use this herbal tonic in my recipe for Malabar Honey Syrup (page 344), which is mixed into the Malabar Silver Corn Fizz (page 74). YIELDS TWO 5½-OUNCE SERVINGS

MALABAR BLEND

- ☐ 40g (⅓ cup) chopped dried ginger root, sifted
- ☐ 27g (¾ cup) finely cut dried lemongrass
- ☐ 13g (1 tablespoon) chopped dried turmeric root, sifted
- ☐ 13g (2 tablespoons) chopped dried licorice root
- ☐ 6.7g (1 teaspoon) Malabar black peppercorns

MALABAR INFUSION

- ☐ 6g (2 tablespoons) Malabar Blend
- ☐ 340g (12 ounces) filtered water, heated to 205°F

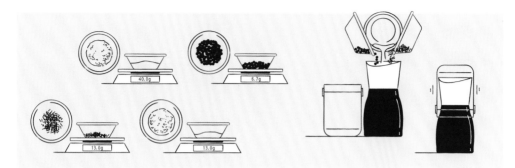

To make the Malabar blend, add the ginger, turmeric, licorice root, and black pepper to a blade grinder. Pulse 3 times for a total of 5 seconds of grinding.

Combine the ground spices with the lemongrass in a 5-quart measuring bowl. Stir with a spoon to combine. Store in a sealed, nonreactive container like a tea caddy with an internal plunger. Yields 99.7g (1½ cups; enough for 12 servings).

Place 6g of the Malabar blend in the infuser.

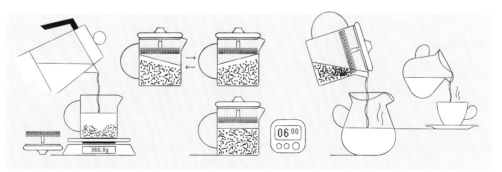

Pour the heated water into the infuser, then give it a swirl to thoroughly hydrate the botanicals. After 6 minutes, pour the infusion into the sharing pitcher. Serve in a prewarmed tempered cup.

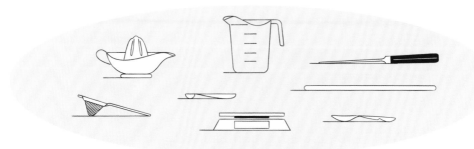

SANGRITA ROJA

from Osvaldo Vázquez

Sangrita is prepared from a mix of juices and spices that are served alongside agave spirits throughout Mexico. Many families have their own recipes prepared with the juice of oranges, pomegranates, or tomatoes. For this reason, the beverage serves as a window into the soul of a Mexican bar program. At Hotel Los Cabos Pedregal, Osvaldo Vázquez served two different types: a Sangrita Roja and a Sangrita Verde. The Roja is made with his homemade grenadine recipe, which includes local pitaya (prickly pear) and hibiscus to replicate the colorful vibrance and piquant tartness of the more commonly used pomegranate juice.

Drink this alongside your favorite agave spirit and add a Sangrita Verde (page 66) to make it a Bandera (page 68). YIELDS 23 OUNCES

- ☐ 17 ounces orange juice (from 5 oranges)
- ☐ 5.5g (1 teaspoon) kosher salt
- ☐ 1 ounce Baja Grenadine (page 32)
- ☐ ¼ ounce Lea & Perrins Worcestershire sauce
- ☐ 0.5g (¼ teaspoon) ground black pepper
- ☐ ¼ ounce Tabasco sauce
- ☐ 1g (⅛ teaspoon) Maggi seasoning sauce
- ☐ 4 ounces lime juice (from 4 limes)

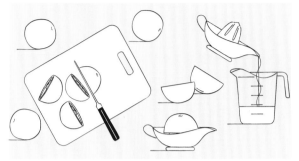

Prepare the orange juice and add it to a measuring cup.

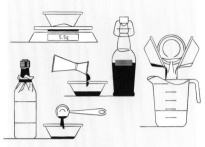

Add the salt, Baja Grenadine, and Worcestershire sauce to the orange juice.

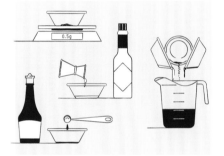

Add the pepper, Tabasco sauce, and Maggi sauce to the mixture.

Prepare the lime juice and add it to the mixture, stirring to combine.

Fine-strain the mixture into a nonreactive jar with a lid.

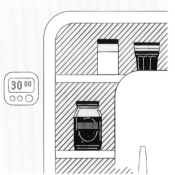

Cover and chill in the fridge for no longer than 30 minutes.

Serve fresh, that day.

SANGRITA VERDE

from Osvaldo Vázquez

Osvaldo Vázquez, the founder of Bitter & Barrel cocktail bitters, created his green sangrita—the second version of the classic Mexican recipe he served at Hotel Los Cabos Pedregal—as part of an "agave experience" pairing in 2010. His goal was to complement the unique flavors and aromas of tequila and raicilla (an agave spirit from the state of Jalisco). The grapefruit and pineapple buttress the jalapeño splendidly in this verdant agave sidecar, which also features the proprietary celery bitters he formulated before they were widely available in Mexico.

Drink this alongside your favorite agave spirit, and add a Sangrita Roja (page 64) to make it a Bandera (page 68). YIELDS 20 OUNCES

- ☐ 9 ounces grapefruit juice (from 2 Ruby Red grapefruits)
- ☐ 3½ ounces lime juice (from 3 limes)
- ☐ 1 bunch (120g) fresh cilantro
- ☐ 1 (24g) jalapeño, seeded
- ☐ 9 ounces pineapple juice (from 500g peeled and cored pineapple)

- ☐ 5.5g (1 teaspoon) kosher salt
- ☐ ¾ teaspoon Lea & Perrins Worcestershire sauce
- ☐ 4 dashes Bitter & Barrel celery bitters
- ☐ ⅛ teaspoon Maggi seasoning
- ☐ ¼ teaspoon ground black pepper

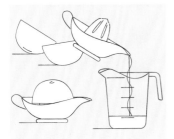

Prepare and measure the grapefruit juice.

Prepare and measure the lime juice.

Seed the jalapeño.

Prepare, extract, and measure the pineapple juice.

Measure the salt, Worcestershire, bitters, Maggi seasoning, and pepper.

Pour the spices and juices into the blender, then add the cilantro and jalapeño. Process until smooth, about 20 seconds.

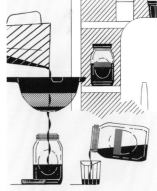

Fine-strain the mixture, cover, and chill in the fridge for no longer than 30 minutes. Serve fresh, that day.

BANDERA

from Osvaldo Vázquez

Tequila used to be synonymous with shots. When you ordered one, it would come in a squat glass with a wedge of lime and a shaker of salt on the side. Today, many tequila drinkers prefer sipping the spirit alongside spicy sangrita to complement its character. In many Mexican bars, a shot of lime juice is also included with the tequila and sangrita roja, in which case the trio is called a Bandera. In this rendition, Osvaldo's Sangrita Verde serves as a stand-in for the lime juice. The three colors of the ingredients—*verde, blanco, and roja*—echo the colors of Mexico's flag. YIELDS 1 SERVING

☐ 2 ounces Sangrita Verde
(page 66), chilled

☐ 2 ounces blanco tequila

☐ 2 ounces Sangrita Roja
(page 64), chilled

Pour the Verde, the tequila, and the Roja into their own veladora glasses. Arrange the glasses with the Verde to the left, the tequila in the middle, and the Roja to the right.

BLOODY MARION

by Jim Meehan

This is one of four signature Bloody Marys that use the spice blends Lior Lev Sercarz and I co-developed (see page 60) to accentuate the flavor profiles of vodka, gin, tequila, and aquavit. Lior sourced, blended, and milled high-quality salt, pepper, celery salt, cayenne, paprika, and chile to refocus the imbiber's appreciation of the beverage itself, instead of the cornucopia of garnishes typically arranged above it. For my aquavit-based Bloody Mary, Lior added anise, caraway, and coriander seeds to the base blend to accentuate the botanicals commonly found in the spirit. YIELDS 1 SERVING

- ☐ 4 ounces tomato juice
- ☐ 1½ ounces Krogstad aquavit
- ☐ ¼ ounce Lea & Perrins Worcestershire sauce
- ☐ ¼ ounce lemon juice
- ☐ ¼ ounce orange juice

- ☐ ½ teaspoon B-Marion Spice Blend (page 60)
- ☐ ½ teaspoon prepared horseradish
- ☐ ¼ teaspoon Cholula hot sauce
- ☐ ⅛ teaspoon toasted sesame oil
- ☐ Ice cubes
- ☐ Dill pickle spear, for garnish

Add the tomato juice, aquavit, Worcestershire, lemon and orange juices, spice blend, horseradish, hot sauce, and oil to a Boston shaker. Add a scoop of ice cubes. Roll the mixture back and forth between the tins. Double-strain through a Hawthorne and a fine-mesh strainer into a chilled Collins glass filled with ice cubes. Garnish with a dill pickle spear and serve with a straw.

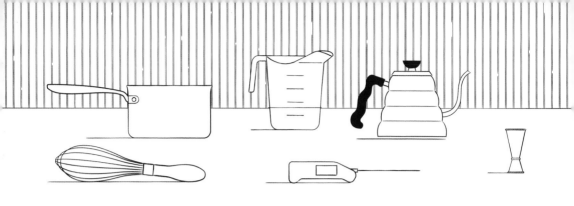

CHILDREN OF THE CORN

by Noah Small

At Empellón Cocina in New York City, corporate beverage director Noah Small created this warm champurrado-based nightcap as part of an "Art of Masa" dinner in 2014. He paired it with a mignardise (small confection) served by chef Rick Bayless. Noah likes to use pop-culture references in his recipe titles, and this one refers to the popular early 1980s horror movie. He adds, "Kids love hot chocolate . . . and this is a sort of hot chocolate from a weird and delicious dream." YIELDS FOUR 4¾-OUNCE SERVINGS

- ☐ 16 ounces Champurrado (page 58)
- ☐ 2 ounces Fidencio Clásico mezcal
- ☐ 1 ounce Casa D'aristi Xtabentún liqueur
- ☐ 22g (four 4-inch quills) Ceylon (canela) cinnamon

Add the Champurrado to a medium saucepan over medium heat and warm until it reaches 140°F, about 2 minutes. Turn off the heat and add the mezcal and liqueurs while whisking. Transfer the warm mixture to a prewarmed service vessel or directly into tempered mugs. Garnish each with a cinnamon quill.

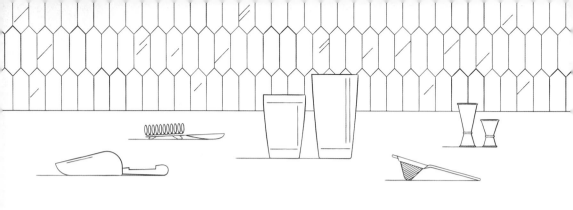

MALABAR SILVER CORN FIZZ

by Jim Meehan

Using spices to enhance a syrup is a simple but impactful strategy to employ during recipe development. The original version of this recipe—the Silver Corn Fizz, created in the summer of 2009 for PDT—used honey syrup and a Tennessee whiskey with a corn-forward mash bill. When I began exploring how I could amplify the cocktail's "corniness," chef Wylie Dufresne steered me toward canned corn because it's easier to work with and just as good (or better, in his opinion) than fresh kernels. I enhanced the elemental honey syrup in the original recipe with a Malabar infusion. The new iteration—now called the Malabar Silver Corn Fizz, owing to its shift in preparation—features a more flavorful corn-based whiskey and a local sparkling wine I've come to prefer over many Champagnes.

YIELDS 1 SERVING

- ☐ 1½ ounces Mellow Corn bonded corn whiskey
- ☐ 1 ounce Corn Water (page 196)
- ☐ ½ ounce Malabar Honey Syrup (page 344)
- ☐ 1 large egg white
- ☐ Ice cubes
- ☐ 1 ounce Argyle vintage brut sparkling wine, chilled

Add the whiskey, corn water, syrup, and egg white to a Boston shaker. Shake without ice. Add a scoop of ice cubes and shake again. Add the sparkling wine, then double-strain through a Hawthorne and a fine-mesh strainer into a chilled 8-ounce coupe.

CHOKED UP

by Leo Robitschek

Salt is a mineral, not a spice, but it can be used as a seasoning element in mixed drinks too. That is the case with this riff on a classic gin smash featuring Cynar (derived from the Latin name for "artichoke," hence the title). Leo Robitschek created this recipe for the 2018 opening of the NoMad Los Angeles rooftop bar. He says the drink really pops with a touch of salt that's not discernable, but brings down the bitterness and brightens the other flavors. The half-salt rim gives imbibers the option to enjoy more salt on their own terms. **YIELDS 1 SERVING**

- ☐ 1 (20g) kumquat, cut in half
- ☐ 2 slices cucumber, about ¼ inch thick
- ☐ 5 leaves fresh mint, plus a plouche (2 to 3 large mint sprigs) for garnish
- ☐ ½ ounce Cane Syrup (page 337)
- ☐ 1 ounce Beefeater gin
- ☐ 1 ounce Cynar
- ☐ ¾ ounce lemon juice
- ☐ 2 dashes Mineral Saline (page 340)
- ☐ Ice cubes
- ☐ 1 lemon wedge, to moisten the rim
- ☐ 1 tablespoon kosher salt, for the rim

Add a kumquat half, 1 cucumber slice, the 5 mint leaves, and the cane syrup to a Boston shaker, and muddle. Add the gin, Cynar, lemon juice, saline, and a scoop of ice cubes to the Boston shaker, and shake. Double-strain through a Hawthorne and a fine-strainer into a chilled, half-salt-rimmed old fashioned glass filled with ice cubes. Garnish with the mint plouche speared through the center of the other half of the kumquat and remaining cucumber wheel.

Dairy

From medieval possets, syllabub, Hot Buttered Rum, and clarified milk punches to more recent recipes like the Ramos Gin Fizz, Irish Coffee, and Grasshopper, dairy has been mixed into cocktails for centuries. While dairy's use in cocktails and Irish cream liqueurs remains popular, bartenders are increasingly reaching for other forms like yogurt and sweetened condensed milk as drinks like the Lassi and Coquito gain popularity beyond their cultural diasporas. The fats in dairy products smooth the tannins in tea, tame the astringency of coffee, and provide a creamy canvas for spices, making them versatile partners for these popular drink preparations.

Since the Middle Ages, the English word *dairy* referred to the farm building where women processed milk into butter and cheese. Nowadays, it refers to products made from milk—a liquid produced by the mammary glands of mammals. "Before humans invented dairying, milk existed only as part of an exclusive two-party, one-way flow shielded from external forces," writes Anne Mendelson in *Spoiled*. "The complementary gateways formed by the mother's nipple and the suckling infant's mouth allow the living fluid to travel straight from mammary system into digestive system with no detours."

The milking story beyond mother and child (or cow and calf, in this case) began with relationships between dairy animals and humans that were facilitated by microbes. At some point long ago, nomadic herdspeople on the Eurasian Steppe discovered that milk soured using ambient lactic acid bacteria killed off harmful microbes, making dairy products safe and digestible. Mendelson posits that "the headlong expansion of the drinking-milk trade into a gigantic industry has done much to obscure this knowledge."

In modern times in the United States, cows (typically Holsteins) are the primary source of dairy, but in other countries water buffaloes, camels, goats, and sheep are also milked. Each animal's milk has a different flavor, fat content, and acidity level based on what it grazes upon that day. In this chapter, I'll focus on cow's milk, which is the most widely available milk for preparing beverages in North America. Insights and recipes for plant-based nut and grain "milks" are included in the Grains & Nuts chapter beginning on page 110.

Milk

Before dairy was industrialized, milk was only available seasonally—during spring and summer when cows breed and fresh grass grows. In *Spoiled,* Mendelson identifies silage—plants that are harvested fresh then left to ferment with naturally occurring bacteria—as the scientific breakthrough that made year-round milk production feasible. "Partly preserved by fermentation, [silage] could see cattle through the winter more reliably than untreated hay," she explains.

With a steady source of year-round milk, technological innovations like cold chain refrigeration from farm to shelf have helped make unsoured drinking-milk a staple of North American diets. Mendelson contextualizes the marvel of its ascendance: "no other food product is as staggeringly difficult and expensive to get from source (in this case, a cow) to destination (milk glass on table) in something loosely approximating its first condition. If one existed, it would be treated as an astounding luxury."

Most commercial milk is pasteurized and homogenized before being packaged and shipped to the store.

Pasteurization In 1862, Louis Pasteur developed the pasteurization process that used heat to kill the bacteria that spoiled wine. The technique confirmed and convinced health experts of the germ theory of disease, and was later used by scientists for many other beverages, including milk, by the beginning of the twentieth century. Three different pasteurization methods are used today in large-scale commercial operations—each method affects the shelf life of the milk and influences its flavor.

- Batch pasteurization (also known as vat pasteurization): agitates and heats milk at a minimum of 145°F, for a time period of 30 minutes to four hours. Today, many small regional dairies use this pasteurization method to kill bacteria while preserving nutrients and flavor.

- High-temperature, short-time method (HTST): the most common approach, pumps milk continuously through a heat exchanger at higher temps (a minimum of 161°F) for around 15 seconds before rapid cooling, which denatures 10 percent of the whey proteins and creates hydrogen sulfide. The higher temperatures reduce the complexity of the flavor and aroma of the milk.

- Ultra-high temperature method (UHT): a radical departure from the original pasteurization principle where the liquid being pasteurized remains well under its boiling point, UHT heats milk to the highest temperature (more than 280°F) for the shortest time period (one to two seconds), then rapidly cools it to room temperature. This is the most aggressive approach, and it has the greatest impact on flavor, aroma, and nutrition.

Homogenization In its natural state, milk separates into a top layer of heavy cream and a layer of thinner milk beneath (a division called creamline). Historically, the skim milk and cream separation wasn't seen as a defect, as it is sometimes perceived today. "A deep, conspicuous creamline in a bottle of milk indicated superior quality going back to the beginning of the nineteenth-century," writes Mendelson.

Homogenization—a process invented in the late 1800s—uses high pressure to break up the fat globules of cream so they disperse more evenly throughout the liquid, creating a uniform texture. According to Mendelson, one of the goals of homogenization was to eliminate the ability to guess the amount of cream in a milk based on the visual cue of the creamline. "Homogenization also allowed the standardization of milk fat and 'solids nonfat' (SNF) content to continue imposing the effect of industrial uniformity, obliterating most evidence of the subtle or dramatic distinctions that can exist between the milk of different breeds, different cows of the same breed, or even one cow under different conditions," she writes.

SOURCING

In response to a well-publicized University of Minnesota study of the relationship between dietary fats from animal-based foods, blood serum cholesterol, and coronary artery disease by nutrition researcher Ancel Keys, the Senate Select Committee on Nutrition and Human Needs published its Dietary Goals for Americans in 1977, which recommended citizens cut down on animal-based fats including whole milk (except for children).

Milk-processing companies responded to the proposed overhaul by promoting nonfat milk and creating homogenized versions of reduced-fat milk. We now have a classification system based on butterfat content, which ranges from skim milk, clocking in around 0.5 percent butterfat, to "whole" milk, which usually contains around 3.5 percent butterfat. When choosing what type of milk to use for drink making, know that milk with a higher fat content has more flavor and a thicker texture.

I source creamline milk for use in cocktails when I can find it, because of its complex flavor and full-bodied creaminess. While whole creamline milk in a glass jar is available in some markets in the United States, people raised on homogenized milk might find the presence of milk solids in their glass off-putting. The longer it takes for the milk to travel from the farm to a consumer's refrigerator, the more solid the creamline fats become—the fats float like icebergs in coffee and form buttery chunks of milk fat in morning cereal. When I can source creamline milk, I strain and discard the solids, and reserve the rich, flavorful milk for mixed drinks and my morning granola.

If you can't source whole creamline milk, look for organic milk from grass-fed cows, Dana Cree, author of *Hello, My Name Is Ice Cream,* told me during a phone interview. "Cows that eat grass are healthier because that's what they were meant to eat. And the flavor of what they're eating is transferred into the milk. When they eat fresh grass, that's when the milk gets the really beautiful flavors."

STORAGE
Dairy products should be stored in the coldest part of the fridge. Pasteurized milk stored below 40°F should remain drinkable for up to 18 days. Avoid storing milk in the freezer, which causes the fat and protein to clump and separate.

Cream

Fresh milk that has not been homogenized will separate into a layer of liquid on the bottom and a float of less dense fat globules on the top, known as cream.

Like milk, the classification system used for cream is based on butterfat content.

Half-and-half is a mixture of whole milk and cream containing between 10.5 and 18 percent butterfat. Light cream contains between 18 and 30 percent butterfat, while light whipping cream varies between 30 and 36 percent butterfat. Heavy cream (sometimes labeled heavy whipping cream) must contain at least 36 percent butterfat.

Generally speaking, the fat content of the cream determines its culinary application. Half-and-half and light cream are commonly poured into coffee drinks to mitigate bitterness and buttress texture. Heavy cream is used to enrich drinks like the Brandy Alexander and the Ramos Gin Fizz and can be churned into ice cream. For cocktails, cream must have at least 30 percent butterfat in order to hold a whip when shaken, so use light whipping cream or heavy whipping cream for applications like the wet-whipped cream on an Irish Coffee.

SOURCING

Cream is also typically pasteurized before sale. Ultra-pasteurized heavy cream loses viscosity in the high heat, so stabilizers and emulsifiers such as glycerides and carrageenan are added to simulate creaminess, which represents another reason to reach for lesser processed cream. UHT cream has a longer shelf life than regular cream, but it doesn't whip as well. Temperature also influences how well cream whips, so chill it thoroughly for best results.

STORAGE

Cream lasts around ten days if well-sealed in the refrigerator, while ultra-pasteurized cream can last up to four weeks.

Ice Cream

Ice cream is made with milk or cream, sugar, and sometimes eggs, and it can be flavored with any number of ingredients. Harold McGee posits that "most good ice cream recipes produce a mix with a water content around 60 percent, a sugar content around 15 percent, and a milk-fat content between 10 percent—the minimum for commercial U.S. ice cream—and 20 percent."

Ice cream's character and consistency depends on the ingredients and techniques used to prepare it. Here are the most common types sold in U.S. grocery stores.

Philadelphia-style ice cream Also known as American or New York ice cream, Philadelphia-style ice cream is typically made without eggs, so the texture and color are usually light. Lightweight ice creams make for light, fluffy cocktails.

Custard This French style of ice cream that can include up to 12 egg yolks per quart—or a minimum of 1.6 percent egg yolk solids, according to the FDA. It has a smoother texture, lower fat content, and higher water level than egg-free ice cream. Custard is a good option for Midwestern-style boozy milkshakes—the lightweight ice cream integrates seamlessly with the other ingredients.

Gelato Churned at a much slower rate than American ice cream—hence the density of its texture—Italy's gelato has a higher percentage of milk and a lower percentage of cream and eggs (and sometimes no eggs). It is the richest and smoothest of the three most popular styles, often sold freshly churned instead of hardened like American ice cream. In Dana Cree's book *Hello, My Name Is Ice Cream,* she explains that pints labeled "gelato" in American grocery stores are not actually true to form because the designation isn't regulated. "Ask any gelato maker worth their salt, and they will insist to you that gelato is made fresh daily, never hardened," she adds. Gelato works well in affogatos and ice cream floats.

SOURCING

Because the art of mixing with ice cream is the same as making a great latte or cappuccino or cocktail—their quality depends on the ideal aeration and texture—the density, texture, and amount of air incorporated into the ice cream are key factors in deciding which style to use. Dana Cree recommends looking for ice creams that have a high fat content and short list of ingredients, with no whey (which adds a sandy texture and graham cracker flavor) and no calcium sulfate, which is typically used to firm up texture and reduce melting rates. "Good quality ice cream can be dense or light depending on the stylistic preference of the ice cream maker, but it will often list cream ahead of milk, and will list flavor inclusions by name or as extracts instead of 'natural flavor' or 'artificial flavor,'" she told me. "For a true measure of a brand's quality, pick up their vanilla and look at that list of ingredients; if they pay the price for real vanilla extract or beans, and not natural flavor, it's more likely to be made with good quality ingredients."

STORAGE

Ice cream is best kept as cold as possible to preserve its texture. Scrape all the ice cream from the sides of the container and smooth the top, then press a sheet of plastic wrap or parchment paper onto its surface before resealing the container to prevent it from absorbing odors from the rest of the freezer compartment or from drying out. Cree says this method helps prevent unwanted freezer burn.

Butter

Butter is churned cream, historically combined with salt for storage when cows stopped producing milk over the winter.

U.S. butter is between 80 and 82 percent butterfat, with the percentage of fat depending on manipulations that occur after churning. Annatto, a natural dye made from the pulp of fruit from the *Bixa orellana* tree, is often added seasonally for color when the cows aren't eating fresh grass.

Unsalted butter This is sometimes labeled "sweet cream butter" because the only ingredient is cream. Natural flavorings may also be added, so check the label before buying to avoid them.

Salted butter As the name suggests, this is sweet cream butter with salt added. The amount of salt in salted butter is not standardized, so if consistency matters, use unsalted butter, which you can salt to taste.

Cultured butter Like yogurt, cultured butter is made with cream that includes live cultures. When churned to 82 percent butterfat or higher, it is called European-style (here, the minimum is 80 percent). It has a more tangy flavor and richer texture than other butters. Use cultured butter to bring creamy lactic acidity to Monica Berg's Buttered Martini (page 104).

SOURCING

A cow's diet determines the quality and character of its milk, so terroir—the combination of growing conditions that give foods their distinct character, including the vegetation a cow forages upon and the cultural customs of its farmer—may be an inspiration for storytelling in cocktails. Because butter is less perishable than drinking-milk, it's exported from celebrated dairy regions like France, Ireland, or Norway (the latter is where Berg's original gin butter fat wash recipe originated).

STORAGE

Butter should be stored in foil in the coldest part of the fridge, as it will readily absorb the aromas of other wrappings. It can also be frozen to extend shelf life.

Yogurt

In *Spoiled,* Mendelson traces milk's journey back thousands of years to the cradle of prehistoric dairying in southeastern Europe and the Middle East, where she pointedly reminds readers that nobody had to "invent" yogurt: daytime temperatures during late spring and summer exceeded 95°F in "Yogurtistan," where ambient lactic-acid bacteria spontaneously colonized freshly drawn milk, transforming it into the thick and slightly tangy gel we know as yogurt. Many different sour milk preparations became important parts of those early herdspeople's diets thanks to lactic acid bacteria (LAB), which broke milk's lactose down into digestible sugars and acidulated it to a pH that warded off harmful pathogens.

Here are three popular styles of commercial yogurt currently found in many American grocery stores.

Traditional If a yogurt is labeled "yogurt" it's probably your traditional whole milk, low-fat, or nonfat variety.

Greek This has a thicker texture than "traditional" yogurt, and a more tart flavor. "Greek" yogurt contains no whey and does not need to be produced in Greece to use the classification.

Icelandic skyr Traditionally made from skim milk, skyr is thick and tart and does not contain whey, like Greek yogurt.

SOURCING

In recent years, health experts have posited that gut health is transformative for overall health, with prebiotics and probiotics playing key roles in the discussion. To take advantage, some companies add them; but they can change yogurt's acidity—and their health benefits remain contested—so it's best to avoid formulations that include them when making mixed drinks. You can always add sugar, fruit, or other microbes later if you'd like.

STORAGE

Keep yogurt covered in the fridge. It's ideally served cold, but not freezing, because when it freezes, the water crystallizes and the yogurt won't reconstitute uniformly.

Concentrated Milks

During the industrial revolution in North America and Western Europe, new technologies were developed that extended the shelf life of milk dramatically by condensing or dehydrating it, then distributing it powdered or concentrated in cans with sweeteners and other texturizing stabilizers. These products—evaporated milk and sweetened condensed milk—are shelf-stable, which is one of the main reasons they were used prolifically during times of war, and in parts of the world where fresh dairy is impractical.

For many people around the world—particularly billions living in tropical regions—this is the only milk available. In some Latin American and Asian countries, concentrated milks play a prominent role in beverages such as Coquito (page 108), Cà phê sữa đá (Vietnamese coffee), and Cha yen (Thai iced tea). During the postwar U.S. occupation of Japan, millions of pounds of nonfat dry milk—once used to feed soldiers—were sold as part of a school lunch program. Today, nonfat powdered dried milk continues to find its way "around the world as a mainstay of U.S. food policy and global trade," according to Mendelson.

Powdered milk also turns out to be a problematic driver of recurrent domestic surpluses of drinking-milk, which are taking a toll on farmers everywhere as oversupply drives prices down and leaves farmers with excess milk they cannot sell. "U.S. per capita annual consumption of fluid milk and cream peaked at 399 pounds in 1945 and has been declining ever since. Meanwhile, most years since 1980 have seen increases in total production," Mendelson explains in *Spoiled*. "As things now stand, chronic overproduction of milk is the single most serious problem of the industry and seems likely to remain so indefinitely."

Knowing how pervasive lactase-nonpersistence is globally, combined with an awareness that concentrated milks, which are made with surplus milk that farmers receive less money for, contributes to the excesses of the industrial dairy complex, I think bartenders from the global north should be careful to embrace them like the superfoods they must have seemed like to soldiers on the battlefields in the 20th century. With that said, denigrating concentrated milks widely enjoyed in desserts and beverages created by and for people who live outside the Global North is equally fraught.

Evaporated milk This viscous product is made by heating milk until 60 percent of the water is removed, then the remaining liquid is homogenized and heat-sterilized before canning, thus rendering the milk shelf-stable. Evaporated milk does have some natural sweetness (about 10 percent sugar by weight) although there is no sugar added during the production process. The color tends to be darker than condensed milk due to a lack of added sugar. Pablo Moix uses both evaporated and sweetened condensed milk in his Coquito recipe (page 108).

Sweetened condensed milk Like evaporated milk, sweetened condensed milk is made by heating milk until 60 percent of the water is removed. Then sugar is added so the concentration of sweetness reaches 55 percent, and the resulting reduced liquid is homogenized before packaging. Because the sugar helps stabilize the liquid, it doesn't need to be heat-sterilized like evaporated milk, which is why Harold McGee says the thick, shelf-stable fluid "has a milder, less 'cooked' flavor than evaporated milk, a lighter color, and the consistency of a thick syrup." And as the name suggests, the texture of condensed milk is more dense than evaporated milk.

Powdered milk This is milk that is first pasteurized at a high temperature, then dried via evaporation.

SOURCING

Concentrated milks are typically sold in the baking goods aisle of the grocery store. If you can't find adequate options at your local grocery store, ask a clerk to speak with the buyer about this, as they are a staple of many popular global cuisines.

STORING

Concentrated milk can be stored for years in a cool, dry place. Once opened, store it covered in the fridge and plan to use it up within a few weeks.

The environmental costs of industrial dairy farming are staggering. Every element of bringing milk from cows to market—from growing and harvesting the forage they eat, to milking, processing the milk, cleaning animals and facilities, and maintaining the integrity of the cold chain—is carried out on huge vertically integrated operations where water and energy needs are unimaginable. So is the havoc wreaked on local waterways, water tables, aquifers, and our airways due to the air pollution (methane) generated by the cows themselves.

In Greta Thunberg's *The Climate Book,* contributor Michael Clark writes that modern food systems "produce 30 percent of all greenhouse gas emissions, occupy 40 percent of Earth's land surface, use at least 70 percent of Earth's fresh water and are the leading driver of biodiversity loss and nutrient pollution." Dairy production contributes to every one of those categories as forests, grasslands, and savannahs are being cleared to create pastures, and waterways are diverted to irrigate the fields needed to raise cows for dairy and meat all over the world.

The human toll of dairy farming is similarly fraught. In the early 1970s, the rise of major agribusiness coincided with U.S. Secretary of Agriculture Earl Butz's "get big or get out" mantra, which urged farmers to focus on commodity crops versus diverse plantings. This changed the landscape of farming in America, and now the occupation is widely agreed to be one of the most physically and mentally grueling, with dairy farming being especially relentless for small to mid-sized operations. "One all-too-usual escape route is simply giving up and selling off the herd, often followed by selling off the land. Another is much darker," Mendelson writes in *Spoiled.*

A sizable post-hippie backlash against mass-produced food and factory farming in the past few decades has renewed interest in raw milk (milk that has not been pasteurized). Raw milk is prominently featured in many artisan cheeses, which were one of the first opportunities that provided alternatives to the commodity milk market, allowing farmers to begin changing the narrative around both milk and their personal fortunes. Now, many farmers sell milk—both raw and pasteurized—and other dairy products directly to artisanal cheese, yogurt, and butter producers, and to customers at farmer's markets, where they can set their own prices and sell through CSAs.

Note: In the absence of government oversight and regulation, consuming raw milk poses relative health risks.

Mendelson hopes that as demographics continue to shift in our country—and the ability to digest full-lactose milk goes from a majority condition to the minority—fermented milk can assume the central role that it had previously held in the earliest ages of dairying. She reassures that "this does not mean banishing drinking-milk from the table of anybody who likes and can digest full-lactose milk. It means demoting it from a uniquely—and falsely—privileged position and making it simply one option among many others that have never before reached Western consumers." I think bartenders can certainly get behind this.

KADAK SPICY CHAI
from Sana Javeri Kadri

The quality of the spices, sweeteners, tea, and milk used to bind the complex medley of flavors in chai is important. This recipe was adapted by Diaspora Co. founder Sana Javeri Kadri from the masala chai served at London's Dishoom (and shared in their eponymous book). Sana's adaptation involves blending a flavorful spice base before adding the milk and tea. She brings the mixture to a boil three times to create a luscious, creamy texture. While she prefers to make her chai with oat milk, I recipe-tested with whole milk because I prefer the platform it provides for her spices.

Use this spicy chai in the Masala Milky Tea Punch (page 102), or enjoy on its own. YIELDS 12 OUNCES

- ☐ 8 ounces filtered water
- ☐ 2.5g Baraka cardamom pods (12 to 14 pods)
- ☐ 2.5g (1 teaspoon) Aranya black peppercorns
- ☐ 1g (½ teaspoon) ground Makhir ginger
- ☐ 1.25g (½ teaspoon) Peni Miris ground Ceylon cinnamon

- ☐ 1.5g (½ teaspoon) Hariyali fennel seeds
- ☐ 0.5g Kandyan whole cloves (about 5)
- ☐ 4g (1 teaspoon) Madhur jaggery powder
- ☐ 8 ounces whole milk
- ☐ 5.5g (1 tablespoon) Chota Tingrai Assam broken pekoe tea

• CONTINUED •

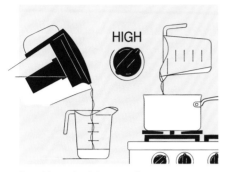

Pour the water into a medium saucepan and bring to a boil over high heat.

Meanwhile, measure the spices and jaggery.

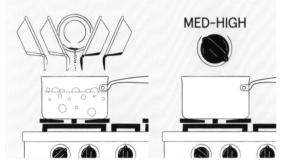

Add the spices and jaggery to the boiling water and reduce the heat to medium-high.

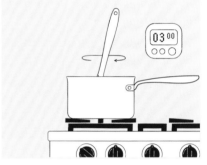

Simmer for 3 minutes, constantly stirring with a spatula to dissolve the jaggery.

Add the milk and the black tea and bring back to a boil.

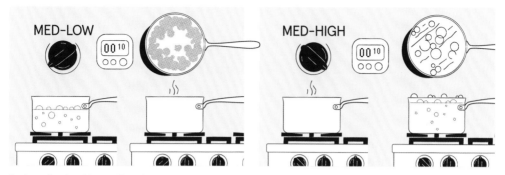

MED-LOW

00 10

MED-HIGH

00 10

Reduce the heat to medium-low, and simmer for 10 seconds.

Increase the heat again to medium-high and bring the mixture back up to a boil, 10 seconds.

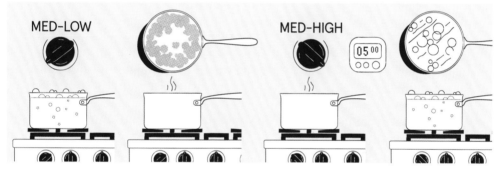

MED-LOW

MED-HIGH

05 00

Repeat the last 2 steps, bringing the mixture from a simmer to a boil for a third time, for a total of 5 minutes.

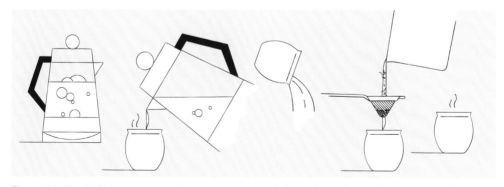

Fine-strain the chai into a prewarmed ceramic mug. The chai may be refrigerated for up to **2 DAYS** and then served over ice or reheated.

Dairy

93

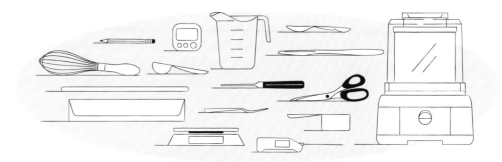

BARTENDER'S ICE CREAM

from Dana Cree

Dana Cree, co-founder of Chicago's Pretty Cool Ice Cream and author of *Hello, My Name Is Ice Cream,* developed this ice cream recipe to be used in mixed drinks. She describes it as "light, airy, and meant to disintegrate, unlocking its flaky ice crystals and releasing its creamy body into the liquid as it's shaken, or pulled apart by the bubbles of a carbonated beverage." The trick to achieving this fluffy texture is to withhold the cream from the early stages of the recipe. By adding it slowly at the end, while the ice cream machine is running, it whips instantly, adding air in the process.

Use Dana's ice cream in the Wondermint Malted (page 106), or in other classic ice cream drinks like the Grasshopper, Pink Squirrel, Golden Cadillac, or Brandy Alexander. YIELDS ABOUT 4½ CUPS

☐ 150g (¾ cup) white cane sugar
☐ 20g (2 tablespoons) nonfat milk powder
☐ 3g (½ teaspoon) kosher salt
☐ 1 (4.5g) whole vanilla bean
☐ 15g (1½ tablespoons) cornstarch

☐ 15 ounces whole milk
☐ 50g (2½ tablespoons) glucose syrup
☐ 425g (3 cups) ice cubes
☐ 14 ounces heavy whipping cream

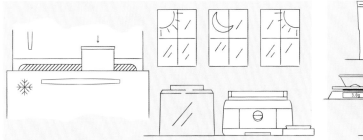

Chill the bowl of the ice cream maker in the freezer overnight, or at least 12 hours before you start making the ice cream.

In a small bowl, combine the sugar, milk powder, and salt.

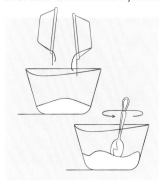

Stir to combine.

Split the vanilla bean with a knife and scrape out the seeds, retaining all parts.

In a separate bowl, combine the cornstarch and 2 tablespoons of the milk.

Whisk the cornstarch and milk into a slurry.

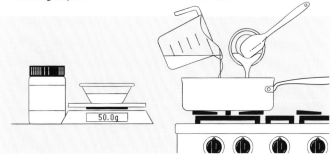

In a heavy-bottomed medium saucepan, add the glucose syrup and remaining 1¾ cups milk together.

· CONTINUED ·

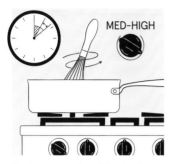

Heat over medium-high heat, whisking constantly, until the glucose syrup dissolves and the milk starts to simmer, 5 to 8 minutes.

When it reaches 195°F, add the sugar mixture and whisk to combine.

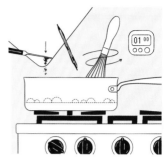

Add the vanilla pod and seeds and continue whisking until the mixture comes to a boil, about 1 minute.

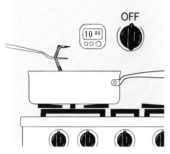

Turn off the heat and let sit for 10 minutes. Remove the vanilla pod and discard.

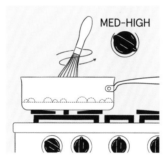

Over medium-high heat, bring the milk mixture back to a boil, whisking constantly.

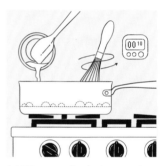

Add the cornstarch slurry and continue whisking until the mixture thickens and bubbles, about 10 seconds.

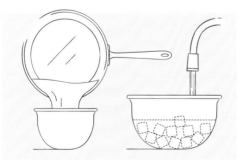

Pour the hot mixture into a shallow metal bowl. Fill a large metal bowl with ice cubes and add enough water to come up to the top of the ice.

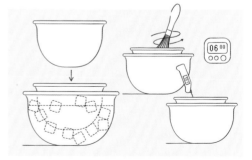

Place the bowl with the milk mixture into the ice bath and whisk until the mixture has cooled down to 50°F, about 6 minutes.

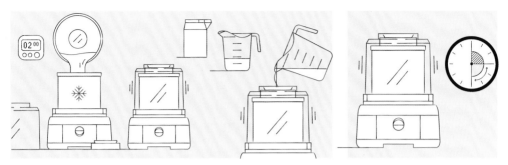

Add the cooled mixture to the ice cream maker and turn the maker on. After 2 minutes, slowly pour in the cream.

Continue to churn until the ice cream is the texture of soft serve, between 15 and 30 minutes.

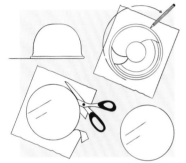

Trace the outline of a freezer-safe storage bowl over a piece of parchment paper. Cut the pattern out and set aside.

Transfer the ice cream to the freezer-safe bowl with a spatula. Press the parchment paper directly on the surface of the ice cream to prevent ice crystals from forming.

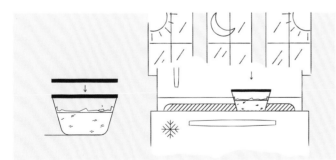

Cover the bowl with a tight-fitting lid and freeze for at least 8 hours; preferably overnight.

Store, covered, in the freezer for up to 3 WEEKS.

YOGURT

from Mony Bunni

Mony Bunni grew up with homemade yogurt. When I asked her about it, she told me she didn't have a written recipe for it, so she documented her mother Samia's and aunt Janette's process. "As a first-generation Arab American, I believe food was one of the main ways we kept connected to our homeland and traditions," she says. "One of those traditions was making homemade yogurt, labneh, and cheese." Use a high-quality whole milk yogurt as your starter (she prefers Kalona SuperNatural), then "retain a portion of your homemade yogurt as the starter for the next batch. Continue to do this for future batches," she advises.

Use Mony's yogurt to make her Cultural Consumption (page 100). **YIELDS 36 OUNCES (4½ CUPS)**

☐ 1 quart whole milk

☐ 150g (⅔ cup) plain whole-milk yogurt

Pour the milk into a Dutch oven.

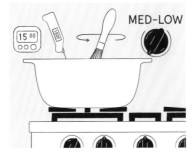

Bring to a simmer over medium-low heat, whisking constantly, until the milk reaches 180°F, around 15 minutes.

Turn the heat off and let the milk cool to 110°F, whisking intermittently, around 30 minutes.

Add the yogurt to a large bowl.

Add the warm milk to the bowl, 1 ladle at a time, whisking to combine.

Transfer the mixture to 3 pint-sized mason jars. Seal tightly.

Fill an 18-liter sous vide tank three-quarters of the way with water. Using an immersion circulator, heat the water to 95°F.

Submerge the jars in the water, cover the tank, and heat for at least 12 hours, until the yogurt is firm and has a layer of cultured water floating in the tops of the jars.

Remove the jars from the tank, let cool briefly, then store, still covered, in the fridge for up to 1 MONTH.

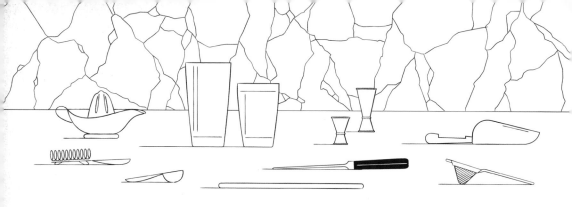

CULTURAL CONSUMPTION

by Mony Bunni

This recipe is inspired by two of Mony Bunni's favorite uses for homemade yogurt: laban ayran, a salted yogurt drink consumed throughout the Arabic-speaking world; and kh'yar bi laban, a cucumber-yogurt-mint sauce that's often part of the mezze portion of meals. "In addition to backing up the mineral notes of the tequila," says Mony, who took first place in Speed Rack's national competition in 2017, "the grassy green banana notes of the rhum agricole complement the cooling green notes of the cucumber and mint." **YIELDS 1 SERVING**

☐ 1½ ounces ElVelo blanco tequila

☐ 1 ounce (2 tablespoons) Yogurt (page 98)

☐ 1 ounce Cucumber-Mint Cordial (page 34)

☐ ½ ounce Rhum J.M. Blanc rum (80 proof)

☐ ½ ounce lime juice

☐ Ice cubes

☐ 1 mint leaf, for garnish

Add the tequila, yogurt, cordial, rum, and lime juice to a Boston shaker. Shake without ice. Then, add a scoop of ice cubes and shake again. Double-strain through a Hawthorne and a fine-mesh strainer into a chilled coupe. Garnish with a mint leaf, gently clapped to release its aroma.

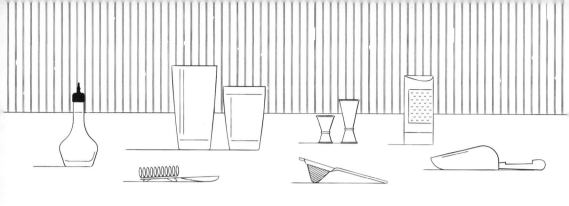

MASALA MILKY TEA PUNCH

by Jim Meehan

For the opening menu at PDT Hong Kong in the winter of 2018, bartender Adam Schmidt and I created a riff on the classic New Orleans milk punch called the Milky Tea Punch, prepared with Hong Kong's popular milky tea (black tea sweetened with condensed milk). I've updated the recipe here, by substituting Sana Javeri Kadri's Kadak Spicy Chai in place of the Hong Kong milky tea. The chai maintains the tannin and sweetness of the original recipe but adds a more complex spice component. YIELDS 1 SERVING

- ☐ 1½ ounces Kadak Spicy Chai (page 91), chilled
- ☐ 1 ounce Ron Zacapa No. 23 rum
- ☐ 1 ounce Hine V.S.O.P. Cognac
- ☐ ½ ounce Demerara Syrup (page 337)
- ☐ 1 large egg
- ☐ Dash of Angostura bitters
- ☐ Ice cubes
- ☐ Nutmeg, freshly grated, for garnish

Add the chai, rum, Cognac, syrup, egg, and bitters to a Boston shaker. Shake without ice cubes, then add a scoop of ice cubes and shake again. Double-strain through a Hawthorne and a fine-mesh strainer into a chilled tea cup. Garnish with the freshly grated nutmeg.

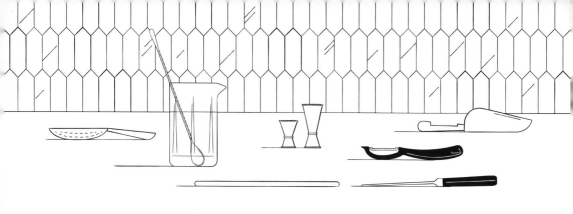

BUTTERED MARTINI

by Monica Berg

Monica Berg co-owns Tayēr + Elementary with Alex Kratena in London. She created this recipe in 2016 for Credo, a restaurant in Trondheim, Norway, led by chef Heidi Bjerkan, which Monica hails as her favorite farm-to-table restaurant in the world. The use of butter from a nearby Norwegian dairy farm in her Martini is "the ultimate expression of the ecology of drinking," she says. "My aim was to create the smoothest, gentlest version of the drink, which would allow guests to test out a Martini without being overpowered by its strength." YIELDS 1 SERVING

- ☐ 2 ounces Butter-Washed Gin (page 347)
- ☐ ½ ounce Martini bianco vermouth
- ☐ Ice cubes
- ☐ 1 lemon peel, for garnish

Add the gin and vermouth to a chilled mixing glass. Add a scoop of ice cubes. Stir and strain into a chilled martini glass. Garnish with a lemon twist.

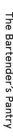

WONDERMINT MALTED

by Christopher Marty

Christopher Marty, the co-owner of Chicago bar Best Intentions, created this recipe for a 2014 *Chicago Reader* spring cocktail competition (which he won). At the bar, he serves the drink with high-butterfat dairy from Fox Valley Farms. Instead of blending each order individually, Christopher uses a Taylor 428 frozen drink machine that produces a consistent *stand-up-the-straw* viscosity at high volume. Since most of us can't afford this machine or source the high-butterfat dairy that's available to Christopher in the Midwest, ice cream and a blender will suffice. **YIELDS FOUR 13-OUNCE SERVINGS**

- ☐ 300g (2 cups) crushed ice
- ☐ 70g (½ cup) Carnation malted milk powder
- ☐ 700g (3½ cups) Bartender's Ice Cream (page 94)
- ☐ 8 ounces Death's Door Wondermint schnapps
- ☐ 4 ounces Broker's gin
- ☐ 3 ounces Luxardo Angioletto hazelnut liqueur
- ☐ 3 ounces heavy whipping cream
- ☐ 1 drop green food coloring
- ☐ 8 dashes acid phosphate
- ☐ 4 mint sprigs, for garnish

Add the crushed ice, malt powder, and ice cream into a blender pitcher, then add the spirits, cream, food coloring, and acid phosphate. Pulse 2 or 3 times to homogenize the mixture, then use medium and then high speed to whip the mixture into stiff peaks, about 1 minute. Pour into chilled sundae glasses. Garnish each glass with a mint sprig and serve with a straw.

COQUITO

from Pablo Moix

For Pablo Moix, a Los Angeles–based restaurateur and bar owner, Coquito symbolizes happiness, good times, and "Puerto Rican family reunions during the Christmas season," he says. "Each recipe is passed along from one generation to the next, who make their own twist upon the family formula." This recipe is an adaptation of the Coquito served at his wife Roxanna's family holiday gatherings.

YIELDS FIVE 4½-OUNCE SERVINGS

- ☐ 10 ounces Carnation evaporated milk
- ☐ 3 ounces Nestle La Lechera sweetened condensed milk
- ☐ 6 ounces Cream of Coconut (page 160)
- ☐ 20g (4 teaspoons) Coquito "Tea" Infusion (page 354)
- ☐ 4 ounces Bacardi Superior rum
- ☐ 22g (four 4-inch quills) Cassia (Indonesian or Vietnamese) cinnamon

Add the evaporated milk, condensed milk, and cream of coconut to a medium saucepan. Over low heat, whisk the mixture to integrate and warm the ingredients, about 2 minutes. Add the infusion and rum, and continue to whisk over low heat for 2 minutes to prevent the milk from curdling. Turn off the heat and let cool to room temperature, approximately 45 minutes.

Transfer to a large jar, add the 4 cinnamon quills, cover, and store in the fridge for up to 2 weeks.

Serve chilled, neat, in stemless wine glasses, with no garnish.

Grains & Nuts

Whole grains have long been used to make beer, saké, and spirits such as whiskey and shochu. Nuts are almost nowhere to be found in mixed-drinks history, beyond bowls filled with free snacks to stimulate thirst and via orgeat—which isn't typically formulated with actual almonds unless it is housemade (see page 118). Outside of these popular applications, American bartenders have only recently started to harness the savory qualities of toasted grains and nuts in syrups and infusions. Nuts and seeds are also used as thickening agents in a number of global cuisines, which, when applied behind the bar, bring creamy full-bodied mouthfeel to preparations such as the sunflower seeds in Lydia Parsley's Oat Milk (page 124) and the cashews in Yana Volfson's Cashew Horchata (page 126).

Grains and nuts are both types of seed—that is, "structures by which plants create a new generation of their kind," writes Harold McGee in *On Food and Cooking*. "Seeds gave early humans both the nourishment and the inspiration to begin to shape the natural world to their own needs. Ten thousand turbulent years of civilization have unfolded from the seed's pale repose."

In beverage history, grains and nuts served a functional purpose before they became prized for flavor. From medieval times until about the nineteenth century, when modern water-treatment facilities were invented, people purified water with grains to make a low-proof ferment (1–3 percent alcohol by volume) called "small beer." Some historians suggest that this was done to transform bacteria-riddled water into something potable, while other sources suggest it was done simply to create a tasty source of sustenance. This drink was "brewed both domestically and by commercial brewers, was drunk throughout the day at meals by all classes and ages of the population," writes Ray Anderson in *The Oxford Companion to Spirits & Cocktails*. The origins of chicha morada (corn), kvass (rye), and orgeat (almonds) are comparable to small beer.

Seeds continue to nourish and captivate us today, as major crops like corn, wheat, and soy are grown, shipped, consumed, and used in innovative and traditional food and beverages enjoyed around the world. "From our morning coffee and bagel to the cotton in our clothes and the cup of cocoa we might drink before bed, seeds surround us all day long," writes Thor Hanson in *The Triumph of Seeds*. "They are quite literally the staff of life, the basis of diets, economies, and lifestyles around the globe."

The categorization of seeds can be confusing. Grains grow into grasses like wheat, oats, and rice; nuts grow into trees like walnut and pecan; and legumes like beans are also seeds. The generic term *seed* can apply to any number of plants, including flowers, herbs, and vegetables. For this chapter, I focus on grains and nuts only, since they are the most common seeds used in beverages. One could also employ pumpkin seeds, sesame seeds, and sunflower seeds to make syrups, alternatives to dairy-based milk, and orgeat—in those cases, prepare them the same way you would grains and nuts: buy fresh, store properly, and toast before infusing to coax out delightful umami flavors. Several other seeds, like coffee, coconut, anise, cardamom, coriander, and nutmeg, are featured elsewhere in the book, based on how they are used in praxis and not how they are categorized.

Grains

The word *grain* is often defined as a seed from a cereal crop, one of several types of grasses cultivated by humans. Roxana Jullapat, author of *Mother Grains: Recipes for the Grain Revolution,* names eight that serve as foundational to cooking, à la Escoffier's "mother sauces": barley, buckwheat, corn, oats, rice, rye, sorghum, and wheat. These grains are made up of three layers: bran, endosperm, and germ. When all components are intact, it is a "whole" grain. When any are removed, the grain becomes "refined," which typically extends shelf life. Refinement diminishes nutritional value and flavor quality.

Here are some of the most relevant grains used in mixed drinks.

Oats Oats are commonly used to make oat "milk" as an alternative to dairy. Commercial oat milks are made with milled oats combined with water to yield a slurry-like suspension that is heated and sometimes mixed with enzymes to break the starches down into smaller components. The solids are strained out, and the "milk" is sometimes pasteurized and homogenized before packaging. At home, many folks take the less laborious route of soaking oats in water, which is what Lydia Parsley does with her recipe (see page 124).

Corn Most of us are familiar with corn from the fresh ears that appear at farmer's markets in the height of summer, but there are multiple varieties: sweet corn, which is edible off the cob; dent corn (also known as field corn), used as livestock feed and for producing ethanol; and flint corn, a low-moisture, tough-textured corn (hence the name) with fewer soft starches, typically used to make cornmeal, flour, masa, and grits. Corn is a staple ingredient in Peruvian Chicha Morada (page 128) and in Mexican preparations like atole and Champurrado (page 58).

Barley This mildly flavored, chewy grain is processed to bake bread, infused into hot liquid as an infusion (such as boricha in Korea and mugicha in Japan), or malted to serve as the base for many whiskies. Two forms of barley—pearl and hulled—are widely available. For the former, the husk and bran layers are polished off the seed, so it is not a whole grain anymore (and this type cooks quickly). The latter is less processed—the outer husk is simply removed, leaving the bran and the seed intact—so it offers more flavor and nutritional value. Boricha cold brew appears in the Pomme and Circumstance (page 36).

Rice As a foodstuff and the base for fermented beverages like saké and distilled beverages like shochu, rice comes in over 120,000 varieties. Each is classified by size (long, medium, and short grain) and has unique texture and aromatics, so choose a variety based on its distinctive characteristics. For example, Indian basmati rice and jasmine rice have some of the same aromatics as pandan, so they pair well together. Jasmine rice brings an ethereal floral note to the Cashew Horchata (page 126), and roasted, popped brown rice is used to flavor genmaicha, a Japanese green tea that brings a savory note to recipes like the Riot Act (page 140).

Buckwheat A pseudo-grain—which means it "comes from a leafy flowering bush or shrub rather than a grass," Roxana Jullapat explains—buckwheat is also used to make infusions like memilcha in Korea, sobacha in Japan, and kuqiaocha in China. It is naturally gluten free. When toasted and infused in syrups or spirits (like in the apple brandy infusion used in the Thunderbird on page 138), it brings an aromatic nutty quality to drinks.

SOURCING

Before bread baking was commercialized in the twentieth century, many towns had their own grist mills, where recently harvested grains were freshly ground. Today, most consumers only have access to refined grains that have sat on a grocery shelf for far longer than they should. If whole grains aren't available locally, they can be mail ordered from reputable suppliers such as Anson Mills, Camas Country Mill, and Grist & Toll.

STORAGE

Nuts, seeds, and whole grains with the germ and endosperm intact (and thus their volatile oils) are perishable if stored at room temperature. They should be labeled, dated at the time of purchase, and stored in a cool, dark, dry environment in an airtight container. In the pantry, grains can be kept for up to

Grains & Nuts

six months; in the freezer, uncooked grains will last for up to a year. In *Grist,* Michigan chef Abra Berens says she keeps seeds in jars on her pantry shelf so she can "see what I have and remember to be excited about using them."

PREPARATION

"Grains are hard, dry seeds, and usually need both water and heat to make them soft enough to eat with pleasure," writes Harold McGee in *Keys to Good Cooking*. The same goes for preparing grains for use in cocktail applications: soaking grains is the first step toward making non-dairy "milks," syrups, and infusions.

TOOLS

To make syrups and infusions with grains, I recommend using a high-powered professional blender, a nut-milk bag to extract and filter liquid from solids, and a fine-mesh strainer. Most grains are toasted first to coax out their savoriness. Do this in the oven or in a skillet, making sure the temperature is low and the grains are agitated often so they don't burn.

Allergy note: The gluten protein in wheat, barley, and rye can trigger harmful reactions in people with celiac disease.

Nuts

Nuts are oil-rich, edible seeds nestled inside a hard exterior shell. "The role of nuts in the North American and European vegan diet is vital, for they offer a delectable source of protein, minerals, and other nutrients; they provide umami, or the savory sensation that also comes from meat; and they thicken in a similar way to flour and butter," writes Susan Herrmann Loomis in *Nuts in the Kitchen*. Nuts are often partially dried before shipment to the grocery store because their inherent moisture is susceptible to mold. Many producers roast and salt nuts to prepare them to be served as snacks.

You can use almost any commercially available nut in cocktail applications. One of the most important considerations is fat content; because the core of the nut is so rich in oil, this translates to a thick, creamy texture when the nut is ground into a paste (nut butter) or emulsified with liquid to create a syrup or nut milk. A rule of thumb is that the more oil, the creamier the texture of its "milk." The following are nuts commonly used in beverages, arranged from lowest to highest fat content.

Cashews Originally from the Amazon region, cashews are about 44 percent fat and have a high starch content, which means they are good for thickening syrups. The juice of the cashew apple (the stem connected to the nut, which looks kind of like a bell pepper) is sometimes used to make feni, an Indian spirit, or is sold as fruit juice in countries like India, Brazil, and Thailand. Yana Volfson uses the nut to bring smoothness and slight acidity to her unique version of horchata (see page 126).

Pistachios Like cashews, pistachios are 44 percent fat. Some bartenders use the nut to make orgeat alternatives, and the nuts have found a home in lattes and matcha drinks in the form of syrup. The vibrant green color comes from chlorophyll; if used in a drink for that purpose, Harold McGee recommends toasting the nuts at low temperatures to minimize color deterioration.

Almonds Native to the Mediterranean, sweet almonds (49 percent fat) are used to make orgeat (see Sean Hoard and Daniel Shoemaker's recipe on page 118), and sometimes amaretto, an Italian liqueur. Bitter almonds and stone fruit pits generate the aroma of almond extract, but also toxic cyanide, so work with them cautiously, using expert guidance. Today, California supplies almost 80 percent of the world's almonds, which have a high water footprint, so it's worth considering alternatives.

Walnuts Most mixologists know walnuts from nocino, the Italian liqueur prepared from unripe, green walnuts. Persian walnuts (also called English walnuts) are easy to find in stores and online, while black walnuts aren't as widely cultivated—they impart a more earthy flavor and have the same amount of fat (65 percent). Infuse walnuts in syrups or aged whiskey or brandy; the tannins in the nuts bring depth of flavor and balance some of the richness of the spirits.

SOURCING

Buy raw nuts and seeds—that is, "untoasted, unsalted, the way nature made it," writes Susan Loomis. You can toast or salt to your heart's desire, but starting with an unadulterated nut gives you control of those elements. Also look for signs of freshness—vacuum-sealed packages preserve oils better than bulk bins. "When buying fresh nuts, look for an opaque, off-white interior," adds Harold McGee in *On Food and Cooking*. "Any translucency, or darkening is a sign that the cells are damaged, oil has been released, and rancidity is developing."

Keep in mind that nuts require different amounts of water to thrive, so sustainability should be a consideration. Claire Sprouse, who has done extensive sustainability research, explains: "It takes about 1 gallon of water to make an almond, 4.9 gallons to make a walnut, but only three-quarters of a gallon to make a pistachio. How can we reconsider a traditional ingredient like orgeat and find another way to make it with these things in mind? It should be inspiring, not limiting."

STORAGE

"The same high oil content that makes nuts nutritious and delicious also makes them much more fragile than grains and legumes," warns McGee, which is why, when exposed to light, heat, and moisture, nuts will go stale. Store nuts in the freezer, if possible. If not, shelled nuts should be stored in a cool, dark place and unshelled nuts in the refrigerator. Use airtight vessels like glass jars or vacuum-sealed bags. Label with the date and store for up to six months.

PREPARATION

Most nuts are toasted before use in drinks to bring out their inherently savory qualities. "Dry heat removes moisture from nuts and seeds, crisps them, and creates characteristic nutty flavors as they cook in their own or added oil," according to Harold McGee in *Keys to Good Cooking*. "For the best flavor, heat nuts and seeds until the interior turns golden brown, and just before serving. Cooked nuts lose flavor within a day or two and then become stale and rancid."

TOOLS

If you're making nut milk, I recommend using a high-powered professional blender, nut-milk bag to extract and filter the "milk" from solids, and a fine-mesh strainer.

Allergy note: Nuts can cause allergic reactions, the most severe being anaphylactic shock, which can be fatal.

Today, the U.S. grain industry focuses mostly on bulk production for animal feed and ethanol production. Instead of growing for nutrition and taste, massive industrial farms cultivate monocrops, often with varieties that have been genetically modified to grow in particular regions, so they require pesticides and herbicides to thrive. This makes the plants vulnerable to blight (look up the way phylloxera wiped out vitis vinifera crops in the late nineteenth century, creating lasting problems in the wine industry) and depletes the soil.

Thankfully, producers like Glenn Roberts of Anson Mills are working to resuscitate a pre-industrial, anti-monoculture mentality, cultivating overlooked and undervalued heirloom varieties and breeding plants with flavor as his North Star. As consumers, we can embrace and explore a broader swath of grains from producers like this; examples include sorghum, millet, farro, and pseudo-grains like buckwheat, amaranth, and quinoa. We can learn how to prepare them in new drinks and promote more crop diversity.

Small gestures like this might seem microcosmic, but every buying decision has the potential to create ever-larger waves as more people make their preferences known. "Farmers, producers, and retailers are incredibly smart and adaptable, as we've seen," writes Abra Berens in *Grist*. "Give them the financial incentive they need to make the change you want to see, and tell the elected official who represents you to do the same. There's no more delicious activism than food activism—and no sovereignty can come without food sovereignty."

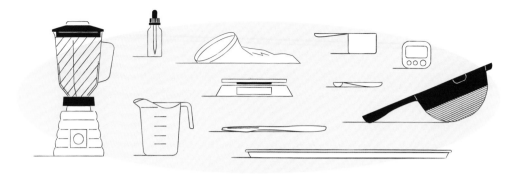

ORGEAT

from Sean Hoard and Daniel Shoemaker

"When I was training to tend bar at PDT, my colleague David Slape described orgeat as sweetened and slightly aromatized almond milk. That always stuck with me," says Commissary PDX co-owner Sean Hoard. "This recipe is just that: almond milk sweetened with sugar and aromatized with orange blossom water." When he and partner Daniel Shoemaker were developing this recipe, the duo wanted to create a syrup sturdy enough to stand up in a Mai Tai but nuanced enough for a Japanese cocktail. "To cover a wide spectrum, the focus had to be on the toasted almond flavor, not the aromatics or the sweetener."

Use this in Sean Hoard's Windowsill Spritz (page 172). YIELDS 30 OUNCES

☐ 300g (2½ cups) slivered almonds
☐ 24 ounces filtered water, cold
☐ 560g (3 cups) superfine sugar

☐ 1.5g (¼ teaspoon) kosher salt
☐ 5 drops orange flower water

TOAST THE ALMONDS

Preheat the oven to 315°F. Spread the almonds on a baking sheet in a single layer.

Toast the almonds in the oven until fragrant and golden in color, about 13 minutes.

BLANCH THE ALMONDS

While still warm, pour the almonds into a large bowl and add water. Let the almonds sit for 30 minutes.

Pour the almond water through a fine-mesh strainer, reserving both the almonds and the blanching water.

PREPARE THE ORGEAT

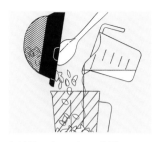

Add the almonds and 1¼ cups of the blanching water to a blender.

Blend until the mixture is the texture of wet sand, about 30 seconds.

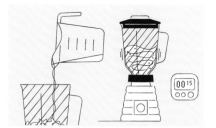

Add the remaining water to the blender and stir with a spatula. Blend again until the mixture is smoother, the texture of wet cement, around 15 seconds.

• CONTINUED •

Grains & Nuts

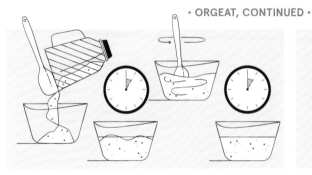

Pour the contents of the blender into a large bowl and let sit for 2 hours, stirring it occasionally to break up any clumps.

After 2 hours, stir the mixture thoroughly one more time.

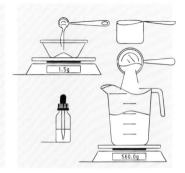

Strain the mixture through a fine-mesh strainer lined with a nut milk bag into another large bowl.

Squeeze the nut milk bag to extract as much liquid as possible. Compost the solids.

Measure the superfine sugar, salt, and orange flower water.

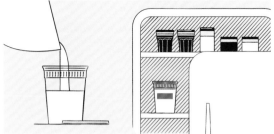

Add the superfine sugar, salt, and orange flower water to the almond milk. Stir until the sugar and salt dissolve.

Store the orgeat, covered, in a nonreactive container in the fridge for up to 1 MONTH.

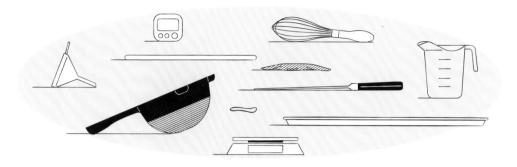

BORODINSKY RYE KVASS

from Bonnie Morales

Bonnie Morales, chef and co-owner of Kachka, in Portland, Oregon, didn't appreciate kvass, a low-ABV fermented drink made with bread, until she tried some traditionally brewed versions in the former Soviet republics. "Kvass was traditionally prepared to use up old bread scraps so nothing went to waste." Her preferred brew is made with Borodinsky rye bread, "a common bread for people to have on hand in the places where kvass is made." While her kvass can be bottled and stored for months in the fridge, Bonnie prefers it on the third day, before all the sugar is converted to alcohol.

Use this in the Castle on a Cloud (page 130). YIELDS 30 OUNCES

- ☐ 170g Borodinsky sourdough rye bread (or similar dark rye)
- ☐ 48 ounces filtered water
- ☐ 40g (3 tablespoons) white cane sugar
- ☐ 8g golden raisins (about 12)
- ☐ 1.5g (1 tablespoon) active dry yeast

• CONTINUED •

Preheat the oven to 350°F.

Cut the bread into ¼-inch slices and set them on a baking sheet.

Toast until crisp, around 20 minutes. Check often to make sure they don't burn.

Place the toast in a large bowl.

Bring 24 ounces (3 cups) of water to a boil.

Pour the hot water over the toasted bread slices.

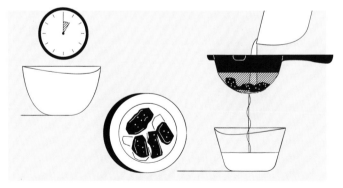

Let the toasted bread sit for 1 hour. Then strain the bread water through a fine-mesh strainer into another large bowl. Reserve the water and soggy bread.

Place the soggy bread back into the first large bowl.

Bring another 24 ounces (3 cups) of water to a boil.

Pour the hot water over the soggy bread and let sit for another hour.

Strain the bread water through the fine-mesh strainer into the bowl holding the already-steeped water. Compost the soggy bread.

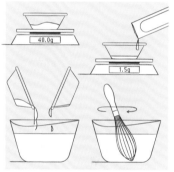

Add the yeast and sugar to the bowl of water and stir to dissolve.

Cover with cheesecloth and let sit at room temperature for at least 8 hours or overnight.

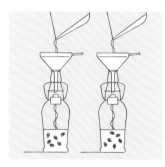

Add 6 raisins to each of 2 flip-top pint bottles. Decant 15 ounces of the kvass into each bottle.

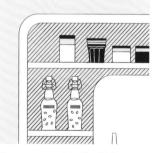

Store, covered, in the fridge, burping the bottles daily, until fermentation is complete.

OAT MILK

from Lydia Parsley

Most commercial oat milk is relatively unremarkable, but with the aromatics of the spices, and the sunflower seeds and dates included for texture, this recipe is anything but. Lydia Parsley (whom I worked with at PDT many moons ago) developed this for a Portland coffee shop in 2019 as part of their raw, plant-based milk offerings. With a nice round mouthfeel—in part, thanks to the sunflower lecithin that serves as a natural emulsifier—this oat milk is great to drink on its own and adds complexity to mixed drinks.

Use in the Dragonfly (page 136). YIELDS 28 OUNCES

- ☐ 85g (⅔ cup) raw sunflower seeds
- ☐ 32 ounces filtered water
- ☐ 85g (¾ cup) old-fashioned rolled oats
- ☐ 2 (42g) pitted dates
- ☐ 0.5g (¼ teaspoon) ground Ceylon cinnamon
- ☐ 0.5g (¼ teaspoon) ground nutmeg
- ☐ 0.5g (¼ teaspoon) sea salt

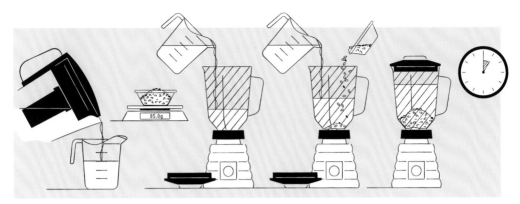

Add the sunflower seeds and water to a blender and let soak for 1 hour.

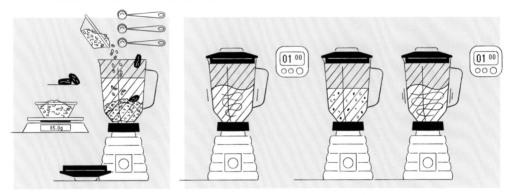

Add the oats, dates, cinnamon, nutmeg, and salt to the blender.

Blend on low for 1 minute, then on high for 1 more minute.

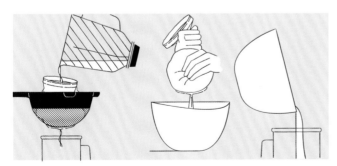

Strain the mixture through a fine-mesh strainer lined with a nut milk bag. Squeeze the nut milk bag to extract as much liquid as possible. (Lydia retains the muesli-like solids for breakfast.)

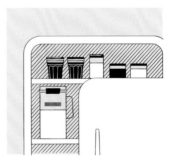

Store the oat milk, covered, in a nonreactive container in the fridge for up to 1 WEEK.

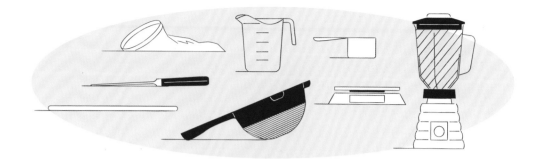

CASHEW HORCHATA

from Yana Volfson

As beverage director for Enrique Olvera's restaurants, Yana Volfson incorporated traditional ingredients from Mexico for her menus. She says horchata is commonly made with rice or condensed milk, canela (Ceylon cinnamon), piloncillo, and water. Her addition of cashews was something that came to mind in lieu of using canned ingredients. "By adding cashews, you create a silkier texture because of the fat content. The cashew nut also offers a hint of acidity, which makes this version taste lighter and more doughy," she says.

Use this in her Arroz con Rum (page 134), or drink it over ice. YIELDS 28 OUNCES

☐ 24 ounces filtered water
☐ 220g (1 cup) brown jasmine rice
☐ 85g (⅔ cup) cashews

☐ 39g piloncillo, broken into pieces (see page 22)
☐ 4.5g (one 3-inch quill) Ceylon (canela) cinnamon

Add the water, rice, cashews, piloncillo, and cinnamon to a nonreactive container.

Cover the container, and place in the fridge for 12 hours.

Transfer the mixture to a blender and blend until smooth, in batches if need be.

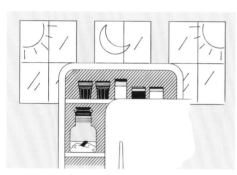

Strain through a fine-mesh strainer lined with a nut milk bag.

Squeeze the nut milk bag to extract as much liquid as possible. Compost the solids.

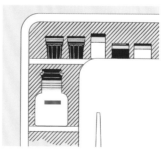

Store the horchata, covered, in a nonreactive container in the fridge for up to 3 DAYS.

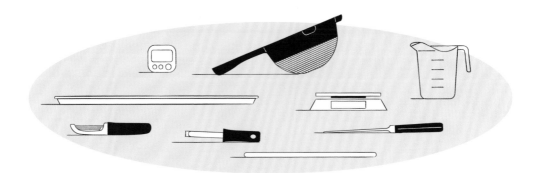

CHICHA MORADA

from Erik Ramirez

Chicha morada typically refers to a lightly fermented beverage from the Andean regions of Peru, but today the purple-corn drink is often made as an alcohol-free infusion. "I guess it could be called the iced tea of Peru," says Erik Ramirez, the chef and owner of Llama Inn and Llama San, in New York City. As Ramirez, who grew up drinking his grandmother's version, explains, "It spans many generations," adding how he introduced a few personal touches to the version he serves at the restaurant. "For example, in Peru they use the peel of the pineapple and throw in whole apples, while I find the flavor more consistent if you use the meat of the fruit only. Little things like that, nothing too major."

Serve this on ice (with or without soda) as a refreshing cooler, or mix it into the Llama del Rey (page 132). **YIELDS 24 OUNCES**

- ☐ 425g (15-ounce bag) dried maiz morado (purple corn)
- ☐ 2 small (350g) Granny Smith apples
- ☐ ½ small (500g) pineapple
- ☐ 13.5g (three 3-inch quills) Ceylon (canela) cinnamon
- ☐ 1g whole cloves (about 14)
- ☐ 40 ounces filtered water

Separate the kernels from the cobs and compost the cobs.

Peel, core, seed, and quarter the apples.

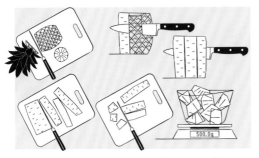

Peel and quarter the pineapple (do not core). Cut half the pineapple into smaller pieces and reserve the other half for another use.

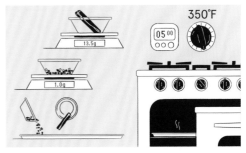

Place the cinnamon and cloves on a baking sheet and toast in a 350°F oven until fragrant, about 5 minutes.

Add the toasted spices, corn kernels, apples, pineapple, and water to a large saucepan.

Simmer over low heat, partially covered, for 2 hours. Remove from heat and let sit, covered, overnight.

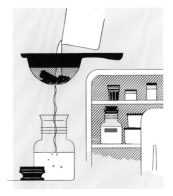

Fine-strain the mixture into a nonreactive container, then cover and store in the refrigerator for up to 1 WEEK.

Grains & Nuts

CASTLE ON A CLOUD

by Maria Davidoff

Bartender Maria Davidoff created this cocktail while working at Kachka in Portland, Oregon. "I wanted to make a twist on a flip that spoke to my heritage—my family immigrated to the United States from Russia in 1995. We are a big family that believes it's important to stay connected with our heritage through food," she says. "Every Russian kid drinks kvass. It's basically Russia's Coca-Cola. The other ingredients are classic flavors of Soviet culture and complement the rich rye flavors of the kvass nicely." **YIELDS 1 SERVING**

☐ 1 ounce Krambambulya (page 349)
☐ 1 ounce Becherovka herbal liqueur
☐ ¼ ounce lemon juice
☐ ¼ ounce Demerara Syrup (page 337)
☐ 2 dashes Angostura bitters
☐ Large egg white
☐ Ice cubes
☐ 2 ounces Borodinsky Rye Kvass (page 121), chilled
☐ Lemon peel, for garnish

Add the Krambambulya, herbal bitters, lemon juice, syrup, bitters, and egg white to a Boston shaker. Shake without ice, then add a scoop of ice cubes and shake again. Add the kvass to the shaker, then double-strain through a Hawthorne and a fine-mesh strainer into a chilled stakan glass. Garnish with a lemon twist and serve with a straw.

LLAMA DEL REY

by Lynnette Marrero and Jessica Gonzalez

When Lynnette Marrero tasted chef Erik Ramirez's Chicha Morada at Llama Inn, she knew it would mix well with wine—an inspiration that led to this complex and delicious collaboration. "We committed to putting pisco in 90 percent of the drinks at the restaurant, so we blended Italia (an aromatic grape varietal akin to Gewürztraminer) pisco with aged rum and incorporated grilled pineapple to pair better with the *anticuchos* [grilled meats] on the menu." Marrero's colleague Jessica Gonzalez rounded out the mix with the Peruvian pink peppercorn tincture, which she used to accentuate its mouthfeel and to tie together the diverse ingredients. YIELDS FIVE 5-OUNCE SERVINGS

- ☐ 6½ ounces South American malbec wine
- ☐ 5 ounces Chicha Morada (page 128)
- ☐ 4 ounces juice extracted from Grilled Pineapple (page 158)
- ☐ 3½ ounces Zacapa No. 23 rum
- ☐ 3 ounces Barsol Italia pisco

- ☐ 2½ ounces lime juice
- ☐ ¼ ounce St. Elizabeth allspice dram
- ☐ 2 dashes Pink Peppercorn Tincture (page 350)
- ☐ Ice cubes, plus 1 large ice block, tempered for 30 minutes
- ☐ 15 seedless red grapes, for garnish

Add the wine, Chicha Morada, pineapple juice, rum, pisco, lime juice, allspice dram, and peppercorn tincture to a nonreactive container and stir to incorporate. Chill for at least 1 hour.

Add the tempered block of ice to a punch bowl (or large tempered ice cubes to a pitcher) and fill with the punch. Ladle or pour into chilled old fashioned glasses filled with ice cubes. Garnish each glass with 3 red grapes on a cocktail pick.

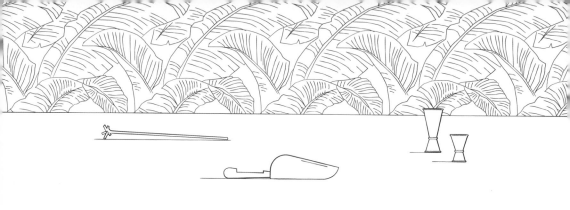

ARROZ CON RUM

by Yana Volfson

Yana Volfson invented this boozy agua fresca to showcase her cashew horchata on the opening brunch menu for chefs Enrique Olvera and Daniela Soto-Innes's restaurant Cosme, in 2015. With subtle nods to a classic New Orleans milk punch, the unique character of the cachaça, chile liqueur, and Mexican fernet "add an earthy, spicy, and savory component that keeps it grounded, preventing it from tasting too sweet," Volfson says. **YIELDS 1 SERVING**

- ☐ 2 ounces Cashew Horchata (page 126)
- ☐ 1 ounce Santa Teresa 1796 rum
- ☐ ¾ ounce Avuá Amburana cachaça
- ☐ ½ ounce pure maple syrup
- ☐ ¼ ounce Fernet Vallet
- ☐ ¼ ounce Ancho Reyes Original chile liqueur
- ☐ Crushed or pebble ice
- ☐ Mint sprig, for garnish

Add the horchata, rum, cachaça, maple syrup, fernet, and liqueur to a chilled highball glass. Add a scoop of crushed or pebble ice. Swizzle, then add more ice, forming a mound. Use a straw to create a hole for a sprig of mint. Garnish with the mint sprig and serve with a straw.

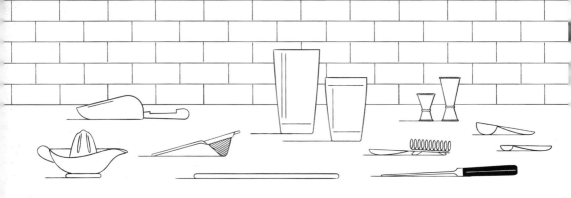

DRAGONFLY

by Jim Meehan

A dragonfly's levity inspired the title of this ethereal riff on the Ramos Gin Fizz. This recipe is remarkable for a few reasons: it has a pleasant creaminess, like the original cocktail, but the mouthfeel is lightened significantly by the substitution of oat milk for heavy cream; the celery-spiced gin tastes better with the grain-based milk than with dairy; and because there is no dairy involved, this is a great go-to for lactase non-persistent imbibers. YIELDS 1 SERVING

☐ 1¾ ounces Rutte celery gin

☐ 1¼ ounces Oat Milk (page 124)

☐ ½ ounce Giffard white crème de cacao

☐ ½ ounce prepared Usucha Matcha (page 252)

☐ ½ ounce lemon juice

☐ ½ ounce Simple Syrup (page 339)

☐ ¼ ounce lime juice

☐ 1 large egg white

☐ Ice cubes

☐ 1 ounce force-carbonated water (see page 282), chilled

☐ ⅛ teaspoon Kettl Tea Hanaka matcha powder, for garnish

Add the gin, oat milk, crème de cacao, matcha, lemon juice, simple syrup, lime juice, and egg white to a Boston shaker. Shake without ice, then add a scoop of ice cubes and shake again. Add the soda water to the shaker and double-strain through a Hawthorne and a fine-mesh strainer into a chilled Collins glass. Garnish with a light dusting of the matcha powder striped across the center of the drink.

The Bartender's Pantry

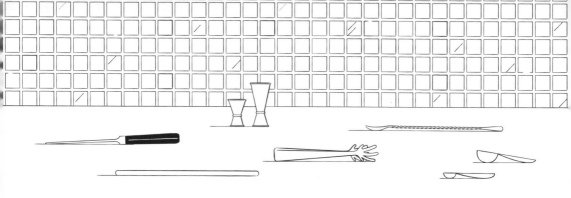

THUNDERBIRD

by Masahiro Urushido

This recipe was inspired by ingredients from Katana Kitten co-owner Masahiro Urushido's home prefecture in Japan. "Soba, or Japanese buckwheat—which is made into soba noodles, as well as the infusion in this drink—is well known in Nagano, along with apples, as the land is full of orchards," Masahiro told me. The pseudograin is ideal for people with celiac disease because it is naturally gluten-free. When toasted, soba gives off a pleasant, savory aroma. In regard to the title, Masahiro explains, "Thunderbird is the translation of the ptarmigan called raichō, that flies 3,000 meters above the city in the Japanese Alps."

YIELDS 1 SERVING

- ☐ 3 ounces Doc's Hard Pear Cider, chilled
- ☐ 1¼ ounces Sobacha–Infused Apple Brandy (page 350)
- ☐ 1 teaspoon Honey Syrup (page 338), prepared with buckwheat honey
- ☐ 1 large (2-inch) ice cube, tempered for 1 to 2 minutes
- ☐ 1 slice of Fuji apple, for garnish
- ☐ ½ teaspoon sobacha (buckwheat tea), for garnish
- ☐ ½ teaspoon Maldon sea salt, for garnish

Add the cider, brandy, and syrup to a chilled old fashioned glass. Add the tempered ice cube and stir to blend and chill the ingredients. Evenly coat the apple slice with the sobacha and salt, and use it to garnish the drink.

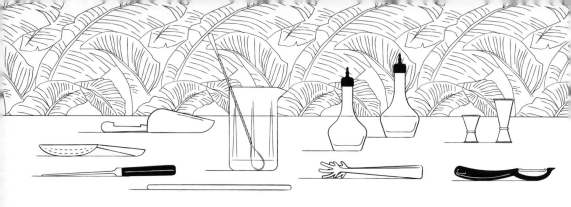

RIOT ACT

by Jillian Vose

The idea of using toasted rice in a drink came to Jillian Vose, a co-owner of Hazel and Apple in Charleston, after ordering toasted rice ice cream at Van Leeuwen on East 7th Street in the East Village of New York City. Genmaicha, a Japanese green tea blended with toasted puffed rice, was the perfect way to bring that character to the glass. "I started thinking of ingredients that would go well with that, and my former Dead Rabbit colleague Gregory Buda's grilled pineapple genever came to mind. The combination yielded a fruity, malty, nougat flavor; the drink developed from there." YIELDS 1 SERVING

- ☐ 1 ounce Torres 15-year brandy
- ☐ 1 ounce Grilled-Pineapple-Infused Genever (page 348)
- ☐ ½ ounce Amaro Nonino
- ☐ ½ ounce Genmaicha Syrup (page 342)
- ☐ 2 dashes Mineral Saline (page 340)
- ☐ Dash of Bitter Truth aromatic bitters
- ☐ Ice cubes, plus 1 large (2-inch) ice cube, tempered for 1 to 2 minutes
- ☐ 1 lemon peel, for garnish

Add the brandy, genever, amaro, syrup, mineral saline, and bitters to a chilled mixing glass. Add a scoop of ice cubes. Stir and strain into a chilled old fashioned glass filled with a large clear ice cube. Twist a lemon peel over the drink, then discard the twist and serve.

Fruits

Fruits are the most archetypal produce in mixed drinks. From citrus in punch to berries in cups, apples in wassail, and tropical fruits in tiki drinks, their alluring flavor, peppy acidity, and bright colors have drawn us to mix with them since at least the 1600s. After a regressive period in mixology at the end of the twentieth century, when fresh fruits all but disappeared from cocktails, bartenders like Dale DeGroff and Tony Abou-Ganim reintroduced fresh-squeezed juice to large-scale beverage programs, kickstarting the earliest stage of the modern American cocktail renaissance. Now, as new preservation technologies emerge, bartenders are challenging the orthodoxy of the "fresh-squeezed" paradigm by replacing certain fruits with preserved versions that work equally well—or even better—in their recipes.

Fruits are the parts a plant grows to propagate their species by attracting animals—like us—to eat them and disperse their seeds. Fruit develops from a flower's ovary into three layers: a thin outer protective skin, an inner coating around the maturing seed, and a thick layer in between that's endowed with a mixture of sugars and acids, among other qualities.

The final stage in the life cycle of fruit is called ripening, in which starch and acid levels decrease as sugar increases, aroma builds, and the skin softens and changes color from green (typically) to a vibrant hue to entice us to consume them. Harold McGee says ripening was long viewed as the first step toward rotting, but "now it's clear that ripening is a last, intense phase of life," he writes in *On Food and Cooking*. "As it ripens, the fruit actively prepares for its end, organizing itself into a feast for our eye and palate." It's no wonder that fruits are one of the primary ingredients bartenders use to attract customers to their drinks.

All fruits ripen in one of two ways, which is key for bartenders to consider when sourcing and prepping them for drink service:

Climacteric Fruits like bananas, avocados, and apples are climacteric. That is, they continue to ripen after being harvested, producing a natural hormone called ethylene, which causes their flavor, texture, and color to change. These fruits store their sugars in the form of starch, which enzymes convert to sugar as the fruit ripens. They are picked early to minimize physical damage during shipping, then gassed with ethylene to ripen them for sale. Months of cold cellaring (done by the wholesaler or buyer), slows the ripening process significantly, which allows for changes in flavor over a longer period of time and facilitates inventory control so grocery stores can sell fruit year-round.

Non-climacteric Fruits like raspberries, cherries, and pineapples do not continue to ripen after harvest. This means they don't store sugars as starch and instead rely on their connection to the plant to maximize sugar levels. Once harvested, they get no sweeter, though enzymatic action may continue to soften their flesh and heighten their aroma, in some cases. This means they're best when picked and shipped as ripe as possible. They decline after purchase, if unprocessed.

Following is a non-exhaustive list of many fruits, grouped imperfectly by family, that are used throughout the book in various forms. While produce comes in and out of season at different times all over the world, I've contextualized the seasons here for fruit grown primarily in the Northern Hemisphere for the North American market.

Apples and Quinces (climacteric)

Apples, quinces, and pears are members of the rose family and are known as "pomes," whose fleshy portion forms from the tip of the original flower stem.

Apples Apple trees, which do not reproduce reliably from seed, are propagated by budding and grafting. There are three types of apples, which are not mutually exclusive: bittersweet cider apples; dense-fleshed cooking apples like Granny Smiths; and "dessert" apples, which require no preparation to enjoy. Around a hundred varieties—mostly selected for appearance and shelf stability instead of flavor—are produced by commercial growers in the United States, with more flavorful heirloom apples appearing each year at farmer's markets. Many late-harvest apples are hard and starchy when picked and require a number of weeks to soften in cold storage. At home, apples should be stored in the coldest part of the fridge to keep them fresh. Apple slices are used as garnish in the Pomme and Circumstance (page 36) and the Thunderbird (page 38).

Quinces In *Fruit,* Alan Davidson observes that "quince resembles a large, lumpy, yellow pear. It has hard flesh, many pips and is too sour and astringent to eat raw; but it has a delicious fragrance and, when cooked with sugar or honey, develops a fine flavor and turns pink." That's exactly what is done in Spain, where quinces are formed into a paste called membrillo, which is prized as a cheese condiment but also works well when dissolved as a flavorful sweetener. Use quince paste to make the Q.P. Warmer (page 270).

Stone Fruits (climacteric)

"Stone" refers to the hard shell that surrounds a single large seed. McGee explains: "Stone fruit seeds (including almonds) are protected by an enzyme system that generates the aroma we associate with almond extract, and at the same time cyanide." All stone fruits—peaches, apricots, cherries, and plums—are members of the large rose family.

Apricots Like other stone fruits, apricots don't ship well, so farmers tend to ship them underripe or else dry them, which concentrates their flavor and sweetness. The fruit is dried in the sun in early summer for one or two weeks and usually treated with sulfur dioxide to preserve nutrients and flavor. Unsulfured apricots are brown and have a cooked quality. Dried apricots are used to make the Ginger Burns (page 313).

Cherries (non-climacteric) Two types of cherry—sweet and sour—from two different species, vary chiefly in their maximum sugar content. Cherry season begins in the late spring and lasts until mid-summer. Cherry stems should be green and pliable, and the flesh should be firm, with no bruises. Like blueberries, they don't emit an aroma until chewed. While the most famous preserved cherries are sour marasca cherries from Italy's Veneto region, sweet Bing cherries also make great garnishes (see Miles Macquarrie's Preserved Cherries recipe on page 155). A cherry pitter helps expedite this work neatly.

Peaches Two categories of peach—clingstone and freestone—are distinguished by the difficulty or ease with which the flesh comes away from the pit. The peak of the season comes in late July and August and winds down in September, but it can extend into early October if the weather remains temperate. Early peaches from May to June are almost always clingstone, which are the best for eating. Midsummer and fall peaches are usually freestone, which have firmer flesh that separates easily from the pit, and less juice, making them ideal candidates for IQF (individually quick frozen) method, which preserves the ripe fruit's concentrated flavor and aromatics for purées (like the one on page 164). Each type has varieties with both bright yellow and aromatic white flesh. Store fresh peaches at room temperature until they become aromatic and tender to the touch.

Berries and Grapes (non-climacteric)

Grapes and berries—including blackberries, blueberries, cranberries, raspberries, and strawberries—grow on bushes and vines, although some berries grow on trees, too.

Raspberries Red, gold, and black raspberries are cultivated and grow wild in the Northern Hemisphere during the warmer months from May to July in cooler states. A second crop from ever-bearing varieties may be harvested depending on how the canes are pruned. Check the berries' inner cavities for mold before purchase and rinse them delicately before service. Given the short window of ripeness raspberries have before spoilage, sourcing them freeze-dried or IQF are compelling alternatives to fresh for preparations like Martin Hudák's Beet-Raspberry Syrup (page 194). Vinegar is a historic preservation agent for fruit used in Neal Bodenheimer's Raspberry Shrub (page 318).

Blackberries Blackberries grow on thorny bushes on long, arching canes that produce a variety of deep-purple to black berries. They mature from mid-summer to early fall and are fully ripe when their color darkens. Check blackberries for mold, which often starts at the stem end, and rinse them gently with cold water for service. They're only a little more shelf stable than raspberries, which makes Gaby Mlynarczyk's Blackberry Consommé (page 166) perfect to capture and preserve their essence with no pulp, which also allows her to carbonate their juice in house-made sodas.

Blueberries Many growers plant multiple varieties of blueberry that mature at different times so they have berries all summer long. If the berries still have stems attached, it's likely they were harvested indiscriminately by a mechanical harvester regardless of their ripeness. Look for rich color, avoiding any green berries. Size is not an indicator of quality. Blueberries may be stored for up to a week in the refrigerator. They maintain their flavor when cooked, frozen, or freeze-dehydrated in spirit infusions like my Blueberry-Infused Gin (page 346) for the Kind of Blueberry (page 176).

Grapes Most of the world's grapes are used to make wine, while the rest—table grapes grown primarily in California and available from late spring to early winter—are eaten fresh or made into raisins. In the United States, this is usually done by laying the grapes out in the vineyard when it's warm and sunny. Golden raisins, such as those called for in Bonnie Morales's Borodinsky Rye Kvass (page 121), are treated with sulfur dioxide and dried in temperature-controlled facilities to retain their light color and plump texture.

Melons (climacteric and non-climacteric)

All melons are members of the Cucurbitaceae family, which includes pumpkins, squashes, and cucumbers. Except for watermelons, which cannot cross-pollinate, melons fall into two seasonal categories: the aromatic summer melons, which we call cantaloupes (climacteric) in the United States (even though they're genetically distinct from European cantaloupes), and more hearty winter melons, including the Crenshaw, canary, and honeydew (non-climacteric), whose hard rinds facilitate export and ensure a durable shelf life. Many growers use manure as fertilizer to grow nutrient-intensive melons, so the surface of melons should be thoroughly scrubbed before slicing into them. Unlike many other types of fruit featured here, melons are not good candidates for preservation, so enjoy them fresh. Honeydew melon balls are featured in the Lava Lamp (page 174).

Citrus (non-climacteric)

Citrus trees have glossy evergreen leaves and fragrant blossoms. Citrus peel is permeable and prone to drying if left out, which is something to be mindful of if you'll be relying on its oil to be ignited or zested.

Oranges Nearly three-fourths of all citrus grown in the world are oranges, which are typically grouped into two categories: sweet and bitter/sour. Sweet oranges, like Valencia, mandarins, navels, and blood oranges, may be peeled and eaten or squeezed for their juice. Bitter/sour oranges, such as Bergamots, are prized for their aromatic peel, and are typically seedy, with little juice.

- Navel oranges are popular because they're easy to peel and are seedless, but juice from navel oranges becomes noticeably bitter after 30 minutes, according to Harold McGee in *On Food and Cooking,* because "acids and enzymes convert a tasteless precursor molecule into an intensely bitter terpene compound called limonin." The thick, smooth peel of navel oranges makes them ideal for twists and half-orange wheel garnishes.

- Valencia oranges, which have seeds, a smooth blossom end, and do not develop limonin bitterness like navels, are the most commonly planted orange tree in the world. The sweet juice of Valencia oranges makes for a flabby cocktail mixer, so most bartenders either avoid mixing with it or adjust its pH with food-safe acids. Bartender Naren Young famously reconstitutes orange juice for his version of the Garibaldi, served at Dante in New York City, by running peeled oranges through a masticating juicer (instead of reaming it), which gives it a "fluffy" texture.

- Blood oranges come in many varieties—such as Moros—which are sweet and deeply colored, and whose flesh has classic citrus notes with distinct raspberry aromas.

- Mandarin oranges include both a specific orange—a historic hybrid used to create numerous modern citrus fruits—and a group of easy-peeling sweet oranges, such as tangerines, tangelos, and clementines. Mandarins have a distinctive aroma, and some varieties, such as the satsuma, are seedless.

- Sour/bitter oranges, also known as Seville oranges, are too astringent to be peeled and eaten fresh. Orange blossoms from this family of citrus are harvested to make orange flower water. Their aromatic peel oil is used to flavor orange liqueurs, sodas, and Earl Grey tea.

Yuzus These are a distinctive citrus celebrated in Japan and Korea that are often grouped with bitter oranges because they're prized more for their peel than for their juice. Yuzu trees bear mandarin-sized fruit with a thick, uneven peel. Their zest's unique fragrance is used as a flavoring agent for soda and saké, and as a garnish for Shingo Gokan's Speak Low (page 268).

Grapefruits So-called because the fruit grows in clusters like grapes, grapefruits are available year-round from Florida, Texas, Arizona, and California. There are three types: the tart, aromatic white grapefruit (sometimes called a yellow grapefruit); the tangy-bittersweet pink grapefruit (derived from the Duncan grapefruit); and the sweet Ruby Red grapefruit, which is a much-beloved mutation of a pink grapefruit first discovered on a tree in Texas. Grapefruits flatten a little on the shelf but should not look pushed out of shape. Unlike lemons and limes, the presence of blemishes on the peel is not an indicator of the quality of the flesh and juice, so you can use unsightly peels to make sherbets (see page 343), but not eye-catching garnishes (like the one used in the Grail Ale (page 302). Grapefruits keep well for up to a week at room temperature or two to three weeks when refrigerated. Grapefruits contain a precursor of limonin, which, as with navel oranges, makes the juice taste bitter if not imbibed shortly after squeezing.

Allergy note: Grapefruit can alter the activity of certain drugs, like statins taken to lower cholesterol, so always list it clearly on bar menus.

Limes The smaller, more fragrant and highly acidic Key lime was the dominant variety until hurricanes wiped out Florida's trees in the late 1920s. Persian limes came into favor thereafter and are now the most commonly used type of lime for mixed drinks. Both varieties gradually turn yellow and lose acid during storage. Avoid limes that have dull, dry skin, soft spots, or brown patches.

· Key limes are grown throughout Mexico and other parts of the tropics. They are small, round, pale green, thin-skinned fruits with seeds. Their season runs from early summer to late fall, although there is continuous availability throughout the year in certain regions. Key limes should be kept at room temperature, out of direct sunlight, and used within a week. The size and flavor of Key limes make them ideal for juicing with an "elbow" squeezer.

· Persian limes are available year-round, with the peak of the harvest in summer. Seedless, with shiny, dark skin and pale green flesh that can be stingy with its juice, they lack the aromatics of Key limes. The size, firm peel, and eye-catching color make Persian limes ideal to slice into wedges and wheels for cocktail garnishes. They may be refrigerated for several weeks.

Lemons There are over 25 cultivated varieties of lemon, which grow from small, thorny trees with white, purple-tinged fragrant flowers. The lemon thrives in cooler coastal climates than limes and can be harvested as many as ten times a year. The fruit reaches maturity while green, at which time it's frequently picked and (uniquely for citrus) stored off the tree at high humidity in a cool warehouse for up to three months. Eureka and Lisbon varieties, which are virtually indistinguishable, are the two most common varieties of lemon, supplemented with aromatic Meyer lemons from November through spring on the West Coast. Lemons can be stored at room temperature for up to a week and in the refrigerator for up to a month.

Kumquats This tart, bite-sized citrus, which may be eaten whole, is available from November through March. Kumquats may be stored at room temperature for up to a week or for several weeks loosely covered in the refrigerator. Their size and edibility make them ideal garnishes for drinks like Leo Robitschek's Choked Up (page 76).

Tropical Fruits

Most tropical fruits grown in temperate climates are available year-round.

Bananas (climacteric) The banana plant is a giant herb that grows from an underground rhizome into a 10- to 12-foot false trunk, with a large flower spike that bends downward, where bunches of bananas grow. While many varieties of bananas are still grown in the tropics, the only one you're likely to see exported for sale in the United States is the Cavendish, which replaced the Gros Michel in the 1950s when fusarium wilt threatened the whole species. Bananas are picked and shipped green, when they're less susceptible to bruising and may be ripened uncovered at room temperature until brown flecks appear on the skin, indicating higher sugar levels. Avoid dark areas of the creamy flesh, which indicate bruising. Bananas are well preserved frozen and dehydrated for infusions such as the coconut banana bourbon for Kevin Diedrich's Banana Stand (page 178).

Passion Fruits (climacteric) Passion fruits come from a group of climbing vines that produce egg-sized fruits with a brittle outer shell, whose yellow or purple skin wrinkles when ripe. Purple passion fruits have black seeds; yellow passion fruits—often a little larger and more acidic—have brown seeds. Both varieties have yellowish pulp, whose flavor is concentrated and frequently diluted and sold as a purée for drinks like Chanel Adams's Penny (page 236). Smaller passion fruits can be sliced in half and perched on top of icy tropical drinks as garnishes.

Pineapples (non-climacteric) Pineapples are aggregate fruits, like raspberries, developing from tiny purple flowers clustered around the cone of a stalk. Almost all U.S. pineapple production occurs in Hawaii, which cans, juices, and freezes a large proportion of their yield. Look for firm, aromatic pineapples with deep green leaves and no soft patches on the skin.

There are many applications for pineapple in cocktails. The fruit's dense flesh stands up to grilling in Lynnette Marrero and Jessica Gonzalez's Llama del Rey (page 132) and Jillian Vose's Riot Act (page 140). The richness of the juice is reinforced when cooked down to a cordial for Paul Calvert's Welcome Mother (page 330) and Erik Ramirez's Chicha Morada (page 128), while its high tones are retained when freshly extracted and strained in Osvaldo Vásquez's Sangrita Verde (page 66). Pineapple typically has enough native yeast on its skin to ferment tepache naturally, but Rosio Sánchez supplements hers with a cultivated yeast at Hija de Sanchez in Copenhagen (see page 320).

Palm Fruits

Coconuts and dates are the only fruits of the palm tree cultivated for commercial use.

Coconuts (non-climacteric) A palm tree yields thousands of coconuts over its long life span. Each coconut has several layers: a smooth, tan outer covering; a hard, dark brown husk with three indented "eyes" at one end; thin brown skin; creamy white meat; and opaque coconut water in the center. Upon ripening, the flesh becomes white and firm. Dried coconut meat, called copra, is pressed into coconut oil, which Kevin Diedrich infuses in bourbon with dried bananas for his Banana Stand (page 178).

Fresh coconuts are available year-round, with the peak season October through December. "Young coconuts" are harvested early—when their meat is soft and they still have their husks. "White coconuts" are young coconuts with the husks removed. The smooth outer shell is typically removed in preparation for sale. When buying a whole coconut, choose one that feels heavy for its size and sloshes when shaken. The coconut water inside—which Julie Reiner uses in her Dragon Pearl Punch (page 262)—is extracted by puncturing two of the three "eyes" with a pick. As a coconut matures, its "water" becomes cloudy and more nutty.

Canned coconut milk—mixed into Nico de Soto's L'Alligator C'est Vert (page 208) and cooked into Jen Colliau's Cream of Coconut (page 160)—is available at most supermarkets. Cream of coconut—which is sweetened and called for in recipes like the Piña Colada—is not the same as unsweetened coconut milk or coconut cream. Unopened cans can be stored at room temperature for up to 18 months and should be refrigerated and covered after opening. Small plastic squeeze bottles are ideal to dispense it for service.

Dates (climacteric) The date palm, which can reach a height of 100 feet, produces berries after its eighth year and can continue to do so for over a century. More or less oblong, they vary in size, color, shape, quality, and consistency according to their variety and environment. A single large bunch, weighing over 20 pounds, can contain as many as 1,000 fruits that ripen between August and December. Dried dates can be ground into a fibrous sugar and are used to sweeten and thicken beverages like Lydia Parsley's Oat Milk (page 124).

SOURCING

While the service window between ripeness and rot ranges from fruit to fruit, there's little doubt that societal preference for fresh fruit leads to an unethical amount of fruit needlessly rotting in the fields or on supermarket shelves. The USDA estimates that retail food waste in the U.S. averages between 30 and 40 percent. To combat this, excellent modern innovations such as IQF—the individual quick-frozen method of preservation during which each piece of fruit gets frozen separately so it doesn't stick to the rest of the batch—represents a way to preserve fruits at their peak ripeness and support farmers by giving them the opportunity to sell at a competitive price in bulk, without risking spoilage.

STORAGE

Decisions about the best ways to store fruits should be made on a case-by-case basis. *The Waste-Free Kitchen Handbook* by Dana Gunders is a compact but commendable guide for all types of vegetables, herbs, and fruits.

PREPARATION

All non-organic fruit should be washed and scrubbed before service to remove pesticides, herbicides, and wax (an FDA-approved natural coating sometimes used to stop mold and slow rot). Find a good colander for rinsing delicate berries, which can be carefully placed on a towel to dry afterward.

TOOLS AND MACHINERY

There are different ways to extract juice such as citrus presses that express the oil in the peel in addition to the juice (like an elbow juicer), and citrus reamers that bypass the peel's oil altogether. For garnish work, a Y-peeler, vertical peeler, cheese slicer, or utility knife are all useful. Use knives that feel comfortable in your hands, such as a paring knife, utility knife, or chef's knife with a sharp blade for safety. Large volumes of pulpy juice should be filtered through strainers of different gauges to expedite the process. Stock a collection of cutting boards in various sizes, too—small ones for citrus and berries, medium ones for apples and cantaloupes, and large ones for watermelons and pineapples—so you can adjust your workspace and equipment requirements accordingly.

Thanks to contemporary cold-chain technology throughout our global economy, citrus and other fruits are available "fresh" any time of the year. In *On Food and Cooking,* Harold McGee contextualizes the relative whiplash our society has experienced since the days when fresh fruit was available only when it was in season regionally: "Barely a century ago, oranges were special holiday treats; now, much of the Western world starts its day with orange juice."

In a capitalist system farmers plant what sells, and in countries (like our own) where unscrupulous agribusiness operates with profit as the first priority, this can be disastrous for both citizens and the land. Knowing that our buying practices are influential, bartenders should menu-plan with discretion, prioritizing local, organic, heirloom varieties of fruit in season to encourage biodiversity and sustainably minded global agriculture.

For bartenders, "discretion" can mean not putting certain fruits on a menu, even if they can be afforded and there's a market for them. For example, when recipes like Douglas Ankrah's Porn Star Martini—made with vanilla vodka, fresh passion fruit, passion fruit liqueur, vanilla syrup, lime, and sparkling wine—goes from being a modern classic from a London cocktail bar to one of the most popular cocktails on the planet, we should ask ourselves if shipping tropical passion fruit all over the world is prudent, or if another more sustainable recipe should be chosen for the spotlight instead?

Today, the use of freshly squeezed citrus is once again declining in cocktail bars. Specious new preservation technologies such as HPP (high pressure processing) are touted as alternatives to extend "freshness" for operators balking at the cost of preparing it in-house daily. While this could reasonably be framed dispassionately as a generational value shift, a boom-or-bust economic pattern, or one more example of how cocktails reflect the zeitgeist; it also represents an opportunity to reevaluate historic and modern preservation techniques to meet the enduring needs of our time.

By learning a fruit's best qualities—sweetness, acidity, aromatics, texture, and tannin—we can candy, cook, can, distill, air-dry, ferment, freeze, freeze-dry, and purée these characteristics before rot begins. This not only minimizes spoilage but also cuts down on the excessive energy costs involved in rushing non-climacteric fruit to market—a move analogous to fishing boats blast-freezing fish at sea and continuing to fish, instead of rushing the catch back to shore to sell fresh. Applying food technology in this manner with discretionary menu planning is a progressive practice bartenders should use to help preserve the availability of sustainable fruit.

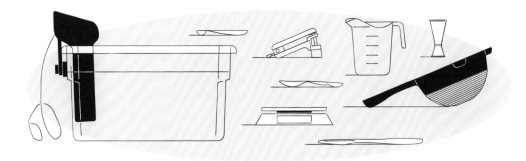

PRESERVED CHERRIES

from Miles Macquarrie

Miles Macquarrie started experimenting with canning cherries the summer before Kimball House in Decatur, Georgia, opened to ensure the bar was well-provisioned from the get-go. He uses Bing cherries for their sweetness and adds Cherry Heering for its baked cherry aroma. At the bar, they use a sous vide canning method to speed up the process. The added benefit of canning in-house is all the leftover syrup, Miles observes. "Commercial cherries come in a thick, heavily sweetened syrup that's hard to work into cocktail recipes. The liquid from canning these cherries works really well, especially in stirred drinks, as the acid helps cut through the sweetness."

Use this to garnish Penny (page 236) or a classic Manhattan. YIELDS APPROXIMATELY 18 OUNCES SYRUP AND 3 TO 4 PINTS OF CHERRIES

- ☐ 1000g (2–3 quarts) fresh Bing cherries
- ☐ 1000g (1 liter) filtered water
- ☐ 20g (1 tablespoon) kosher salt
- ☐ 500g (13½ ounces) Rich Simple Syrup (page 339)
- ☐ 5g (1½ teaspoons) malic acid
- ☐ 5g (1 teaspoon) acid phosphate
- ☐ 1 ounce Cherry Heering

• CONTINUED •

DAY 1

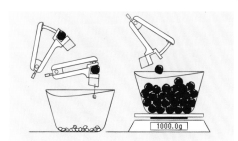

Pit the cherries with a cherry pitter, separating the cherries and the pits into 2 different bowls.

Pour the water and salt into a third bowl and stir until dissolved.

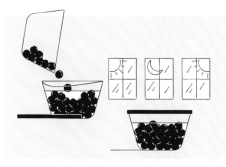

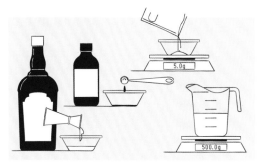

Add the cherries to the bowl filled with salt water, cover, and let sit overnight.

Measure out the rich simple syrup, malic acid, acid phosphate, and Cherry Heering into a measuring cup.

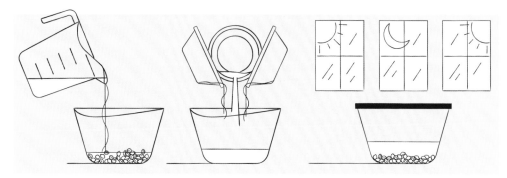

Add the rich simple syrup, malic acid, acid phosphate, and Cherry Heering to the bowl with the cherry pits, cover, and let sit overnight.

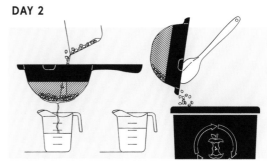

Pour the cherries into a fine-mesh strainer and discard the brine. Rinse the cherries with water to remove any remaining brine.

Strain the cherry pits from the syrup, reserving the syrup and composting the pits.

Add the cherries to 4 pint-sized mason jars. Fill each jar with syrup, leaving a bit of headspace. Be sure to use new lids and rings to ensure the jars are airtight. (Any extra syrup may be bottled or frozen.)

Add water to an 18-liter sous vide tank until three-fourths full. Using an immersion circulator, heat the water to 190°F. Submerge the mason jars in the bath for 2½ hours.

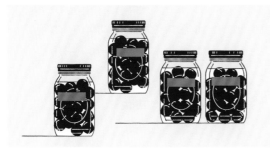

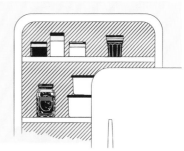

Remove jars from bath, let cool, then store in a cool, dark place for later use.

Once a jar is opened, store it covered in the fridge for up to **2 MONTHS**.

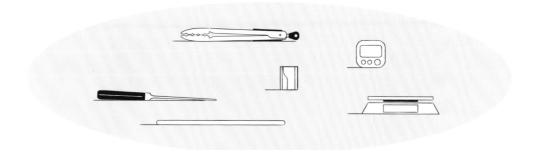

GRILLED PINEAPPLE

from Gregory Buda

For Gregory Buda, a partner in Bisou Bisou in Montreal, fresh pineapple juice can be too bright and fruity for some cocktails, but the char and caramelization from grilling dramatically changes how pineapple presents in a drink. "It mellows the bright candy fruit quality of fresh pineapple and adds darker, smoky notes," says Buda. This recipe is delicious in its own right and shows how grilling is a great way to coax different flavors from fruits and vegetables.

Use Buda's recipe for the juice needed in the Llama del Rey (page 132) or infuse the grilled fruit into barrel-aged genever (see page 348) to bring a charred smoky note to drinks like the Riot Act (page 140). YIELDS 625G (4¼ CUPS)

☐ 625g (half of one large) pineapple

Preheat the grill to high.

Cut the pineapple in half horizontally, and set aside half for another use.

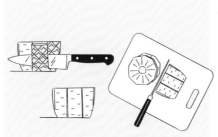

Slice the rind off one half, and cut the pineapple into 1½-inch-thick rings.

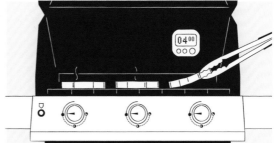

Place the rings on the grill for 4 minutes on each side, turning once with grill tongs.

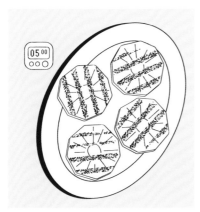

Set aside the pineapple rings; cool for 5 minutes.

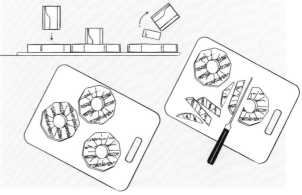

Core and cut the grilled pineapple rings into spears or cubes.

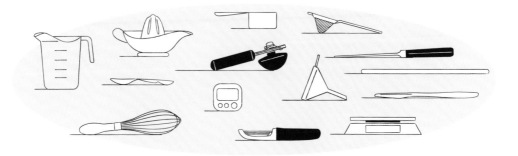

CREAM OF COCONUT

from Jennifer Colliau

Cream of coconut is essentially a sweetened, thick coconut syrup made with either coconut cream or coconut milk. Coconut cream is made with less water than coconut milk, so it's richer and fattier. Jennifer Colliau, founder of Small Hand Foods (a cocktail ingredient company), says that you can use either in this recipe. "Find one with as few emulsifiers as possible," she says, "because you want to discard extra water and emulsifiers keep it bound up." Jennifer prefers organic cane sugar for this recipe, which adds to its richness and complexity.

Use in a classic Piña Colada or the Coquito (page 108). YIELDS 26 OUNCES

- ☐ 2 (13-ounce) cans Thai Kitchen organic unsweetened coconut milk
- ☐ 6¼ ounces young coconut water
- ☐ 1½ ounces lime juice
- ☐ 325g (3 cups plus 2 tablespoons) organic cane sugar

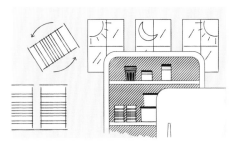

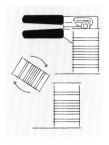

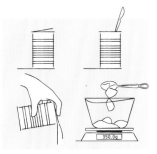

Place the cans of coconut milk upside down in the fridge overnight.

The next day, turn the cans right side up and remove the tops.

Carefully pour out and discard the liquid separated from the solid cream. Scoop the solidified cream out of the can with a spoon and reserve.

Add the solidified cream (around 1½ cups) to a medium saucepan. Stir in the coconut water, lime juice, and sugar.

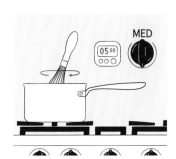

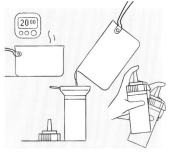

Cook over medium heat, whisking constantly, until the sugar dissolves, around 5 minutes.

Let the mixture cool for about 20 minutes. Funnel it into squeeze bottles (shake before each use with your finger over the opening).

Store, covered, in the fridge for up to 1 WEEK.

Fruits

161

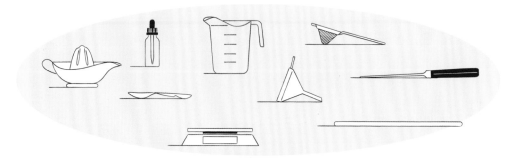

"ENHANCED" RUBY RED GRAPEFRUIT JUICE

from Chad Solomon

The idea for this recipe came to Chad Solomon, the co-founder of Cuffs & Buttons, when he was working on a way to serve Hemingway Daiquiris without lime juice, where it's relied upon for its acid instead of its flavor to balance the drink. For Solomon, the acidity of the lime juice "steps on" the grapefruit, so he replaced it with phosphoric acid. The acid helps sharpen flavor by adding a dry, aroma-free tang, and serves as a preservative that slows the growth of bacteria and mold. Note: Phosphoric acid is corrosive in large quantities, so it must be used judiciously, with food safety protocols meticulously observed.

Use this to make Chad's elemental Paloma (page 170) or Enhanced Grapefruit Sherbet (page 343), which serves as the base for my Grapefruit Soda (page 288).

YIELDS 20 OUNCES

- ☐ 20 ounces (from 3 to 4 grapefruits) Ruby Red grapefruit juice
- ☐ 2g (1 tablespoon) citric acid
- ☐ 3 drops phosphoric acid

Ream 20 ounces of juice from 3 to 4 Ruby Red grapefruits.

Fine-strain the grapefruit juice into a measuring cup.

Add the citric and phosphoric acids, and stir to combine. Pour into a bottle or mason jar.

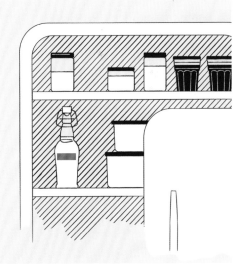

Store, covered, in the fridge for up to 3 DAYS.

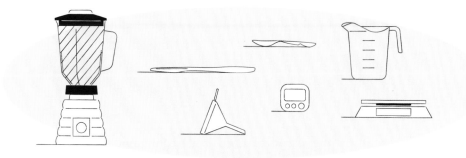

PEACH PURÉE

from Sean Hoard and Daniel Shoemaker

When Sean Hoard and Daniel Shoemaker opened The Commissary in Portland, Oregon, they prioritized development of a reliable peach purée that would work well year-round in a Bellini. When it comes to summer produce with an unpredictable growing season like peaches, they gravitate toward individual quick-frozen (IQF) fruit. "IQFs allow us to support local farms year-round and yields a delicious, consistent product," says Sean. "They work great because I know they're ripe and ready when I need them, so there's no guesswork."

Use the purée to make Sean's Windowsill Spritz (page 172), or in a classic Bellini. YIELDS ABOUT 34 OUNCES

- ☐ 620g (5 cups) IQF white peaches, thawed
- ☐ 3.5g (1 teaspoon) citric acid
- ☐ 12 ounces Simple Syrup (page 339)

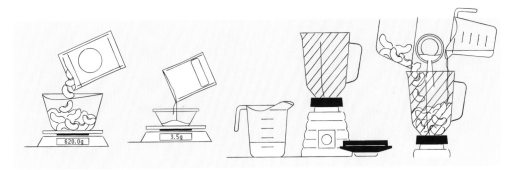

Add the peaches, citric acid, and syrup to a blender.

Blend on high until the mixture is smooth, about 30 seconds.

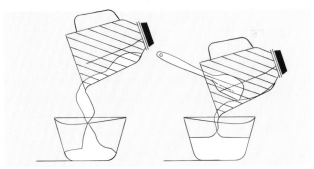

Transfer the mixture to a nonreactive container, using a rubber spatula to scrape out any remaining purée from the sides of the blender bowl.

Stir to integrate the remaining purée. Funnel it into squeeze bottles (shake before each use with your finger over the opening).

Store, covered, in the fridge for up to 1 WEEK.

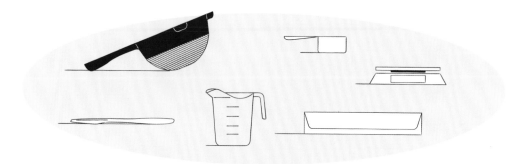

BLACKBERRY CONSOMMÉ

from Gabriella Mlynarczyk

While at Ink, *Clean + Dirty Drinking* author Gabriella Mlynarczyk was encouraged by chef Michael Voltaggio to make fruit consommé to capture ephemeral produce at its peak of ripeness for a house soda program. "The pulp in the fruit base was diminishing the soda's carbonation, so he showed me how to make consommé," she recalled. Mlynarczyk uses fresh, ripe fruit from the farmer's market and freezes surplus consommé in vacuum-sealed bags laid flat in the freezer to extend their availability beyond the fruit's natural growing season.

Use this to make her "Pimm's" Cup (page 168). YIELDS 14 OUNCES

- ☐ 500g (2 cups) fresh blackberries
- ☐ 8 ounces filtered water
- ☐ 125g (½ cup) superfine sugar
- ☐ 425g (3 cups) ice cubes

Add the blackberries, water, and sugar into a medium heat-resistant bowl and stir gently with a spatula to evenly coat the berries with the sugar.

Wrap the entire bowl in plastic wrap.

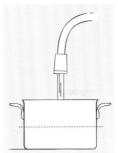

Fill a medium saucepan halfway with water and place on the stove.

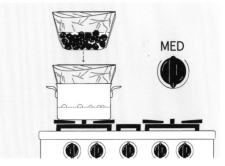

Position the wrapped bowl in the top of the pan (it should fit snugly but not touch the water). Bring the water to a simmer over medium heat.

Steam the berries for 2½ hours, then remove the bowl from the pot.

Set the bowl in a larger bowl filled three-quarters with ice to cool more quickly.

Remove the plastic wrap. Gently strain the blackberry liquid through a fine-mesh strainer (do not press the berries).

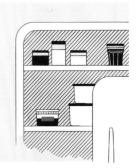

Compost the berries and store the liquid, covered, in a nonreactive container in the fridge for up to 5 DAYS.

"PIMM'S" CUP

from Gabriella Mlynarczyk

Gabriella Mlynarczyk developed this recipe at Birch, in Los Angeles, in 2015, at the request of an English chef who wanted a Pimm's Cup as the signature drink for the cocktail menu. "I love the idea of Pimm's, but I hate the muddy flavor," she says. "I did a little research and discovered Pimm's was based on a claret cup recipe that's been drunk for centuries. The basic recipe is 2 parts claret to 1 part gin, and Pimm's uses fortified wine or vermouth, fruits, and spices." Her first experiment was with rhubarb and cinnamon, though she has also made versions with beets, pineapple, pears, and more. I tested this with Katie Rose's Szechuan ginger beer—which works fine—but the original recipe calls for Fever-Tree ginger beer.

YIELDS 1 SERVING

- ☐ 1½ ounces Fords gin
- ☐ 1½ ounces Blackberry Consommé (page 166)
- ☐ 1 ounce Dolin blanc vermouth
- ☐ ¾ ounce lemon juice
- ☐ ½ ounce Rich Simple Syrup (page 339)

- ☐ Ice cubes
- ☐ 2 ounces Szechuan Ginger Beer (page 284), chilled
- ☐ 1 mint sprig, for garnish
- ☐ ½ fresh blackberry, for garnish
- ☐ 1 cucumber slice, for garnish

Add the gin, consommé, vermouth, lemon juice, and syrup to a Boston shaker. Add a scoop of ice cubes, then shake the mixture. Add the ginger beer to the shaker, then double-strain through a Hawthorne and a fine-mesh strainer into a chilled wine glass filled with ice cubes. Garnish with a mint sprig poked through half a blackberry on a cucumber wheel.

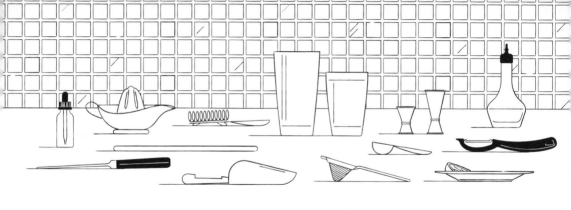

PALOMA

from Chad Solomon

Chad Solomon observed that most of his customers at Midnight Rambler in Dallas expected their Paloma to be made with fresh grapefruit juice rather than grapefruit soda. In this elemental version of the recipe, he acidulates the juice and harmonizes it with grapefruit bitters. Solomon also served a more complex Rio Star Paloma at Midnight Rambler that added maraschino and pamplemousse liqueurs and substituted grapefruit oleo saccharum for simple syrup and Rio Star juice in place of Ruby Red. "I wanted to take fresh grapefruit juice, which is a bit thin on its own, and turn it into a four-note chord," he told me. YIELDS 1 SERVING

- ☐ 2 ounces Tapatio reposado tequila
- ☐ 1 ounce "Enhanced" Ruby Red Grapefruit Juice (page 162)
- ☐ ¾ ounce Rich Simple Syrup (page 339)
- ☐ ½ ounce lime juice
- ☐ 2 dashes Bitter Truth grapefruit bitters
- ☐ 2 drops Mineral Saline (page 340)
- ☐ Ice cubes
- ☐ 1 ounce force-carbonated water (see page 282), chilled
- ☐ 1 lemon wedge, to moisten rim
- ☐ 20g (1 tablespoon) kosher salt, for rim
- ☐ 1 grapefruit peel, for garnish

Add the tequila, grapefruit juice, syrup, lime juice, bitters, and saline to a Boston shaker. Add a scoop of ice cubes and roll the mixture between the 2 tins. Add the soda water to the shaker, then double-strain through a Hawthorne and a fine-mesh strainer into a chilled, half-salt-rimmed Collins glass filled with ice cubes. Garnish with a grapefruit twist. Serve with a straw.

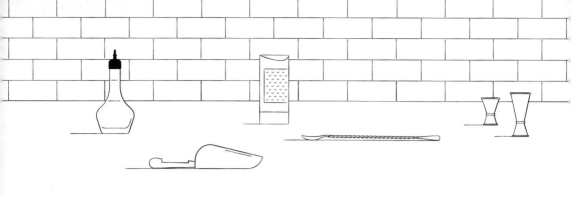

WINDOWSILL SPRITZ

by Sean Hoard

Sean Hoard created this drink, a "Bellini with the windows rolled down and the AC all the way up," for Ringside, the iconic steakhouse in Portland, Oregon, in 2014. The recipe "revolves around the natural affinity between peaches and almonds," he says. It's "somewhere between an almond croissant and a peach hand pie." The name is a reference to "that moment in a cartoon when someone places a pie—fresh from the oven—on a windowsill to cool and the main character (usually someone like Yogi Bear) gets a whiff." **YIELDS 1 SERVING**

- ☐ 1½ ounces Domaine Landrons Atmosphères sparkling wine, chilled
- ☐ 1½ ounces force-carbonated water (see page 282), chilled
- ☐ ¾ ounce Wheatley vodka
- ☐ ¾ ounce Peach Purée (page 164)
- ☐ ¾ ounce Orgeat (page 118)
- ☐ Dash of St. George absinthe
- ☐ Cracked or pebble ice
- ☐ Nutmeg, freshly grated, for garnish

Add the wine, soda water, vodka, peach purée, orgeat, and absinthe to a chilled wine glass. Add a scoop of cracked or pebble ice to the glass and stir gently. Garnish with some freshly grated nutmeg.

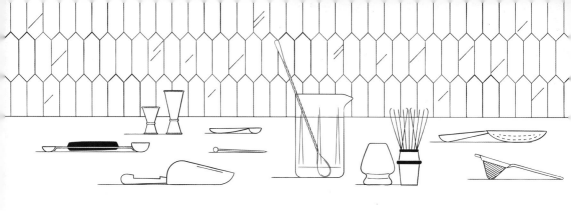

LAVA LAMP

by Sam Anderson

Sam Anderson created this aptly titled recipe for Mission Chinese Food in 2016. It has, as he describes, "the appearance of a lava lamp in the glass once the melon balls are floated in the richly textured cocktail, frothy with matcha and pét-nat." Sam suggests a disgorged pét-nat, whose lees (dead yeast and other particulate matter) have been released from the bottle, facilitating more clarity. Les Capriades is his favorite. **YIELDS 1 SERVING**

- ☐ 1 teaspoon Kettl Soukou matcha powder
- ☐ ¾ ounce Chareau aloe liqueur
- ☐ ½ ounce Rich Simple Syrup (page 339)
- ☐ Ice cubes
- ☐ 4 ounces pétillant-naturel (natural sparkling) wine, ideally Chenin Blanc–based (such as Les Capriades)
- ☐ 3 (1-inch) honeydew melon balls, for garnish

Add the matcha powder, liqueur, and syrup to a chilled mixing glass. Whisk with a chasen to thoroughly blend, then add a scoop of ice cubes and stir. Add the pét-nat sparkling wine and stir briefly. Double-strain through a julep and a fine-mesh strainer into a chilled coupe. Garnish with the melon balls on a cocktail pick or float them in the glass, like Sam does.

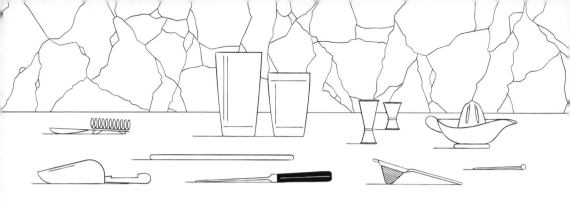

KIND OF BLUEBERRY

by Jim Meehan

The original recipe for the Aviation in Hugo Ensslin's *Recipes for Mixed Drinks* (1916) calls for crème de violette—presumably to give the cocktail a purplish tinge, resembling the sky. I find the liqueur also gives the drink a soapy quality that likely precipitated its absence from *The Savoy Cocktail Book,* published fourteen years later. In my modern take on the drink, freeze-dried blueberries provide both the color and the character to complement the other ingredients, helping the recipe fly high once again. YIELDS 1 SERVING

- ☐ 2 ounces Blueberry-Infused Gin (page 346)
- ☐ ¾ ounce lemon juice
- ☐ ½ ounce Simple Syrup (page 339)
- ☐ ¼ ounce Luxardo maraschino liqueur
- ☐ Ice cubes
- ☐ 3 fresh blueberries, for garnish

Add the gin, lemon juice, syrup, and liqueur to a Boston shaker. Add a scoop of ice cubes, then shake. Double-strain the mixture through a Hawthorne and a fine-mesh strainer into a chilled coupe. Garnish with 3 blueberries on a cocktail pick.

BANANA STAND

by Kevin Diedrich

Coconut and coffee are common in Hawaii, where Kevin Diedrich travels to frequently; and he's always loved pairing banana with bourbon. To incorporate all these elements into a cocktail for the menu at Pacific Cocktail Haven in San Francisco, Kevin combined a coconut-banana infused whiskey with coffee liqueur, using the classic Brooklyn cocktail as the template upon which to layer the flavors. The name of the drink is an allusion to *Arrested Development* character George Bluth's vehement insistence that "there's always money in the banana stand." YIELDS 1 SERVING

- ☐ 2 ounces Coconut-Banana–Infused Bourbon (page 346)
- ☐ ¾ ounce Lustau Jarana fino sherry
- ☐ ½ ounce Kahlúa liqueur
- ☐ 2 dashes P.C.H. Orange Bitters (page 349)
- ☐ Ice cubes
- ☐ 1 lemon peel, for garnish

Add the bourbon, sherry, liqueur, and bitters to a chilled mixing glass. Add a scoop of ice cubes. Stir and strain into a chilled martini glass. Garnish with a lemon twist.

Vegetables, Flowers & Herbs

Flowers and herbs have frequently found their way from the garden into classic cocktails—particularly mint, in drinks like the Mint Julep and Mojito. But vegetables, less so. Besides a fresh cucumber slice to garnish a Pimm's Cup or the use of tomatoes—which are botanically a fruit but usually considered a vegetable—in a Bloody Mary, vegetables only tend to appear in cocktails at restaurants with a culinarily-minded bar staff with a forward-thinking chef. What vegetables, flowers, and herbs all share is the ability to bring appealing savory and herbaceous qualities to mixed drinks—traits that depend on whether they are used fresh, dried, or preserved.

n the introduction to *The Drunken Botanist,* Amy Stewart writes, "Around the world, it seems, there is not a tree or a shrub or delicate wildflower that has not been harvested, brewed, and bottled." And in turn, I imagine there are few vegetables, flowers, and herbs that intrepid bartenders have not also tried to incorporate into their cocktails.

The plant kingdom is so vast and varied that it's prudent to preface this section with notice that botanists don't all agree on plant classifications, and the science remains fluid as new information emerges. With other plant parts like fruits, seeds, nuts, grains, and spices covered elsewhere in the book, what remains for use in beverages are a plant's leaves, flowers, roots, and rhizomes. That is what this chapter features.

Anatomical groupings might seem to be an ideal organizing principle for these ingredients, but I found *Vegetable Literacy* author Deborah Madison's decision to group and survey plants by their botanical family quite useful culinarily, as it gives cooks and bartenders inspiration for pairings they may not consider unless they know how these ingredients are related. "Once you become familiar with them, you suddenly see them differently in the kitchen, more relatedly and more confidently," Madison says.

Herbs

Throughout history, herbs—the tender leaves or flowering parts of plants—have been favored for flavoring food and drinks. For bartenders, herbs are relied upon for their lively freshness and transportive aromatics, which is why they are most commonly used as garnishes. Dried herbs are also an option for brewing or infusing into spirits and syrups, which adds an herbaceous quality to a drink.

The world is brimming with opportunities to incorporate herbs into cocktails, but because some can be unsafe to imbibe (like wormwood in high doses), it's wise to follow the advice of authors Selena Ahmed, Ashley Duval, and Rachel Meyer in *Botany at the Bar: The Art and Science of Making Bitters.* "We only use botanicals that have a long history of common use in traditional cultures and then cross-check their safety through databases and scientific literature."

Some of the most commonly used herbs in beverages include the following.

Basil The Genovese variety, which is famous for its role in pesto and brings peppery complexity to Joerg Meyer's Gin Basil Smash (page 206), is the most common type of basil used in cocktails, but aromatic Thai basil also works well, particularly with savory spirits like gin, mezcal, and tequila.

Lavender Favored for its cooling, calming qualities in spa treatments, lavender is frequently used in soaps; so use it judiciously as a garnish. Some craft distillers use lavender to soften the botanical profile of gin, and lavender pairs well with it in mixed drinks for the same reason.

Mint Of the many types of mint available—including yerba buena, lemon mint, peppermint, chocolate mint—spearmint is the most widely available and what most drink recipes call for (even without specifying it by name). To keep mint as vibrant as possible, follow Lydia McLuen's conditioning method (see page 190). Use bouquets to make a statement garnish for drinks like Chris Marty's Wondermint Malted (page 106) and Leo Robitshek's Choked Up (page 76).

Rosemary A remarkable cold- and heat-resistant plant that thrives in many parts of the country, rosemary is valued for its piney aroma and flavor. Also a member of the mint family, its leaves are slender and its stems are thicker and more woody than many other herbs. Some bartenders brûlée a sprig of rosemary before adding it as an aromatic garnish.

Shiso A member of the mint family known as perilla, shiso is most commonly found in cocktail programs with Japanese influences. There are two types: the red variety is typically used in cooking and adds a peppery quality, while the green variety offers a more refreshing mint-like aroma with anise notes.

Thyme Favored for infusions or as a garnish, thyme has a woody stem (similar to rosemary but thinner) and minuscule leaves. According to author Amy Stewart in *The Drunken Botanist,* "English thyme is the standard culinary thyme, but lemon varieties are also excellent." She adds a notable caveat: "Creeping, woolly varieties are not as tasty."

SOURCING

For delicate herbs like mint, look for loose-leafed bunches at the grocery store if you don't have some growing in your garden. Avoid the mint in the tiny clamshells sold in some markets, which are fine for heartier herbs like rosemary or sage, but not for delicate leaves that will be arranged in a bouquet as a garnish. Even more sensitive than mint, basil—which is part of the mint family—should be purchased as a plant and placed near a window, if you can't make space for it in your garden.

Many tea purveyors stock well-dried herbs and flowers if you don't have the time or space to dry your own. If you prefer to prep them yourself, mint can be dried in a dehydrator, by hanging bunches of it upside down in a well-ventilated area, or by spreading the leaves on parchment paper and letting them dry at room temperature. Use dried mint to prepare the cordial called for in Mony Bunni's Cultural Consumption (page 100).

STORAGE

For freshly picked herbs, *In Praise of Veg* author Alice Zaslavsky suggests that "if you plan on using the herbs within a few days, store them as you would decorative flowers—in a vase with plenty of fresh water, in a shady spot on the counter. Just make sure that none of the leaves are touching the water." Fresh herbs will keep for a week or so in a vase, or you can arrange them in a single layer on a damp paper towel, roll them up, and store them in a resealable bag or quart container in the crisper drawer of the fridge, where they should last for a couple weeks.

Woody and waxy herbs—like pandan leaves, makrut lime leaves, and spruce tips—freeze well. Only defrost what you need by letting them warm up at room temperature on the counter. Use pandan to make L'Alligator C'est Vert (page 208) and spruce tips to make the mint syrup in Light as a Feather (page 202).

As with spices, store dried herbs in an airtight, nonreactive container in a cool, dry place.

PREPARATION

Before mixing, submerge fresh herbs in plenty of water if they need to be cleaned. After draining, spin the leaves dry and store them wrapped in a lightly dampened towel in a resealable container or plastic bag in the fridge.

Flowers

While most flowers are typically reserved as a garnish to add a striking visual element to a drink, many bartenders have begun incorporating them for their flavor, which is the case with hibiscus, chamomile, cherry blossoms, and elderflowers. A particularly theatrical bartender might also freeze flowers into ice cubes or offer them spontaneously to guests from a vase, as I've seen Colin Field do at the Hemingway Bar at the Ritz Hotel in Paris.

Most organic flowers seem safe for consumption, but a handful can cause health complications, so it is crucial to confidently identify edible varieties before serving them. Camper English offers a long list of unsafe flowers at the website cocktailsafe.org/flowers, including (but not limited to) baby's breath, marigold, yarrow, and morning glory.

Some of the most commonly used flowers behind the bar include the following.

Hibiscus Also known as roselle and sorrel in the Caribbean, hibiscus may be infused either fresh or dried to prepare and garnish drinks such as Fortuna Anthony's Sorrel (page 192) and Osvaldo Vásquez's Baja Grenadine (page 32). As with tea leaves, dried flowers should be as close to fully intact as possible, with lively aromatics and color, which are signs that they've been carefully handled. Sometimes hibiscus is candied or coated in sugar, which makes them useful for a memorable garnish.

Nasturtium Basic garden nasturtium come in a rainbow of colors, with flowers a little larger than a quarter. They are beautiful to look at and can be used as an edible garnish, though they are somewhat lacking in flavor.

Orchids Remarkable for their vivid colors and perchable anatomy, organic orchids are also edible. They make striking garnishes (see the Longball on page 260).

SOURCING

In *Edible Flowers*, Mary Newman and Constance L. Kirker recommend seeking out organic options because "flowers from florists will almost certainly have been sprayed with pesticides and should not be eaten, as they may contain up to fifty times the pesticides and fungicides permitted on food crops."

STORAGE

Store flowers like fresh herbs; wrap them in a wet towel and store in a clamshell in the fridge.

PREPARATION

Flowers may also be used to perfume a drink, such as the orange flower water that aromatizes orgeat. Orange flower water is a water-based extraction of orange oil from its blossoms. Water-based distillations of ephemeral flowers and herbs can be made by distilling at low temperature under pressure, using a Rotovap evaporator to preserve delicate aromatics, by supercritical fluid extraction, or through traditional distillation in copper-pot stills.

Vegetables

In addition to imparting a savory quality to drinks, vegetables like peppers add heat, cucumbers contribute melony notes, beets bring earthy geosmin, and celery has grassy tones. Vegetables also broaden the typical color spectrum of cocktails with their deep greens, bright oranges, inky reds, and earthy browns.

There are too many cocktail-friendly vegetables to detail completely, but here are some commonly used options featured throughout this book.

Beets Beets come from the goosefoot and amaranth family, which also includes peppery epazote. In *The Chef's Garden,* Farmer Lee Jones writes that beets' flavor "comes from a compound called geosmin—the same chemical responsible for the smell of fresh soil after the rain." In *Vegetable Literacy*, author Deborah Madison notes that, "beets are also full of sugars—think of sugar beets, from which sugar is made—and these two qualities, the earthy and the sweet, oppose one another and confuse the mouth." Beet juice is employed in the raspberry syrup featured in Back to the Roots (page 238).

Celery Part of the carrot family, which also includes angelica, anise, caraway, cilantro (coriander), cumin, dill, fennel, lovage, and parsley, celery is sturdy enough to store alone in a crisper drawer or wrapped in a moist towel in a mesh bag. Limp celery can be revived with a short dip into an ice-water bath.

Cucumbers Part of the cucurbit family, which also includes squash, melons, and pumpkins, cucumbers are officially classified as a vegetable, even though they bear the hallmarks of a fruit (formed from a flower and containing seeds that can be used to grow more). English cucumbers have thin skin, tiny seeds, and are typically sold shrink-wrapped in supermarkets. Garden cucumbers are more girthy, with thicker skin that some producers coat with wax to extend their shelf life. Persian cucumbers are smaller, thin-skinned, and typically packaged in plastic wrap. Each may be stored in the crisper drawer of the fridge, preferably wrapped but not airtight, for up to a week.

Ginger The young rhizome of ginger—a plant which has its own botanical family called Zingiberaceae—is juicy and fragrant, with a sweetness that diminishes as it matures. Ginger's thin skin is edible and may be left intact depending on its condition and cleanliness. If you prefer to peel the rhizome, use a sharp paring knife or spoon to scrape it off. Fresh ginger may be stored at room temperature for up to a week, but it lasts longer—about 1 month—when wrapped loosely in a paper towel in a sealed container in the fridge.

Horseradish Horseradish comes from the cabbage family, which also includes arugula, cabbage, mustard, and wasabi. The prepared horseradish used in the Bloody Marion (page 70)—which is traditionally preserved with salt and vinegar—should be refrigerated after it's opened. It will store well for a few months if securely sealed.

Peppers *Chile* is a Nahuatl word for what many Americans call sweet or hot, fresh or dried peppers. Hot peppers are used in small proportions like a spice, such as habaneros or the jalapeños used in Osvaldo Vásquez's Sangrita Verde (page 66). Sweet bell peppers, which do not contain the capsaicin that gives chiles their signature heat, are, like hot peppers, part of the nightshade family, which also includes tomatoes and tomatillos. Capsaicin is concentrated in the pithy white ribs of the chile, which provides the chile with structure and the seeds with a place to grow. If you want the flavor of a hot chile, but not all its heat, carefully cut out the ribs with a sharp knife and discard the seeds. Wear gloves if you're especially sensitive to capsaicin and avoid touching any part of your body, especially your eyes, until you've thoroughly washed your hands. Peppers can be stored in a paper bag in the crisper drawer of the fridge for up to a week.

Radicchio Radicchio is part of the sunflower family, which also includes artichokes, chamomile, chicories, chrysanthemums, daisies, echinacea, goldenrod, lettuces, marigolds, milk thistles, sunflowers, and tarragon. Loose-headed lettuces should last at least five days wrapped in a plastic bag in the crisper drawer of the fridge, while the firm heads will remain fresh for several weeks there. Kristina Magro runs radicchio through a masticating juicer to yield its "juice" (see page 357) for Salad Bar (page 210).

SOURCING

In addition to the recommendations made in Sourcing Suggestions (page 6), all of which are especially pertinent when it comes to fresh vegetables, Farmer Lee Jones (author of *The Chef's Garden* and an expert on regenerative agriculture) adds a few questions to consider when making decisions about what to buy: "Am I supporting farmers who are taking care of their soil, their crops, and their team members? Are they treating their vegetables with care after harvest so they retain their nutrients?" Here, he's pointing out that there's a cost—to the land and to the people who pick our crops—that must be paid for agriculture to be sustainable.

STORAGE

Just as with fresh fruits, make decisions about vegetable storage on a case-by-case basis. *The Waste-Free Kitchen Handbook* by Dana Gunders is a compact but commendable source for more specific recommendations regarding all types of vegetables, herbs, and fruits.

PREPARATION

Unlike citrus, vegetables, herbs, and flowers typically require more preparation to mix into drinks. This means extra space at a prep table, more cutting boards and knives, pricey machinery like a masticating juicer, extra refrigerated real estate, and allotment of more prep time.

I n *The Secret Life of Groceries,* author Benjamin Lorr observes that "as a culture, we do a generally excellent to overzealous job thinking about food, a highly conflicted job thinking about its origins in the natural world as a living thing, and spend almost no time thinking about our groceries as retail products." This is especially true for vegetables, flowers, and herbs, as our modern industrial foodways have bent natural cycles out of shape in order to deliver these items to local stores quickly and with regularity from around the world.

"Most of the industrially grown produce is controlled by a few behemoth growers and packers, who have narrowed their offerings down to a few varieties in each category—those that grow fast, large, and uniform in size," write Sam Mogannam and Dabney Gough in their book *Bi-Rite Market's Eat Good Food.* Because these ingredients are meant to look good on a shelf, they are typically not as flavorful or interesting as heirloom varieties grown with care by small and independent farmers.

By design, it is easy to forget that these ingredients are organic matter that live or die depending on the climate, quality of the soil, and stewardship of the farmers that tend them. Restoring these factors to the forefront of our minds is crucial, because when we can trace the way a vegetable or flower comes to market, it becomes easier to understand "how everything from climate collapse, changes in immigration policy, infrastructure, market availability, and a globalized economy affect the already complex challenges facing growers," writes Michigan chef Abra Berens in her book *Pulp.*

When sourced from thoughtful growers, vegetables, flowers, and herbs in top form during peak season deliver a vibrancy of flavor that makes cocktails more memorable. But, with relatively short growing seasons (actual length depending on which part of the country you live in), incorporating fresh vegetables, herbs, and flowers into mixed drinks requires bartenders to be more strategic than they would have to be with shelf-stable ingredients. For those working in a restaurant where the kitchen is already using seasonal produce—and happy to order extra for the bar—this poses few logistical hurdles. Standalone bars need to pay closer attention to economics, as most bar and restaurant owners expect to make up to twice as much profit from a cocktail as a plate of food prepared with the same produce.

Prepping flowers, vegetables, and herbs for drinks generates a fair amount of unusable organic waste, so if you don't already have a composting program in place, this presents a great opportunity to implement one. It's a game-changer for rooftop and home gardens. When properly cultivated, compost adds nutrients and stimulates healthy microbial activity in the soil, which will facilitate more flavorful and nutritious vegetables, flowers, and herbs in the future.

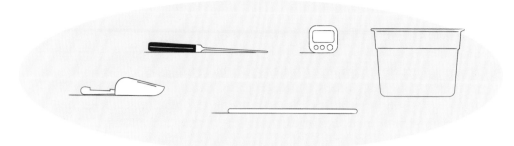

MINT CONDITIONING

from Lydia McLuen

This isn't a recipe per se, rather, a method for keeping mint vibrant and staving off spoilage. Lydia McLuen, who helped me open Takibi in Portland, Oregon, learned this mint-processing method while working for Ricky Gomez at Palomar. Ricky adapted the method from Chicago bartender Peter Vestinos, who popularized it on his *Bar Medic* website in 2016. The original "Vestinos method" calls for storing the shocked sprigs in julep cups filled with hot water, placed on the bar top, to perk them up for display during service. Lydia and Ricky's adaptation is tailored for weekly storage.

Use this method to prepare mint for any recipe that calls for a mint garnish or muddling, like Cultural Consumption (page 100), Wondermint Malted (page 106), Arroz con Rum (page 134), "Pimm's" Cup (page 168), Choked Up (page 76), or Light as a Feather (page 202). YIELDS ABOUT 85G SPRIGS AND 10G FRESH LEAVES

☐ 6 quarts pebble or crushed ice
☐ 6 quarts filtered water

☐ 4 bunches (100g) spearmint sprigs

In a 12-quart food storage container, combine the ice and water. Gently plunge the mint sprigs into the ice bath, being careful not to crush them. Let them sit in the water for 15 minutes, then gently remove and arrange on paper towels to dry.

Sort the mint into 3 piles: brown or black leaves to compost, loose leaves picked from the lower parts of the stems for muddling, and top parts of the sprigs for garnishes. Cut the sprigs to a consistent 5-inch length.

Fill a 1-quart deli container one-fourth of the way with cold water from the ice bath and place the sprigs in the container leaves up, stem ends down (the water level should be below the leaves).

Place the loose mint leaves in another 1-quart deli container and position a damp paper towel on top of them.

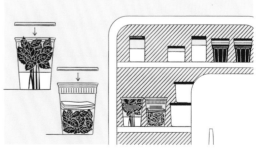

Store both containers, covered, in refrigerator for up to 1 WEEK.

SORREL

from Fortuna Anthony

According to St. Lucia-based cookbook author and chef Fortuna Anthony, "The festive Christmas season in St. Lucia is never complete without families brewing the flower of this red herbaceous annual plant." The typical preparation of sorrel, she says, is to infuse the fresh buds in cold water for three days with spices (like cinnamon, nutmeg, and star anise). In this recipe, I used dried hibiscus flowers, since I don't have access to the fresh sorrel buds Fortuna does. I find a hot extraction makes the flavors more astringent, so I use a long infusion at room temperature to gently coax the flavor from the flowers and spices.

Use this in the Sorrel Rum Punch (page 200) or drink it over ice.

YIELDS 28 OUNCES

- ☐ 34 ounces filtered water
- ☐ 100g (2 cups) dried hibiscus flowers
- ☐ 13.5g (three 3-inch quills) Ceylon (canela) cinnamon
- ☐ 3.5g star anise pods (about 2 pods)
- ☐ 1 dried bay leaf
- ☐ ⅛ teaspoon ground ginger
- ☐ ⅛ teaspoon grated lime zest
- ☐ 70g (5 tablespoons) white cane sugar

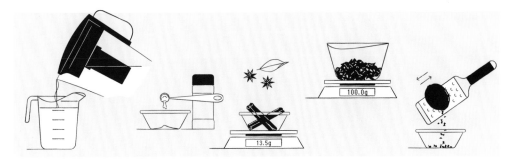

Measure the water, flowers, cinnamon, star anise, bay leaf, ginger, and lime zest.

Add these ingredients to a nonreactive container with a lid.

Cover and let sit at room temperature for 2 days.

Strain the mixture through a fine-mesh strainer. Compost the flowers and spices.

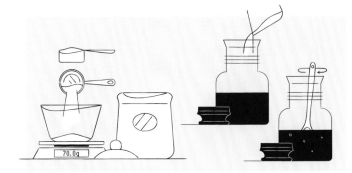

Add the sugar to the mixture and stir until dissolved.

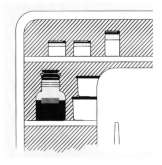

Store, covered, in the fridge for up to 1 WEEK.

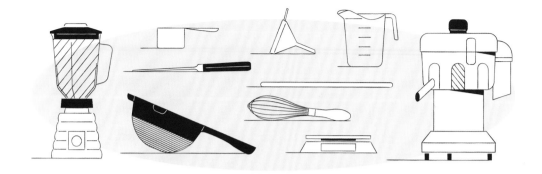

BEET-RASPBERRY SYRUP

from Martin Hudák

Martin Hudák, of Maybe Sammy and Spiritual Coffee (both in Sydney, Australia), told me the inspiration to combine earthy beets with fragrant raspberries came from his time working in specialty coffee, where amid the terrestrial flavors of coffee "you get hints of berry fruits such as raspberries, blueberries, or black currants." The combination is also close to Martin's heart as a native Slovakian, "as these ingredients are widely used in the kitchens where I grew up in Central Europe."

Use this flavorful syrup in Back to the Roots (page 238). YIELDS 12 OUNCES

- ☐ 450g (3 medium) beets
- ☐ 200g (1 cup) superfine sugar

- ☐ 100g (1 cup) raspberries, fresh or thawed IQF (individually quick frozen)

Trim the beets.

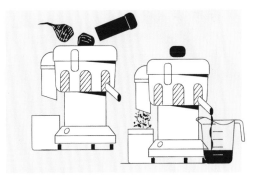

Run the beets through an extractor to yield 6 ounces juice.

Pour the beet juice into a blender pitcher. Add the sugar and raspberries to the blender pitcher.

Blend the mixture until smooth.

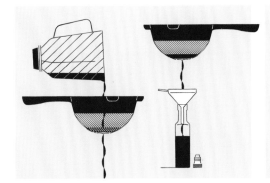

Strain the mixture through a fine-mesh strainer into a nonreactive container.

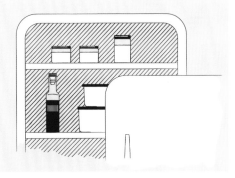

Store the syrup, covered, in the fridge for up to 3 DAYS.

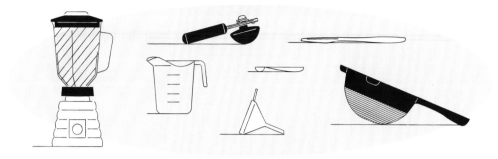

CORN WATER

by Wylie Dufresne

When I asked chef Wylie Dufresne how he'd approach incorporating corn in a cocktail, he surprised me by recommending I use canned corn over fresh kernels cut from the cob. "Corn is high in sugar, but it begins converting to starch as soon as you remove it from the stalk," Wylie said. "Canned corn can be sourced everywhere, and the corn is packed in water, which absorbs the kernel's flavor."

Use this in the Malabar Silver Corn Fizz (page 74). YIELDS 8 OUNCES

- ☐ 1 (15-ounce; 425g) can organic sweet corn, with liquid
- ☐ 5g (1 teaspoon) kosher salt

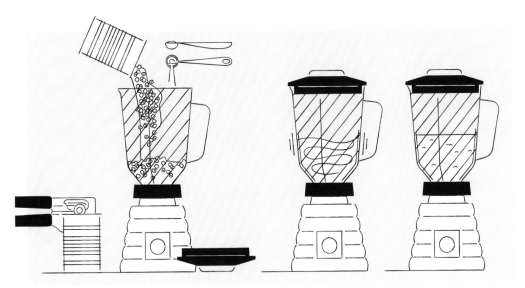

Add the corn, canning liquid, and salt to a blender pitcher. Blend until smooth.

Fine-strain the mixture—pressing the solids with a spatula to extract all the liquid—into a nonreactive container.

Store, covered, in the fridge for up to 5 DAYS.

MINT SPRUCE SYRUP

by Katie Rose

Goodkind co-owner Katie Rose says this recipe was born from her love of gin. "The nuances of the spirit's bold, bright, beautiful botanicals make it my absolute favorite," she says. "Mint is an excellent playmate for gin, and ramping it up with spruce tips lengthens its flavors and ignites my mid-palate." This syrup is also Katie's go-to for nonalcoholic gin and tonics, prepared with fresh lime juice, mint, and tonic water. "It really mimics a gin and tonic beautifully!" If you're not able to source fresh spruce tips, Spruce On Tap ships them frozen via their webstore.

Use this to make Light as a Feather (page 202). It would also make a killer Southside. YIELDS 26 OUNCES

- ☐ 10g (1 cup) mint leaves, rinsed
- ☐ 10g (¼ cup) spruce tips, rinsed
- ☐ 17 ounces filtered water
- ☐ 500g (5 cups) superfine sugar

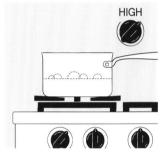

Place the freshly-rinsed mint leaves and spruce tips in a salad spinner and spin until dry.

Add the water to a medium saucepan.

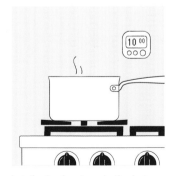

Bring the water to a boil.

Add the sugar to a separate large saucepan and set aside.

Turn off the heat and add the mint leaves and spruce tips to the boiling water.

Let the herbs steep in the hot water for 10 minutes.

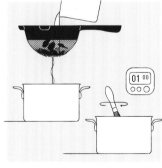

Fine-strain the herbed water into the saucepan with the sugar. Stir until the sugar dissolves, about 1 minute. Compost the herbs.

Let cool, then store, covered, in the fridge for up to 1 WEEK.

SORREL RUM PUNCH

from Fortuna Anthony

Fortuna Anthony told me: "St. Lucians look forward to their sorrel, and many add a shot of rum to give the additional zing." I've adapted the recipe Fortuna shared, in which the sorrel is prepared from fresh flowers, sweetened into a syrup, then spiked with Denros Strong (160 proof) white rum, citrus, bitters, and spices. Here, her sorrel stands in for the syrup and an aged St. Lucian rum takes the place of the overproof bottling, making this much less punchy but delicious nonetheless. YIELDS TEN 4½-OUNCE SERVINGS

☐ 20 ounces Sorrel (page 192)

☐ 15 ounces Chairman's Reserve rum

☐ 5 ounces lime juice (from 6 limes)

☐ 2½ ounces Demerara Syrup (page 337)

☐ 10 dashes Angostura bitters

☐ Ice cubes, plus 1 ice block tempered for 30 minutes

☐ 10 lime wheels (from 2 limes), for garnish

☐ Nutmeg, freshly grated, for garnish

Add the sorrel, rum, lime juice, syrup, and bitters to a nonreactive container and stir to blend well. Cover and chill in the fridge for 1 to 3 hours.

If serving in a punch bowl, add a large tempered block of ice to the bowl. If serving in a pitcher, fill two-thirds full with ice cubes. Add the chilled punch and the lime wheels. Ladle or pour the punch into chilled punch glasses filled with ice cubes. Garnish each serving with freshly grated nutmeg and a lime wheel.

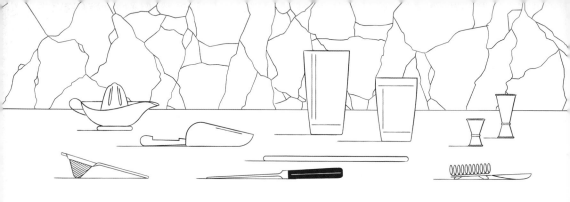

LIGHT AS A FEATHER

by Katie Rose

Katie Rose created this Corpse Reviver-like daisy in the summer of 2014 for her drink menu at Goodkind, in Milwaukee, Wisconsin. "It was a hot summer girls' night out at a friend's house—one that included gin and tonics prepared with mint, stick-and-poke tattoos, texts to boys, and playing light as a feather, stiff as a board," she told me. "In reality," she added, "we were a bunch of mid- to late-thirty-year-olds who all had to be up early the next day. Rational thinking went out the window, but the hangover was worth it." **YIELDS 1 SERVING**

☐ 1 ounce St. George Terroir gin

☐ 1 ounce lime juice

☐ ½ ounce Cocchi Americano aperitivo

☐ ½ ounce Hayman's sloe gin

☐ ½ ounce Mint Spruce Syrup (page 198)

☐ Ice cubes

☐ 1 mint leaf, for garnish

Add the gin, lime juice, aperitivo, sloe gin, and syrup to a Boston shaker. Add a scoop of ice cubes and shake. Double-strain through a Hawthorne and a fine-mesh strainer into a chilled coupe. Garnish with a mint leaf, clapped to release its aroma.

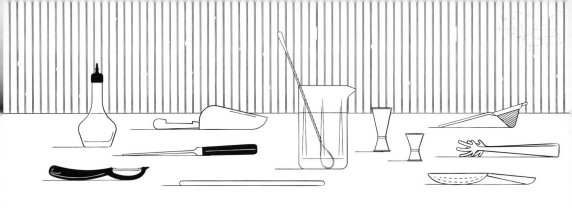

CELERY AND NORI

by Don Lee

When I asked Don Lee about the unusual combination of flavors in this cocktail, he recalled that the inspiration came from a culinary moment at Momofuku Ssäm Bar in 2009, when "Francis Derby was working on a variation of Tien Ho's scallop crudo that was garnished with celery and fried nori." With the traditional pairing of Calvados and scallops in mind, Don developed this recipe as a partner to Derby's dish. "I don't remember if Francis's dish ever made it onto the menu, but it definitely inspired the drink." YIELDS 1 SERVING

☐ 2 ounces Nori-Infused Apple
    Brandy (page 348)
☐ ½ ounce Celery Syrup (page 343)

☐ 2 dashes Bitter Truth celery bitters
☐ Ice cubes, plus 1 large (2-inch) ice
    cube, tempered for 1 to 2 minutes
☐ 1 lemon peel, for garnish

Add the brandy, syrup, and bitters to a chilled mixing glass. Add a scoop of ice cubes and stir. Strain through a julep strainer into a chilled old fashioned glass filled with one large tempered ice cube. Garnish with a lemon twist.

GIN BASIL SMASH

by Joerg Meyer

Two inspirations led to Joerg Meyer's creation of the Gin Basil Smash, which many consider to be the most notable modern classic cocktail from Germany. The first was Dale DeGroff's Whiskey Smash, invented in 1988. The second was a book given to Joerg by Audrey Fort of G'Vine Gin, which featured a drink using basil as a garnish—an unusual application back in 2007—that reminded him of DeGroff's recipe. Joerg substituted Audrey's gin for the whiskey, lime for the lemon, and basil for the mint. He published this recipe on his influential website, *Bitters Blog,* where it quickly caught the attention of cocktailians. The drink can still be found today on menus all over the world, including Meyer's own Le Lion: Bar de Paris in Hamburg, Germany, aka "the cradle of the Gin Basil Smash."

YIELDS 1 SERVING

- ☐ 2½ ounces Rutte dry gin
- ☐ 1 ounce lemon juice
- ☐ ¾ ounce Simple Syrup (page 339)
- ☐ 4 basil sprigs
- ☐ Ice cubes

Add the gin, lemon juice, syrup, and 3 basil sprigs to a Boston shaker. Add a scoop of ice cubes and shake. Double-strain through a julep and a fine-mesh strainer into a chilled old fashioned glass filled with ice cubes. Garnish with the remaining basil sprig, clapped to release its aroma.

L'ALLIGATOR C'EST VERT

by Nico de Soto

Nico de Soto created this decadent twist on Charles Vexenat's absinthe-based Coffee Flip (absinthe, milk, espresso, simple syrup, egg yolk, nutmeg) for Bastille Day, in 2015. "I love sweets and coconuts. After a trip to Indonesia in 2008, where I ate so many rice cakes with pandan, I fell in love with the leaf." As a result, all of his bars stock pandan syrup to prepare this drink. "It goes with everything," he says, adding, "I'm a big fan of coconut milk as well, and reach for it more frequently than cream." YIELDS 1 SERVING

☐ 1 ounce Pernod absinthe
☐ 1 ounce Thai Kitchen coconut milk
☐ 1 ounce Pandan Syrup (page 344)
☐ 1 large egg
☐ Nutmeg, freshly grated, for garnish

Add the absinthe, coconut milk, syrup, and egg (yolk and white) to a Boston shaker. Shake without ice, then add a scoop of ice cubes and shake again. Double-strain through a Hawthorne and a fine-mesh strainer into a chilled fizz glass. Garnish with freshly grated nutmeg.

The Bartender's Pantry

SALAD BAR

by Kristina Magro

Kristina Magro, who worked with me at Prairie School in Chicago, created this drink in February of 2018, after finding inspiration at an indoor farmer's market. "The radicchio's beautiful color caught my attention amongst lots of different lettuces. Its complex, dark purple 'juice' mixes perfectly with the spice notes in the blanc vermouth. The sherry adds a salty green apple note, while the egg white softens the bite of the chicory." I like how the aromatics of the lemon-infused olive oil counterbalance the other ingredients and double as the drink's "salad dressing." **YIELDS 1 SERVING**

- ☐ 1 ounce Alessio bianco vermouth
- ☐ 1 ounce Lustau Fino Jarana sherry
- ☐ ¾ ounce lemon juice
- ☐ ¾ ounce Simple Syrup (page 339)
- ☐ ½ ounce Radicchio "Juice" (page 357)
- ☐ 1 large egg white
- ☐ Ice cubes
- ☐ 5 drops Lemon-Infused Olive Oil (page 356), for garnish

Add the vermouth, sherry, lemon juice, syrup, radicchio "juice," and egg white to a Boston shaker. Shake without ice. Add a scoop of ice cubes and shake again. Double-strain through a Hawthorne and a fine-mesh strainer into a chilled 8-ounce coupe. Garnish with the 5 olive oil drops centered in a circle on the surface of the drink.

Coffee

Setting aside the enduring popularity of the Irish Coffee and Espresso Martini, brewed coffee appears in surprisingly few classic cocktails. In most recipes, coffee's bitterness (to balance sweeteners) and caffeine (to offset booziness) are its most prized attributes. Following the lead of specialty coffee shops, many previously overlooked qualities of coffee beans—like fruity and floral flavor profiles and complex acidity—are now being featured in mixed drinks. As more coffee aficionados cross over to participate in cocktail programs, the influence of coffee's origin, variety, roast level, and extraction method are being highlighted in new coffee liqueurs, spirit infusions, and brewing methods used for mixed drinks. The camaraderie between coffee and cocktail professionals is opening up new horizons for both industries.

C offee is one of the oldest beverages in the world—in *The Coffee Book,* Anette Moldvaer dates it back at least 1,000 years to Africa—and one that is universally beloved, with different preparations and rituals defining its use depending on who is making it and where. Its caffeine rouses in the morning and stimulates throughout the day, and its preparation and consumption conjure powerful memories that influence its imbibers very identities.

The history of coffee traces back to indigenous communities in tropical regions, where people first learned to ferment and prepare beans for consumption. "Even before the seeds were roasted, ground, and brewed to make the coffee we drink today, coffee cherries and leaves were used for their invigorating properties," Moldvaer writes. "Traveling herders in Africa mixed coffee seeds with fat and spices to create 'energy bars' for the long periods of time spent away from their homes. The coffee leaves and cherry skin were also boiled to create an invigorating, caffeine-free infusion."

Now grown in at least seventy countries, "coffee has never been better than it is today," writes James Hoffman in *The World Atlas of Coffee,* adding how over 125 million people depend on coffee for their livelihoods. "Producers know more than ever before about growing coffee and have access to more varieties and specialist growing techniques. Coffee roasters have never before been so likely to appreciate the importance of using freshly harvested coffee beans, and their understanding of the roasting process continues to improve. There are now more cafés selling really good coffee, using the best equipment and training their staff more effectively."

COFFEE SPECIES

Coffee is brewed from the roasted seeds of a flowering evergreen *Coffea* tree, which grows between the Tropic of Capricorn and the Tropic of Cancer. Over 100 species of the *Coffea* tree have been identified, but only two are widely cultivated for coffee consumption: *C. arabica,* or arabica, originating from Ethiopia, and *C. canephora,* or robusta, originating from the Democratic Republic of the Congo.

Arabica This species of *Coffea* thrives at 1,000 to 2,000 meters high. Arabica beans have a higher oil content than robusta, which adds body and a rich mouthfeel when brewed. When roasted, the sugar levels are much higher as well, creating a perceptible sweetness that most find quite pleasing.

Robusta This species of *Coffea* grows best at lower elevations. It has larger yields and twice as much caffeine as arabica, which helps it grow more abundantly in the fields, as caffeine is a natural insecticide. Most coffee connoisseurs denigrate robusta for its woody, bitter taste and prevalence in mass market coffees, but this must be weighed against climate-change considerations ravaging arabica crops worldwide. I'm rooting for Sahra Nguyen, who founded America's first specialty Vietnamese coffee company—Nguyen Coffee Supply—and is boldly ushering in the future for robusta coffee.

COFFEE VARIETIES

There are several hundred varieties of the arabica species, of which two— Bourbon and Typica—can be classified as "original." Bourbon is still grown widely around the world (particularly in Brazil), while Typica is less common, but still cultivated in Mexico, Jamaica, and Hawaii. Geisha, which was originally discovered at the Hacienda La Esmeralda farm in Panama, is another celebrated specialty coffee variety famed for its floral aroma. It sells for notably high prices at coffee auctions.

While most coffee breeding is being done to improve yields without regard for flavor, Kenya's SL28 and SL34—known for their bright acidity and berry aromas— are examples of varieties being selectively bred for flavor too. In response to global warming, many plant geneticists have begun to work on hybrids of robusta crossed with select arabica varieties to yield heat- and draught-resistant plants that produce beans with good character too.

The easiest way to identify a coffee bean's variety is by sight. Geisha beans are tiny compared to varieties like the Pacamara, which are so large they take twice as long to grind. In *The Fundamentals of Excellent Coffee,* the Coffee Collective acknowledges that "it's rare for an ordinary everyday coffee drinker to be able to taste a coffee and say what variety it is, as so many other factors affect the flavor post-harvest, including processing, roasting, and brewing, to name but a few. Keep an eye out for new varieties when you buy coffee, and note down what you think about them, because varieties with distinct flavors are really starting to break through."

HARVESTING AND PROCESSING

It takes three to five years before a coffee tree produces berries (called "cherries"), which are harvested at different times of the year in each hemisphere. The key to good quality is the ripeness of the cherry; the highest sugar development has the greatest potential for flavor.

On small farms located on steep slopes, growers hire experienced pickers to select cherries by hand within a narrow range of color (from ruby red to deep red), leaving immature (green to light orange/red) or overripe (dark purple, black) cherries behind. Immature cherries can be left on the tree to continue developing, and pickers can return for a second or third pass as needed to harvest them when ripe, thus increasing the overall yield. This more costly and labor-intensive process expedites sorting (to remove twigs, or underripe/overripe cherries) and helps ensure the quality of specialty coffee lots.

In countries like Brazil, where much coffee is planted on flat plains in even rows, mechanical harvesters are often used to strip pick cherries from branches indiscriminately. This more cost-effective method of harvesting yields cherries of various ripeness, as well as leaves and twigs, which means that sorting, either by hand, water, or machine (using density, not color, and so not foolproof) is more cumbersome and wasteful, as unripe and overripe cherries must be discarded.

Each cherry has an outer skin, a layer of pulp, a layer of mucilage, a thin parchment covering, silver skin, and two green seeds that become the coffee "beans," once processed. There are four common ways to process a coffee cherry: washed/wet process where the pulp is allowed to ferment before being "washed" off; natural/dry process, whereby the whole berry is dried and its parchment and pulp are removed in one process; honey/pulped natural process, whereby some flesh is left to ferment; and anaerobic, whereby fermentation occurs without oxygen.

The beans are then cleaned, sorted, and graded. Over the next four to six months, the "green coffee" is sold, either to traders who work with other distributors or directly to roasters. Don't assume "direct trade" coffee always means farmers are being treated equitably, though: large roasters can afford to buy direct and may use that power indiscriminately, while many small roasters can work with ethical traders who work transparently.

ROASTING

Roasting creates chemical and physical changes in the green bean (via heat) that influences the bitterness, sweetness, and acidity of a brewed cup. Many roasters maintain a similar level of roast across their offerings for consistency. "Roast level is the number one most important factor when it comes to coffee's final taste," says Matthew Davis, product manager at Breville USA. "So find your favorite roast level and experiment with different coffees of that profile."

Dark roasts During coffee's emergence as one of the most popular beverages in America, dark roasted beans—achieved via exposure to high heat for a long period of time—were most prevalent. "Darker coffees tend to accentuate bitterness and because they're actually roasted for a longer period of time, they become more brittle and therefore grind very differently. This is key with espresso," says Davis. "Because of the brittle nature of dark roasts, they also become more soluble." In other words, they release flavor more readily, which can make lovely espressos but can also lead to over-extraction if you're not careful.

Light roasts Lighter roasted beans maintain more moisture because they're exposed to heat for less time, so more nuanced flavors and light acidity are expressed in the coffee. "Medium roasted beans tend to be a sweet spot, while lighter roasts have the opposite effect of darker roasts. They're more difficult to extract and their taste can range from overly acidic to borderline vegetal without careful attention. All in all, it comes down to personal preference," says Davis. "I think brighter and more acidic coffees work best in a drip brew method while fruity and chocolatey coffees rule as espresso, but that's just my jam."

SOURCING

In *The World Atlas of Coffee,* James Hoffman offers the reminder that "it is fairly safe to presume that if the coffee has been kept traceable, it has the producer's name(s) on it, or at least the name of the farm, cooperative, or factory, which all suggest a better price has been paid."

Single origin vs. blends Single-origin coffees are offered to provide a singular example of one coffee's variety, processing, terroir, and roast according to

Omotesando Koffee's Michael Yung. For that reason, most are available only in limited quantities at a higher price point, and are often reserved for retail. Blends, on the other hand, are formulated with more than one batch of beans to maintain a consistent flavor profile. They are typically less expensive than single-origin coffees, but that doesn't mean the beans used are of lower quality—a lot of effort and ingenuity goes into blending, and a consistent cup is an impressive feat in itself when the components are always changing.

Shelf life Retail coffee should be listed with a roast date instead of an expiration date. In *Specialty Coffee,* Katrien Pauwels recommends buying bags with a one-way valve because beans need time to de-gas after roasting. "The valve ensures that the coffee can de-gas without air entering the bag," she writes. Unlike a ripe raspberry or raw cow's milk, you can't drink coffee right after roasting—this is crucial and widely misunderstood. "In the best-case scenario, the beans rest for four to five days in the packaging—in which they can de-gas—before they are consumed. Only then do they show their true nature." Pauwels adds that the darker the bean, the more gas it will contain. "That is why beans for espresso should rest for a week, while those for filter coffee can be brewed and drunk earlier."

Pauwels recommends consuming roasted coffee within a month. "The coffee will not actually be bad after a month, of course, but the strength of its aromas depletes as time goes by," she writes in *Specialty Coffee.* Once ground, the coffee's quality deteriorates in a matter of hours, so buy whole beans and grind to serve. Ideally, purchase one week's worth of small, resealable bags for your home and 1 kilogram bags for a restaurant or bar.

To prevent beans from going stale, store them at room temperature in an airtight container, ideally in the retail packaging they came in or in a clean inert metal or tinted glass jar with a top that can be plunged to expel oxygen. Place this in a dry, dark, odorless environment. Contrary to popular myth, storing beans in the fridge does not prolong their shelf life, but storing unopened bags of properly sealed beans in the freezer does. Once the beans have thawed and the bag is opened, they should not be refrozen.

COFFEE RELATIVES

Cascara Traditionally cascara—the dried skin and fruit of the coffee cherry—is composted and used as fertilizer after being separated from the beans, but it can also be processed to serve as an infusion that expresses cherry characteristics. After drinking nutty, chocolatey coffee for years, the floral, fruity side of specialty coffee makes much more sense to me after tasting cascara.

Flavored coffee Chicory root has been added to ground coffee since at least the nineteenth century in Europe. It was used to lengthen coffee rations during times of scarcity and hardship in the United States, and is still popular in New Orleans. Cardamom, cinnamon, and other spices have a long history in coffee blends, but purists will remind you they cover up the character of the beans. There's a monumental difference between coffee with freshly ground high-quality spices and coffee with synthetic "natural" flavorings. The former makes for an interesting and complex drink, while the latter tends to taste one-dimensional.

PREPARATION

Before you begin mixing with coffee, it's crucial to understand how to brew a good cup using a variety of preparation methods. With an understanding of the pros and cons of each brewing method, you'll know which one to use to access the full spectrum of coffee's character. This will in turn give you the ability to amplify your selected coffee's qualities during recipe development.

Measure To achieve consistently delicious coffee from batch to batch, you should always measure the weight of your beans before grinding. For espresso, invest in a gram scale that's small and thin enough to place under an espresso cup below the portafilter to measure and time your shots—the Acacia Lunar scale has great accuracy, durability, and legibility.

Grind Invest in a quality burr grinder. The less expensive blade grinders—which work well for grinding spices—don't yield uniform particle size, which is necessary for even extraction of ground coffee. Few burr grinders are calibrated coarse enough for filter coffee and fine enough for espresso, so counter space and financial capital should be considered for both. Oils and particulate matter build up quickly where beans are ground, so brush grinders free of matter fastidiously between each use.

Water source The mineral composition—particularly hardness or softness—of your water source can dramatically influence coffee's flavor. If you live in an area with hard or chlorinated water, you should filter your tap water. Christopher Hendon, who co-wrote *Water for Coffee* with barista Maxwell Colonna-Dashwood, developed a filter pitcher with an adjustable dial, allowing users to adjust the water filtration level to remove unwanted minerals while maintaining the ideal pH to brew delicious coffee.

Tools and machinery An excellent cup of coffee can be brewed relatively inexpensively by hand using a kettle with a gooseneck pour spout and brewer such as a Kalita, Chemex, or AeroPress. A nice drip coffee maker will cost you considerably more, and a café-quality espresso machine will cost you a small fortune. As a general rule of thumb—similar to how audiophiles will tell you to invest in quality speakers if your budget is limited—the more you spend on a coffee grinder, the better the performance. I use a Baratza Encore and Sette at home, a Comandante grinder on the road, and a Mahlkönig Ek43 at the restaurant.

BREWING METHODS

Pour-over When using a Chemex or similar apparatus, ground coffee is placed in a rinsed filter and hot water is slowly poured from the spout of a craning, thin-necked kettle in a circular motion. This maximizes the desirable qualities of the ground beans as they "bloom" up, letting flavor cascade into the pitcher below. The slow method allows greater control over the process because it's done by hand, which helps create a delicate, smooth textured coffee.

Drip coffee This method mechanizes the pour-over process, whereby ground coffee is placed in a filter and hot water is cascaded through it. Michael Yung points out that "while it does not offer the same amount of recipe control as pour-over coffee, it can offer greater consistency from batch to batch with minimal effort or training, and more capacity when large quantities are required." Seek out a machine with an insulated stainless steel carafe that will keep the coffee hot for up to an hour instead of a glass pitcher with a hot plate (which burns the coffee as it sits).

French press Ground coffee is measured into a glass pitcher, hot water is added, the mixture steeps, and then a plunger is depressed to hold the grounds at the bottom while you pour out the coffee. This method creates a full-bodied, flavorful cup because there's no filter paper to hold back the oils, which add rich mouthfeel. Because the grounds remain in contact with the coffee—and because the glass pitcher loses heat rapidly—French press coffee should be consumed relatively quickly or decanted into an insulated carafe to prevent overextraction and temperature loss.

Espresso To make espresso, water is channeled through finely ground coffee at high-pressure to concentrate its flavor and body. Espresso's oil-rich "crema" is preserved when shaken in a cocktail, rivaling only pineapple juice and egg white as a foaming agent. The crema and balance of a shot of espresso deteriorates rapidly, so it should be served or shaken into a cocktail right after it's pulled. Espresso machines and brewers need to be regularly cleaned with eco-friendly solvents to avoid buildup of oils. Wipe the portafilter and steam wand before and after use. Martin Hudák's Espresso recipe (page 228) was developed for Back to the Roots (page 238), but it also works well in an Espresso Martini.

AeroPress This easy to use, affordable, and durable brewing apparatus (that I pack when I'm on the road) allows you to brew concentrated short infusions or longer, pour-over style coffee using a plunger to channel the water through a narrow chamber with a portafilter-sized filter to restrain the oils. The apparatus is designed to perch upon a coffee mug for brewing, making it ideal for single servings.

Flash-brew Coffee is brewed hot first, then rapidly chilled to minimize the acrid, stale flavor that coffee exhibits when allowed to cool at room temperature. In *The Fundamentals of Excellent Coffee,* the Coffee Collective asserts: "This makes for a far more aromatic coffee, as the heat extracts more of the organic acids that give the coffee its liveliness." Flash-brewed coffee should be stored covered in the fridge for up to three days. Check out Michael Yung's Flash-Brewed Iced Coffee (page 224), a method that works wonders for making the Ethiopian coffee I used to make Falling Water (page 240).

Cold-brew Coffee grounds are steeped with cold water for an extended period of time in a brewing apparatus ranging from the larger Toddy system to the more intimate Kinto Casule, which reduces the bitterness of the brew. In spite of the popularity of the method, the Coffee Collective warns that the lack of extraction at high temperatures can yield an "unbecoming woody undertaste lacking in the acidity that makes well-grown coffees so amazing." Their other concern is hygienic: "With cold brew coffee vs. flash brew, the conditions are ripe for the growth of microorganisms." They recommend storing cold brew in the fridge, avoiding as much exposure to air as possible, and enjoying it within three days of brewing.

TROUBLESHOOTING

Martin Kastner, of Crucial Detail, who designed a new brewing apparatus called the Orb, suggests, "if your coffee to water ratio is correct for the method and your coffee is sour or very acidic or just weak (often the case with espresso and very light roasts), use finer grind, and if not already maxed out, then increase water temperature. If it's very bitter, use coarser grind and/or lower water temperature. It's noteworthy that darker roasts release solubles faster and lighter roasts are harder to extract. That's why light roasts aren't the best espresso candidates if one doesn't like very acidic coffee."

SERVICEWARE

In *Coffee*, Tim Wendelboe recommends: "Give the coffee more space in the cup; you'll be able to pick up the aromas more easily and the coffee will cool to drinking temperature faster. Steaming hot coffee really has little taste. Good coffee tastes best when it's slightly warmer than lukewarm. That's when the aromas and flavors are at their most pronounced." Glass is a good choice for this sort of drinking experience, as it diffuses the heat more quickly than ceramic or insulated metal and encourages you to use your sense of sight too.

Wendelboe's advice is reminiscent of Harry Craddock's adage in *The Savoy Cocktail Book* to "Drink your cocktail as soon as possible. Quickly, while it's laughing at you!" This applies to espresso, which becomes acrid the longer it sits; milk drinks, which become flat; and brewed coffee, which oxidizes in the glass. Most recipes recommend serving coffee in a pre-heated vessel, but if your guest plans to drink it right away, this step can be skipped.

The coffee industry has gone through many phases of evolution over the last century in the United States. In the 1950s, mass-production paved the way for coffee to become a daily fixture in households everywhere. About forty years later, coffee drinkers started flocking to cafés like Starbucks for espresso drinks. And in the early 2000s, a new cadre of specialty coffee professionals began encouraging the public's attention toward coffee's migration from bean to cup, centering varietal character and progressive production practices.

"Coffee drinking has evolved from simple morning stimulation into an expression of self, an expression of values or of conscious consumption," writes James Hoffman in *The World Atlas of Coffee*. As we learn more about how coffee is grown, harvested, processed, exported, roasted, and prepared, we gain insights into all the areas in which an extractive system needs to be rebalanced with regenerative, just principles. On the sourcing side, legacies of colonialism persist, including the lack of transparent and equitable trade practices, though now there is more focus on grower and worker compensation and working conditions, along with the long-term ecological sustainability of coffee. In the café, specialty coffee has its own set of issues paralleling what's been called out in restaurants and bars—racism, sexism, pay inequity, and real estate gentrification.

As coffee consumers, we should vote for the changes we'd like to see in the coffee industry with our buying choices.

"It's striking to think about just how many people are needed to get you your morning cup, and it's more astonishing that that cup could still only cost a couple bucks, if not less," writes Ashley Rodriguez, aka the Boss Barista, in a newsletter titled *The Invisible Labor of Coffee*. "Once you pan out and reflect on how true that pricing is of so many other food and drink products you consume—fruit, vegetables, tea, rice, chocolate, and on—a troubling picture begins to emerge."

It might feel unnatural for bartenders to exercise their political capital publicly, but we can support progressive change by respecting picket lines when workers are engaged in collective bargaining on the café side of the industry, and by allocating our bean-buying budgets to suppliers who only use equitable coffee growing and trade practices. When environmental or trade issues are on the ballot, we should educate ourselves and our customers about the stakes for regional and national policies so Americans don't continue to participate in the degradation of land and the livelihoods of workers inside and outside of our borders.

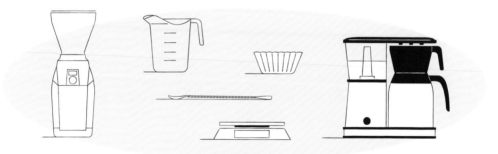

FLASH-BREWED ICED COFFEE

from Michael Yung

Michael Yung, who has judged many international coffee competitions, introduced me to the flash-brew method as an alternative to cold brewing. "Roasted coffee contains more than 800 aroma and flavor compounds. Cold brewing leaves a significant range of the more subtle fruit and floral notes, along with acidity and brightness out," he says. "The remedy is to brew first with hot water (thus attaining a more ideal extraction rate) and then chill immediately using ice. Rapid chilling helps prevent unwanted sourness from oxidation that occurs when you let hot coffee cool slowly on its own or in the fridge."

Use this method for Falling Water (page 240) or drink it over ice. YIELDS 33.8 OUNCES

- ☐ 425g (3 cups) ice cubes
- ☐ 67g (scant ¾ cup) Ethiopian coffee beans
- ☐ 20 ounces filtered water, plus more as needed

Add the ice cubes to the coffee maker carafe.

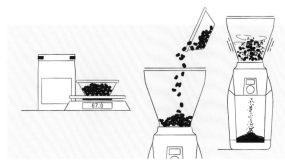

Grind the coffee beans on a medium setting, a little more coarse than sand.

Place an unbleached paper filter in the basket of the coffee brewer and rinse it thoroughly.

Form a level bed of grounds in the filter.

Add the filtered water to the tank.

Turn the coffee maker on (and turn the hot plate off, if there is one).

When brewing is complete, remove the brewing basket and compost the coffee.

Stir the coffee until all the ice melts. Decant the coffee into an airtight container.

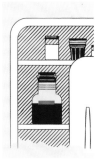

Store, covered, in the fridge for up to 2 DAYS.

TÜRK KAHVESI

from Ria Neri

Ria Neri, co-founder of Four Letter Word Coffee, opened her first coffee shop in Istanbul because she prefers the coffee culture in Turkey. In Turkey, coffee is "slow, intentional, social, and communal," whereas in the United States it is "practical, convenient, fast, and singular," she explains. At the Chicago Four Letter Word Coffee shop, she serves an outstanding rendition of türk kahvesi, or Turkish coffee, that "should be enjoyed slowly in small sips to savor the big flavors," she says. "A single cup of coffee can be a three-hour commitment in Turkey." Four Letter Word serves a lokum, colloquially known as a "Turkish delight," with rose petal, pomegranate, and pistachio alongside this preparation, which is just one of many popular recipes for Turkish coffee. Neri notes that "everyone has their own style" of coffee in Turkey.

Use this coffee to make my Kahvesi Corretto (page 234) or drink it unmixed.

YIELDS 3 OUNCES

- ☐ 15g (2 tablespoons) washed Brazilian coffee beans
- ☐ 2.5g (½ teaspoon) cane sugar
- ☐ Pinch of ground green cardamom
- ☐ 2½ ounces filtered water, brought to 172°F
- ☐ 1 lokum, for serving (optional)

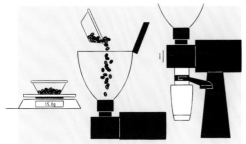

Grind the coffee beans on the finest setting possible.

Place the cezve on a scale and add the ground coffee.

Add the sugar and the cardamom to the cezve.

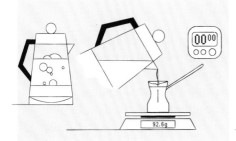

Add the 172°F filtered water and start the timer as you begin pouring.

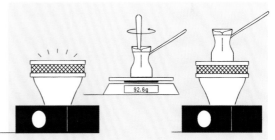

Turn the halogen beam heater all the way up. Stir the coffee to integrate the spices, then add the cezve to the halogen beam heater.

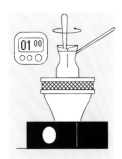

After 1 minute, stir the coffee again to break up any bubbles.

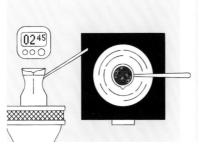

After 2 minutes and 45 seconds, when the coffee begins bubbling, remove the cezve from the halogen beam heater.

Pour the coffee unstrained into a prewarmed Turkish coffee cup. Serve a lokum alongside, if desired.

ESPRESSO

from Martin Hudák

Martin Hudák won the 2017 Coffee in Good Spirits championship while working as a bartender at the Savoy American Bar in London. His espresso recipe, which he calibrated to mix into his Back to the Roots cocktail, calls for a lightly roasted South American coffee. To preserve its character in the cocktail and achieve bigger body and juiciness in the cup, he increases the typical dosage. "It may seem a bit strong—or even over-extracted—but when you make coffee cocktails, you have to bear in mind that the coffee must be stronger, as it will be diluted with ice and the other ingredients," he says. "That's usually the biggest mistake baristas and bartenders make when they start creating coffee cocktails."

Use this to make the coffee needed in the Back to the Roots (page 238) or a classic Espresso Martini. YIELDS ONE 2-OUNCE (60 GRAMS) SHOT OF ESPRESSO

☐ Filtered water

☐ 23g (¼ cup) honey-processed South American coffee beans

Fill the espresso machine (if unplumbed) with filtered water and heat to 200°F.

Wipe the warm portafilter with a clean, dry towel to remove any residual oils, grounds, or moisture.

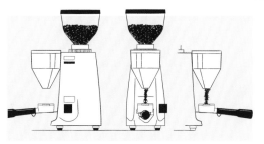

Place the portafilter on the scale and tare it.

Then, place the portafilter in its holder to receive the coffee grinds (an espresso dosing ring helps if you don't have an espresso grinder). Grind the coffee on a fine setting into the portafilter (rotating the portafilter, if necessary, so the grounds fill the basket evenly).

Weigh the portafilter to ensure the correct dosage and remove or add coffee as necessary.

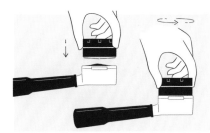

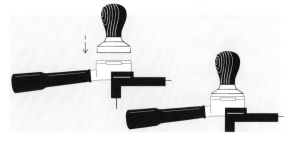

Groom the surface of the coffee bed to evenly distribute the grounds using a distribution tool.

Tamp the freshly ground coffee in the portafilter with a tamper of the same diameter as the portafilter over a sturdy, level surface on top of a tamping pad to create an evenly distributed, level-surfaced coffee bed. (The portafilter should be clean with no loose grinds above the surface of the coffee bed.)

· CONTINUED ·

Flush the group head by dispensing hot water to remove any grounds from the previous shot and ensure a consistent temperature for the proceeding brew.

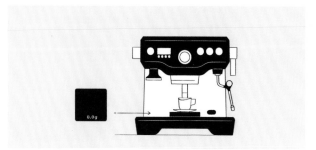

Place the prewarmed espresso cups on top of a digital scale placed underneath the filter outlet or weigh the cup before placing it on top of the clean drip tray below the group head.

If the espresso machine doesn't time the shot, zero your timer.

Carefully latch the portafilter into the group head to avoid dislodging any grounds from the coffee bed.

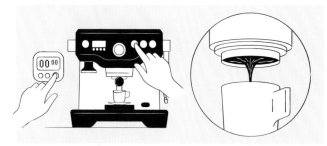

Begin brewing right after latching—to avoid burning the coffee—and start your timer.

When the desired shot weight is achieved—typically after 25 to 30 seconds—stop the brew.

Carefully wipe any drips or splashes from the exterior of the cup with a clean towel.

Place the cup on a warm saucer, stir briefly to integrate the crema, and serve with a fresh espresso spoon.

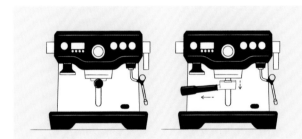

Unlock the portafilter from the group head.

Discard the spent coffee grounds by drumming the portafilter against the padded bar across the strike box to dislodge the ground coffee puck.

Place the portafilter under the group head and flush some water into it.

Wipe clean, then dry the portafilter with a clean towel.

Reset the portafilter to prepare for the next shot.

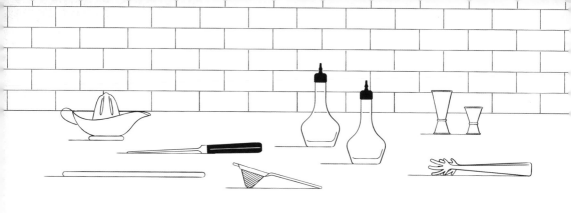

LONDON BRIDGE

by Tyler Kleinow

Tyler Kleinow—who worked as a barista before tending bar—created this Arnold Palmer riff to highlight cascara for Bombay Sapphire's Most Imaginative Bartender competition in 2014. The drink endured as one of the top five best-selling cocktails at Marvel until the Minneapolis bar closed in 2020. In the drink, fruity, floral cascara complements the gin, while licorice root and lemon create a complementary undertone for those botanicals. "I fell in love with this unique ingredient [cascara] so much that we still always have it on hand at Meteor, the bar I helped open after Marvel. It is versatile and can do more than just work in simple refreshing drinks." YIELDS 1 SERVING

- ☐ 3 ounces filtered water, chilled
- ☐ 1½ ounces Bombay Sapphire gin
- ☐ 1 ounce Cascara Infusion (page 354)
- ☐ ½ ounce lemon juice
- ☐ ½ ounce Simple Syrup (page 339)

- ☐ 3 dashes Licorice-Root Water (page 356)
- ☐ Dash of Mineral Saline (page 340)
- ☐ Ice spear, tempered for 1 to 2 minutes

Add the filtered water, gin, cascara infusion, lemon juice, syrup, licorice water, and saline to a chilled Collins glass. Add a tempered ice spear to the glass.

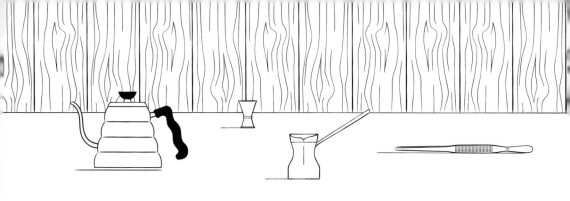

KAHVESI CORRETTO

by Jim Meehan

To create a cartographically appropriate caffè corretto–an Italian espresso drink spiked with a spirit such as grappa or Italian liqueur, whose title translates to "coffee corrected"–with Ria Neri's Türk Kahvesi, I followed the food pairing maxim that "what grows together typically goes together" and landed upon raki, Turkey's most popular spirit, which has an anise flavor profile similar to Italian sambuca. Neri serves her Turkish-style coffee with a lokum, or "Turkish delight," in all her cafés, which contributes a vibrant color contrast and familiar flavors to her cosmopolitan coffee service, which I've playfully "corrected" to add to its delight. YIELDS 1 SERVING

- ☐ ¼ ounce Efe Raki classic
- ☐ 3 ounces Türk Kahvesi (page 226)
- ☐ 1 lokum (Turkish delight), for serving

Add the raki to a prewarmed coffee cup. Pour the Türk Kahvesi into the cup.

Serve with a lokum.

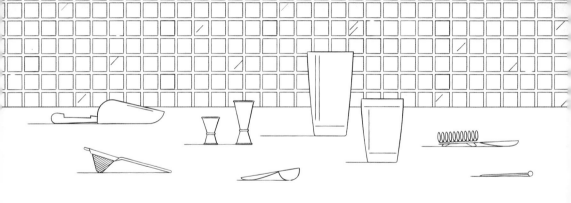

PENNY

by Chanel Adams

Chanel Adams developed this drink named after her colleague Pang "Penny" Yik Nam at Doubleshot by Cupping Room, a short walk from PDT Hong Kong, where we worked together. For the recipe, she chose ingredients that would emphasize the flavors of the coffee: cherry, red wine, and passion fruit. "Coffee can be quite versatile if you are working with medium- to light-roast, single-origin coffees. These tend to be more fruity and sometimes spiced and herbal, rather than the dark roast most people are used to in Espresso Martinis," she says.

YIELDS 1 SERVING

- ☐ 1½ ounces Buffalo Trace bourbon
- ☐ ¼ ounce Mâcon red wine (or a fruit-forward Pinot Noir)
- ☐ ¼ ounce Luxardo maraschino liqueur
- ☐ ¼ ounce Simple Syrup (page 339)
- ☐ 1½ ounces Flash-Brewed Iced Coffee (page 224)
- ☐ 1 barspoon passion fruit purée
- ☐ 1 large egg white
- ☐ Ice cubes
- ☐ 1 Preserved Cherry (page 155), for garnish

Add the bourbon, wine, liqueur, syrup, coffee, purée, and egg white to a Boston shaker. Shake without ice, then add a scoop of ice cubes and shake again. Double-strain through a Hawthorne and a fine-mesh strainer into a chilled glass coffee cup. Garnish with a cherry on a cocktail pick.

BACK TO THE ROOTS

by Martin Hudák

Martin Hudák, who worked in a small Slovakian café before taking the coffee and cocktail world by storm, created this drink for a seminar and guest shift during the 2018 Diageo World Class competition in Moscow. The "roots" in the title refers to beetroot, but also to legendary London bartender Dick Bradsell's Espresso Martini. "I wanted to pay respect to Dick and his creation with ingredients rooted in my childhood in Slovakia. These ingredients were also familiar to bartenders in Moscow." YIELDS 1 SERVING

- ☐ 2 ounces Ketel One vodka
- ☐ 1 ounce Espresso (page 228)
- ☐ ¾ ounce Beet-Raspberry Syrup (page 194)
- ☐ Ice cubes
- ☐ 3 coffee beans, for garnish

Add the vodka, espresso, and syrup to a Boston shaker. Add a scoop of ice cubes, then shake the mixture. Double-strain through a Hawthorne and a fine-mesh strainer into a chilled coupe. Float the 3 coffee beans in the center of the drink.

FALLING WATER

by Jim Meehan

I created this heady flip for my short-lived Chicago bar, Prairie School. It featured coffee from Ria Neri's Four Letter Word, prepared via the slow-drip Kyoto-style cold-brew method. The name "Falling Water" is an allusion to Frank Lloyd Wright's famous house and a literal description of this cold-brew method that helps preserve the stone fruit notes in the Ethiopian coffee. This brewing apparatus is large (and expensive!), so Ria brewed it for us at her roastery and dropped it off in quarts with our whole bean deliveries. To recreate the drink, you can use a Kyoto cold-brew tower if you have one, or the flash-brewed iced coffee method (page 224) also works well. YIELDS 1 SERVING

☐ 1½ ounces Flash-Brewed Iced Coffee (page 224)
☐ 1½ ounces Cardamaro vino amaro
☐ ¾ ounce Rhine Hall plum brandy
☐ ¼ ounce Simple Syrup (page 339)
☐ 1 large egg
☐ Ice cubes
☐ 3 coffee beans, for garnish

Add the coffee, amaro, brandy, syrup, and egg (yolk and white) to a Boston shaker. Shake without ice, then add a scoop of ice cubes and shake again. Double-strain through a Hawthorne and a fine-mesh strainer into a chilled coupe. Float the 3 coffee beans in the center of the drink.

Tea

A cynical argument could be made that the most famous tea cocktail of the twentieth century is the Long Island Iced Tea, which does not include any actual tea. At the turn of the twenty-first century, Audrey Saunders ingeniously course-corrected the trajectory of tea in cocktails with the Earl Grey MarTEAni (page 264) at Bemelmans Bar. Now, thanks to a growing cadre of purveyors importing high-quality loose-leaf teas, and the brewing equipment, techniques, and veneration of the cultural traditions from which they originate, the West has more distinctive options than ever before. From peachy milk oolongs to grassy senchas and smoky lapsang souchong, teas are being incorporated into drinks by bartenders using historic rituals and brewing equipment to help align modern bar service with tea's ceremonial roots.

The origins of tea as a beverage "reflect more than 5,000 years of complex, colorful, and global history," write Brian Keating and Kim Long in *How to Make Tea*. "Tea germinated in ancient China and then spread into Japan, India, and eventually the Western Hemisphere. The story spans legendary Chinese emperors and Japanese monks who revered tea for its uplifting properties, and on to the emboldened British entrepreneurs (colonists) who commercialized tea production in India during the 1800s. Tea has been traded, brewed, and prized worldwide ever since."

Before we explore the intrinsics of tea, here's an important terminology clarification: I'm reserving the term *tea* for beverages made from the *Camellia sinesis* plant, an evergreen shrub native to Southeast Asia. Two varieties are common: *Camellia sinensis* var. *Sinensis*, which has small leaves and is sensitive to seasonal fluctuations in temperature; and *Camellia sinensis* var. *Assamica*, which has larger leaves and is better suited to hot, sunny weather year-round. Tea plants are cultivated in over 49 countries, with most commercial production taking place in tropical and subtropical regions from countries such as China, India, Japan, Sri Lanka, and Kenya.

I include other types of caffeine-free infusions—those prepared with dried flowers, herbs, grains, and leaves, such as mint, hibiscus, lemongrass, and buckwheat—in other chapters. These tisanes, herbals, and infusions (or whatever you prefer to call them) don't have finicky brewing parameters or complex catechins, and can't be steeped multiple times, like some teas.

High-quality tisanes and herbals are fantastic ingredients in mixed drinks, as most people drink cocktails at night when caffeine is unwelcome. They can be prepared with boiling hot water (except for chamomile, which is ideally brewed a little cooler), and because they don't have the tannins and other qualities that make over-steeped tea astringent, you can let tisanes steep without a timer.

HOW TEA IS PROCESSED

It takes *Camellia sinesis* plants approximately three years of maturation to become tea producers. Afterward they may be cultivated for a hundred years or more if well-tended. Most tea is mechanically harvested, while artisan tea is usually hand plucked. Typically, only the bud and the first two or three leaves are harvested, which happens multiple times throughout the season.

Bardo Tea co-owner Ravi Kroesen told me that besides green tea, whose process introduces a heat step to halt oxidation as close to the picking of the leaf as possible, tea production takes place either at an estate where the plants are grown or nearby. The leaves are first dried for several hours via elevated beds, racks, or on the ground. The leaves begin to oxidize as soon as they are plucked from the plant and teamakers further this enzymatic transformation by rolling (sometimes more than once) to shape the leaf. "At the desired level of oxidation, the leaves are fired to halt this process, then dried in ovens or woks to below 6 percent of the original water content of the leaf, to complete the process," says Kroesen. Finally, the leaves are sorted based on size, evaluated, and then packaged.

The method by which the leaves and buds are processed determines the type of tea it becomes, with oxidation being the main factor.

White tea The least-processed type of tea; it's picked then dried. A certain amount of oxidation occurs during the drying process, producing floral, vegetal, and hay-like flavors.

Green tea A heat step is introduced shortly after the leaves are picked to prevent oxidation and allow the leaf to retain most of its natural polyphenols and green color. Shaping and drying complete the process. Green teas typically taste vegetal, floral, and nutty.

Black tea Dark brown to black in appearance, these tea leaves are almost fully oxidized, which creates bold flavors of malt, dark fruits, flowers, and honey.

Pu-erh and dark tea Golden to dark brown in color, these fully oxidized teas include a fermentation step, which produces complex flavors of earth, barnyard, and wood.

Some teas go through additional processing steps before being sold, such as flavoring, scenting, blending, smoking, aging, decaffeinating, and grinding. These are called "altered teas."

Flavored tea These teas are made by adding flavors via inclusions, extracts, or natural and artificial flavoring agents. Earl Grey, infused with bergamot oil, is the most classic example. Audrey Saunders uses this tea in a gin infusion that serves as the base for her Earl Grey MarTEAni (page 264).

Inclusion tea This is tea with the addition of spices, fruit, or flower petals. Masala chai (black tea with spices) and genmaicha (green tea with puffed rice) are examples. The former spices up the Masala Milky Tea Punch (page 102), while the latter brings a green toasted quality to the Riot Act (page 140).

Scenting tea This tea is made by allowing processed tea leaves to take on the scent of their surroundings. Jasmine tea is traditionally made using this process. Ravi Kroesen brews jasmine tea in a teapot (see page 256) to allow the pearls to unfurl in hot water, while Julie Reiner uses a flash-brew method to fully extract its flavor and rapidly chill it for service (see page 262).

Roasted tea For this tea, roasting is used to enhance flavor. This is common among oolongs of East Asia and Japanese hōjicha. Explore this style of tea in the Oolong Tea Syrup (page 344), which features a cold-brewed oolong from Rare Tea Cellar that aromatizes the sweetener for the Longball (page 260). Hōjicha provides an earthy base for Julia Momosé's Comfort's Toddy (page 266), and appears in Arielle Johnson's Hōjicha Kombucha (page 316).

Ground tea Japanese teas like matcha and funmatsucha are ground into a powder and whisked together into suspension with water. Zach Mangan of Kettl Tea showed me how to make Usucha Matcha (page 252), and the grassy tea shines in the Dragonfly (page 136), the Lava Lamp (page 174), and Speak Low (page 268).

Blended tea Batches of tea leaves are blended to create a consistent product year after year. This is common among commodity breakfast teas like English Breakfast, which Nick Bennett relies on for its tannins and earthy complexity in his updated version of the 7 & 7 highball (page 292).

SOURCING

If you have doubts about your tea purveyor's quality, sample their tisanes and herbal infusions. If they are fresh and lively, with flavor that is clear, focused, and natural, chances are the purveyor takes their tea freshness seriously too. If the purveyor doesn't sell tisanes, this is even more encouraging, as it suggests they are solely committed to quality tea.

Source whole-leaf teas (sans sachet), unless you're seeking broken pekoe tea, like the Assam used for Kadak Spicy Chai (page 91), or a ground tea like matcha or funmatsucha—unbroken leaves or buds are preferable. Tea bags—frequently made from bleached paper or non-biodegradable nylon—are not ideal because the leaves have to be cut to fit in the bag, which reduces freshness and flavor. Tea should smell vibrant both dry and wet. If the leaves crumble easily, they have been baked too long or may be old.

STORAGE

Store tea in an airtight container made from a nonreactive material like ceramic or metal, which prevents UV damage, oxidation, and absorption of flavors from other ingredients. I use a glass tea caddy with a plunger that allows me to expel air as I deplete the jar. Glass allows you to verify a tea by sight; you just need to store it in a cabinet away from the light. Most retail bags are also suitable storage vessels. The exceptions are green teas like matcha and gyokuro, which should be stored tightly sealed in the fridge and consumed within two weeks.

PREPARATION

No two teas are exactly alike. The style, origins, and characteristics of the tea you select should influence the brewing method chosen to prepare the tea as an ingredient in a cocktail. For example, every type of tea has an ideal brewing temperature, calibrated to bring out the best qualities in the leaves. The leaf-to-water ratio affects the concentration of a brew, as does time spent infusing. Be mindful of these guidelines—the brewing instructions are typically listed on the retail bag if sourced from a reputable importer—and you'll be rewarded with a consistently delicious cup.

Water source Brewed tea is 98 percent water. The quality and character of your water can vary depending on what part of the country you live in. Mineral content shifts by region and many municipal water sources add chlorine to kill harmful bacteria. Even if you live in a region with great tap water, it's advisable to run it through a filter pitcher such as a Brita to remove any hard minerals or chlorine.

Leaf-to-water ratio As Tony Gebely writes in *How to Make Tea,* "Aficionados banter and debate endlessly about how much tea to use when brewing a cup or pot. There is both art and science involved in this decision, but it comes down to personal preference and little else." Many tea purveyors recommend ratios that work best for each tea, but brewing vessels vary in size and shape, and strength and intensity preferences vary by individual. Gebely suggests experimenting to find the right recipe for your needs. That said, to brew consistently, you'll want to measure your leaves by weight instead of volume, since whole leaves vary in size. This is best accomplished with a high-quality digital scale. I use the Acacia Lunar at home and the Acacia Pearl scale at the restaurant.

Temperature Because different types of tea taste best at various temperatures, in a bar or café with many types of tea on offer, you'll need access to water ranging in temperature from as low as 140°F for gyokuro to 200°F for pu-erh and other black teas. Investing in a kettle with a built-in temperature display and a long-craned spout (such as the Fellow Stagg) makes it easy to brew tea or coffee pour-overs at home or at low-volume cafés. I used a Marco commercial brewer at the restaurant to dispense hot water at three programmable temperatures and volumes.

Time Temperature is important, but so is the amount of time the leaves steep. "Inevitably, under-brewed tea is weak and not satisfying; over-brewed tea is often bitter and too astringent," Gebely writes, recommending the use of a timer for precision. "In general, longer brew times are desirable for black teas and some oolongs, but never for green teas," he adds, suggesting 3 to 5 minutes for oolong, 1½ to 3 minutes for green teas, and 4 to 6 minutes for white tea. I always start with the brewing parameters on the package, and adjust from there.

Brewing vessels Many brewing vessels can be found on the market, but tea is typically prepared in either a large or a small teapot, depending on the tea-drinking conventions of its country of origin and the person brewing it.

- Teapot: Teapots come in many shapes, sizes, and materials, including metal, glass, ceramic, and porcelain. The aesthetics of the pot depend on personal preferences, which are influenced by the tea culture its maker adopts. Look for a teapot with a filter plate that holds back leaves, with enough room inside to allow the leaves to unfurl. My friend Henrietta Lovell sells beautiful teapots of this style at Rare Tea Co. in London.

When picking a teapot, Zach Mangan advises, "It is a tool you will use daily, and it is important that the look and feel of it brings you joy." Porcelain or ceramic teapots retain heat well, while glass teapots, which diffuse heat more quickly, are better for lower-temperature brews. "It is also important that you understand your needs in terms of serving size. And feeling how the lid fits will always give you a good idea about the general quality of a teapot," Mangan adds. "A nice, tight fit with little lateral wiggle is best."

· Small teapot: The Chinese gaiwan or gong-fu teapot and Japanese kyusu allow you to really focus on what's going on in the pot because of the smaller serving sizes. "Unlike Western style steeping, where a minimal amount of tea is used in a larger teapot, steeping in a gaiwan flips this ratio, with much more leaf being used than would be expected for such a small vessel," says Ravi Kroesen. "Almost every type of tea can be enjoyed this way. It is the perfect way to experience the character of single-origin teas, with each steep providing a different experience of the tea in its flavor, body, and finish." Modestly priced utilitarian china, glass, and ceramic versions are suitable for commercial use, while more spendy handmade ceramics from importers like Kettl and Song Tea in San Francisco are the sort of vessels worthy of handing down as family heirlooms.

· Matcha: Unlike whole-leaf teas, matcha, which is both brewed and imbibed unfiltered, requires a set of specialized tools, including a chawan (bowl), chashaku (scoop), chasen (whisk), and a fine strainer. See Zach Mangan's elemental recipe (see page 252) for a demonstration of their use.

Multiple infusions Many teas can (and should) be steeped multiple times. "Multiple steeps allow us to achieve snapshots of the tea as dissolution begins, runs its course, and slowly putters out," writes Tony Gebely in *Tea: A User's Guide*. "As the tea's flavors slowly fade, these snapshots accentuate nuances in the tea that may become muffled during longer infusions. The key is to experiment here; keep adding water and enjoy the tea until the leaves cease to give flavor."

High-quality green teas are good for two steeps and black teas up to three, but there are outliers like certain pu-erhs and oolongs that can be brewed up to fifteen times in a small pot with a high leaf-to-water ratio. This isn't news to knowledgeable tea lovers, but it's crucial for bartenders because it changes the way we work with these ingredients in drinks, serve them to our guests, and enjoy them personally at home. This justifies the value of a high-cost tea and makes sense budget-wise in a restaurant, bar, or café.

Iced tea brewing In instances where cold tea is needed for cocktails, try one of these time-honored brewing methods instead of adding ice cubes to hot tea for service, which just waters it down.

- Cold-brew: Mizudashi is a technique that relies on cold water and a long brew time—ideally for more ephemeral leaves such as green and white tea—to capture rich aromas and flavors along with more body. Zach Mangan says this is a great way to get a sense of how the leaves would taste in their natural state, with layers of nuanced flavor that disappear when brewed hot. Kinto and Hario make the best versions of these infusers. Rodrick Markus of Rare Tea Cellar offers his approach to this method on page 258.

- Flash-brew: For this method—which also works with coffee—tea is brewed hot, then rapidly cooled by adding ice. Since the ice ultimately becomes part of the tea, it's crucial the cubes are made with filtered water in an environment free from food odor contamination. Crushed or pebble ice, versus larger cubes that have smaller surface area, is ideal to bring the temperature of the tea down as rapidly as possible. To accommodate the dilution from the melted ice, extra leaves should be added to brew a concentrated infusion. In my experience, Ravi Kroesen's approach to flash-brewing (see page 355) works for all tea types.

SERVICEWARE

In cities like London, you can spend a whole afternoon—and a week's pay for many of us—at a fancy hotel afternoon tea service. Here, you'll find the finest porcelain cups and saucers with silver spoons, strainers, carafes, and sugar caddies to sweeten your tea (or to merely admire). Alternatively, there are tea cultures such as Japan's, which favors a minimalist environment with rustic, handmade teaware to facilitate your focus on the tea. The wabi-sabi details of the tasting room ground the whole experience. These are just two examples of a broad spectrum of rituals from which to seek inspiration.

As you set out on your tea journey, my advice is to remain open-minded to all cultures' tea rituals, and go with the flow when you're being entertained or on the road as a culinary tourist. At home or in your bar, stock teacups (and saucers if your crowd drinks their tea with milk and sugar) that reflect your aesthetics. Small, 4- to 8-ounce cups are nice if you serve tea with a teapot, while 10- to 12-ounce cups make more sense if you're only offering tea by the cup. Rinsing teacups and equipment with hot water before service helps the tea maintain its temperature.

I n an episode of the *Dig* podcast titled "A Spot of Tea," historian Averill Earls says, "As a product of empire, cultural exchange, medicinal application, immense profitability, social imagination, and agricultural innovation, the history of tea is also the history of millions of intersecting individual lives." Of those millions of intersecting lives, it's estimated that 159 million Americans drink tea, accounting for over 3.9 billion gallons, according to 2022 figures from the Tea Association of the United States. That's almost 80 percent of all households in the country.

And yet, despite its long history and widespread enjoyment, when it comes to caffeinated beverages in the United States, tea's popularity lags behind coffee, soda, and "energy" drinks. Between 75 and 80 percent of all the tea consumed in the United States is iced. So far, traditionally brewed tea hasn't benefited from the halo effect that Starbucks has had on specialty coffee.

In a *Thrillist* article titled "What America Gets Wrong About Tea," Ahmed Ali Akbar poses two theories for this: perhaps its associations with British "tea party" culture have cast too effeminate a reputation upon the drink, or it could be because its association with immigrant communities have kept it simmering under the mainstream. I imagine it is also in part because most retail stores stock it alongside herbals and flavored teas, with little demarcation of the differences in quality, provenance, and character.

Whatever the confluence of causes might be, in *A Little Tea Book,* my friend Sebastian Beckwith offers a useful entryway into the world of tea, if it is new to you. "I often encourage people to think of tea in the same way they think of wine," he says. "For example, you might like Sauvignon Blanc, but not Chardonnay or Pinot Grigio. Maybe at some point you realize your tastes are even more refined: you prefer a Sauvignon Blanc made in California to any from Australia. You might narrow it further to a region (Santa Ynez Valley), and then even to a specific winery. Or not—you could be happy with any and all Sauvignon Blancs and leave it at that."

Keep in mind that whether it's a gong-fu brewed pu-erh, an expertly whisked chawan of matcha, or a cup of my mom's Lipton's with milk and sugar, many tea drinkers view this beverage as part of their identity, so do not disrespect their rituals as you gain connoisseurship. Consult with tea purveyors to ensure you're representing their teas faithfully, and solicit and graciously encourage feedback from knowledgeable customers for all beverages, especially tea.

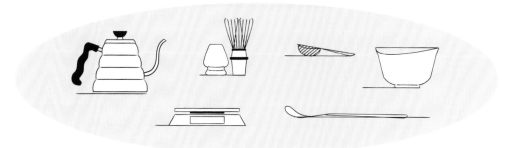

USUCHA MATCHA

from Zach Mangan

Matcha is a Japanese green tea that is milled to a fine powder and whisked into a suspension with hot water, and served unstrained. Zach Mangan, of Kettl Tea, is one of the foremost experts on Japanese tea in the United States, and his recipe for matcha is my benchmark. For Mangan, the key consideration is the leaf-to-water ratio: "If you use either too much water or too little powder, you cannot achieve a rich, meringue-like foam."

Enjoy on its own or mixed into a Dragonfly (page 136), a Lava Lamp (page 174), or a Speak Low (page 268). YIELDS 2¾ OUNCES

☐ 2g (1 teaspoon) Kettl Tea Hanaka matcha powder

☐ 2½ ounces filtered water, heated to 176°F

Tare the scale with a prewarmed chawan with a tea strainer perched across the rim.

Scoop the matcha powder into the tea strainer with the chashaku.

Sift the matcha powder in a circular motion through the strainer into the prewarmed chawan with the chashaku.

Pour the water in a circular motion into the chawan to ensure even contact with the matcha powder.

Hold the chasen with your thumb, index, and middle finger of one hand, and hold the base and sides of the bowl with your other hand.

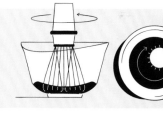

Lower the chasen into the bowl and use a gentle circular motion—both clockwise and then counterclockwise—to integrate the matcha powder.

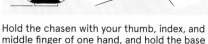

Then, whisk vigorously (from side to side) in a Z pattern for 15 to 20 seconds. Raise the whisk to the surface of the tea and gently whisk to create a fine, fully integrated, bubble-free micro foam. Serve the matcha promptly.

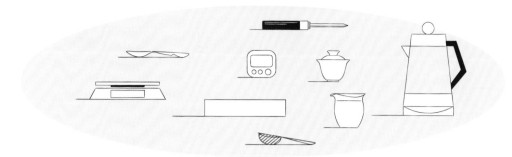

GONG FU SHU PU-ERH
from Sebastian Beckwith

Pu-erh is processed to encourage microbial fermentation after it is dried. The tea is molded into a disc or cake, so the leaves unfurl when submerged in water. To me, it tastes intoxicating, as if you could drink the finest Cuban cigar. Traditionally, pu-erh is enjoyed over the course of multiple short infusions with a gaiwan to showcase the many expressions of the tea's flavor and aroma as it evolves with each steep. Sebastian Beckwith, from In Pursuit of Tea, uses a large proportion of tea leaves to boiling hot water (212°F) for the shu pu-erh. He uses slightly cooler water (200°F) for brewing sheng pu-erh, which is a different variety that ferments over a longer period of time.

After mixing the second infusion into a Q.P. Warmer (page 270) for a guest, I'd suggest pairing subsequent steeps with earthy unaged spirits like mezcal, shochu, baiju, or Batavia Arrack. YIELDS 3½ OUNCES PER INFUSION

- 5g (1½ tablespoons) In Pursuit of Tea shu pu-erh, either cake or loose-leaf
- 3½ ounces filtered water, heated to 212°F (first infusion)
- 3½ ounces filtered water, heated to 212°F (second infusion)

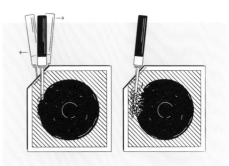

If using a large tea cake, start by bending the cake gently.

Place the cake on a tray.

Use a pick to carefully pry off whole leaves from the cake's edge.

Weigh the tea, then place it in the gaiwan.

Add the first portion of boiling water to the gaiwan to heat the brewer and rinse the leaves.

Place the top on the gaiwan and strain off the first infusion into the sharing pitcher to warm it. Fill the serving cups with the first infusion to warm them, then discard the liquid.

Refill the gaiwan with the second portion of filtered water. Steep the leaves for 10 seconds (or longer to extract more flavor).

Replace the top on the gaiwan and strain off the second infusion into the sharing pitcher. Fill the cups from the pitcher.

Depending on the quality of the tea and your taste preferences, you may repeat this process 5 to 15 times.

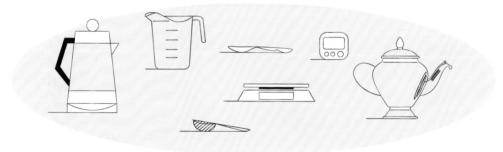

TEAPOT-BREWED JASMINE TEA

from Ravi Kroesen

Jasmine tea is available as both loose leaves and pearls, which are typically made with higher quality tea. Bardo Tea co-owner Ravi Kroesen says quality can be determined by sight and smell—look for delicate pearls with silver buds and clean floral aromas. "Jasmine silver tip [leaves] have a lot more of the green tea's character, whereas jasmine pearls typically feature more jasmine flavor with the green tea providing body and subtle flavor accents." Brewing jasmine pearls in a generously sized teapot is ideal because the extra space allows for the pearls to bloom as they steep, resulting in more even extraction.

I like using jasmine tea as an accompaniment to floral spirits like pisco or botanical spirits like gin. Vodka functions similarly to a blank canvas to let the jasmine flavor shine. Julie Reiner pairs it with an aromatic rum in Dragon Pearl Punch (page 262). YIELDS 7½ OUNCES

- ☐ 3.5g (1½ teaspoons) Bardo Tea jasmine pearls
- ☐ 8 ounces filtered water, heated to 185°F, plus a few ounces more for prewarming the vessel

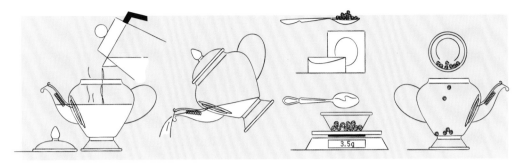

Add hot water to the teapot to warm it, and pour it out. Add the tea to the teapot.

Add the hot water to the teapot and cover.

Steep for 3 minutes.

Fine-strain the liquor into prewarmed teacups for serving and compost the leaves.

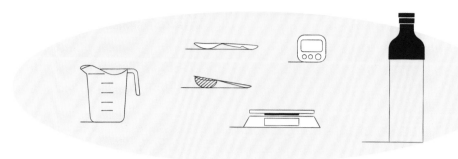

MIZUDASHI COLD-BREWED OOLONG TEA

from Rodrick Markus

"The idea behind cold-brewing is gently extracting flavors, rather than forcing them out with hot water," says Rare Tea Cellar founder Rodrick Markus. Compared to using hot water, cold-brewing doesn't extract as many essential oils and aromas from the tea, but its aroma and flavor last up to three times longer when stored in the fridge. Markus typically brews his proprietary "Freak of Nature" milk oolong (featured in this recipe) in a mizudashi brewer without the basket to facilitate maximum contact between the leaf and water.

Use this method to make the Oolong Tea Syrup (page 344), which sweetens the Longball (page 260). YIELDS 16 OUNCES

- ☐ 6g (1 heaping tablespoon) Rare Tea Cellar Freak of Nature Oolong tea
- ☐ 16 ounces filtered water, at room temperature

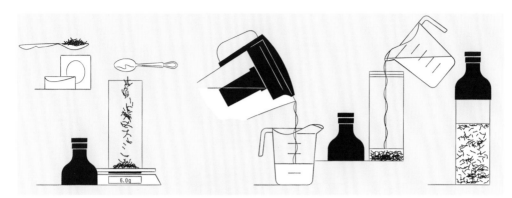

Place the tea in the brewer. Add the water to the brewer and cover.

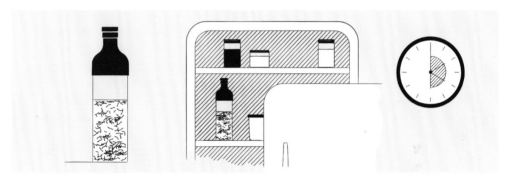

Steep the tea in the fridge for 6 hours.

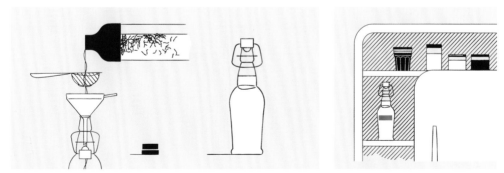

Fine-strain the liquid into a nonreactive container and compost the tea.

Store, covered, in the fridge for up to 3 DAYS.

LONGBALL

by Jim Meehan

This recipe, which was originally developed for a PDT popup in Hong Kong in 2016, features an oolong tea with ripe stone fruit and wildflower honey notes that develop during a huge temperature swing in the space of a single day in the Wuyi Mountains of Southeast China. I paired the rare tea with a subtly flavored floral vodka and lengthened the mixture with dry sparkling wine to add an air of luxury. The title "Longball" is a juxtaposition of the style of drink (highball), and the type of tea (oolong). **YIELDS 1 SERVING**

- ☐ 1½ ounces CÎROC Snap Frost vodka
- ☐ 1 ounce Oolong Tea Syrup (page 344)
- ☐ ¾ ounce lemon juice
- ☐ Ice cubes
- ☐ 2 ounces Argyle brut sparkling wine, chilled
- ☐ 1 edible orchid, for garnish

Add the vodka, syrup, and lemon juice to a Boston Shaker. Add a scoop of ice cubes and shake. Add the sparkling wine to the shaker, then double-strain through a Hawthorne and a fine-mesh strainer into a chilled highball glass. Garnish with the orchid perched on the rim of the glass.

DRAGON PEARL PUNCH

by Julie Reiner

Julie Reiner typically infuses tea directly into the spirit of her drink recipes, but for this punch, she brews it. "I didn't have another recipe to riff from, so I started by combining jasmine and grapefruit—a favorite combination of mine—and took it from there. Serendipitously, I found some coconut water left over from an event at Clover Club in the back room, and thought it would go well in the punch; it did." YIELDS 15 SERVINGS

- ☐ 25½ ounces Banks 7 Golden Blend rum
- ☐ 17 ounces Flash-Brewed Jasmine Tea (page 355)
- ☐ 11¼ ounces coconut water
- ☐ 8½ ounces Grapefruit-Lime Sherbet (page 342)

- ☐ Ice cubes, plus 1 large block of ice, tempered for 30 minutes
- ☐ 2 limes, cut into lime wheels, for garnish
- ☐ 1 Ruby Red grapefruit, cut into half-wheels, for garnish

Add the rum, tea, coconut water, and sherbet to a nonreactive container. Stir to blend well, then cover and chill in the fridge for at least 1 hour.

Add a tempered block of ice to the punch bowl and fill the bowl with the chilled punch. Add half the lime wheels and grapefruit half-wheels to the bowl. Ladle the punch into chilled punch cups filled with ice cubes. Garnish each with the reserved lime wheels and grapefruit half-wheels.

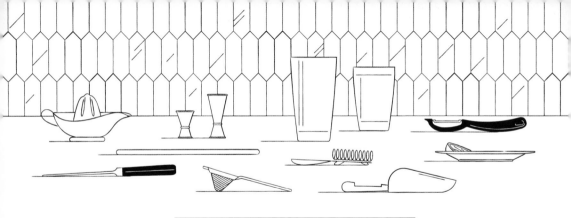

EARL GREY MARTEANI

by Audrey Saunders

This pioneering recipe set the stage for many modern tea cocktails to follow. It was created by Audrey Saunders, my mentor and former boss at the Pegu Club, for a Bemelmans pop-up over Thanksgiving of 2003 at the Rivoli Bar in The Ritz Hotel London. "The name is a play on that whole silly 'tini' business, but the drink is a nod to traditional English tea service," she told me, where tea is "often served with lemon and lumps of sugar on the side. Instead of using milk, I opted for egg white, which provides not only an ethereal mouthfeel but a perfect foil for the tea's tannins." YIELDS 1 SERVING

- ☐ 1 lemon wedge, to rim half the glass
- ☐ 1 tablespoon white cane sugar, for sugaring half the rim
- ☐ 1½ ounces Earl Grey Tea–Infused Gin (page 347)

- ☐ 1 ounce Simple Syrup (page 339)
- ☐ ¾ ounce lemon juice
- ☐ 1 large egg white
- ☐ Ice cubes
- ☐ 1 lemon twist, for garnish

Use the lemon wedge to moisten half the rim of a chilled 8-ounce coupe. Roll the glass rim through the sugar on the saucer, carefully coating only the outside of half the rim.

Add the gin, syrup, lemon juice, and egg white to a Boston shaker and shake.

Add a scoop of ice cubes and shake again. Double-strain through a Hawthorne and a fine-mesh strainer into the coupe. Garnish with a lemon twist.

COMFORT'S TODDY

by Julia Momosé

Julia Momosé uses tea in many different preparations at her bar Kumiko in Chicago. For this recipe, she chose to create a toddy with roots in Japanese tea-drinking traditions. The sweet potato shochu and hōjicha combination represents a classic Chawari, or tea cut with shochu, layered within a classic cocktail template, the Old Fashioned. The hōjicha brings earthiness to the drink. Julia prefers to allow the toddy to cool to around 150°F before serving it, so the heat "gives a sense of warmth without the burn." This is a sound service protocol for all hot drinks served with spirits, as alcohol boils at a lower temperature than water, releasing unpleasant vapors until the mixture cools or is covered by a garnish. **YIELDS 1 SERVING**

☐ 5½ ounces Brewed Hōjicha (page 353)

☐ 1¼ ounces Nishi Shuzo Satsuma Houzan Imo shochu

☐ ¼ ounce Nikka Coffey grain whisky

☐ ¼ ounce Tempus Fugit crème de cacao

☐ ¼ ounce Honey Syrup (page 338)

☐ Azuki Dorayaki, sliced for serving

Add the tea, shochu, whiskey, crème de cacao, and syrup to a pre-warmed tea or shochu cup. Serve unadorned, with the sliced dorayaki.

SPEAK LOW

by Shingo Gokan

Japanese bar entrepreneur Shingo Gokan won the 2012 Bacardi Legacy cocktail competition with this recipe, named after the jazz tune by Kurt Weill. At the time of its creation, it was customary to name cocktails for jazz songs at Angel's Share in Manhattan's East Village, where he tended bar. According to Gokan, the flavor combination of aged rum and PX sherry is reminiscent of the red bean candy (wagashi) served at a traditional Japanese tea ceremony, which inspired this recipe and its preparation. YIELDS 1 SERVING

- ☐ 2g (1 teaspoon) matcha powder
- ☐ 1 ounce Bacardi Superior white rum
- ☐ 1 ounce Bacardi Reserva Ocho rum
- ☐ ½ ounce Osbourne Pedro Ximenez sherry
- ☐ Ice cubes, plus 1 large (2-inch) ice cube, tempered for 1 to 2 minutes
- ☐ 1 yuzu peel, for garnish

Sift the matcha powder through the tea strainer into the chawan in a circular motion with the chashaku. Pour the rums and sherry into the chawan in a circular motion to ensure even contact with the matcha powder. Whisk the mixture as if you were preparing matcha (see page 252).

Pour the mixture into a cobbler shaker. Add a scoop of ice cubes and cover the shaker. Shake, then double-strain through a fine-mesh strainer into a chilled old fashioned glass filled with 1 large, tempered ice cube. Pinch the yuzu twist, skin side down, over the surface of the drink, then compost it.

Q.P. WARMER

by Jim Meehan

In this wintry hot toddy, the quince and persimmon accentuate the stone fruit notes in the Cognac, while the earthy pu-erh reinforces its subtle rancio notes. The ephemerality of fresh persimmons makes this recipe worth splurging on an older Cognac and tea for the holiday season. Note how the clove-studded mandarin wheel is used for a visual and practical purpose; the orange wheel blocks the alcohol aromas that emerge when the Cognac is combined with hot tea, and releases fragrant clove and orange blossom notes in its place. YIELDS 1 SERVING

- ☐ 23g (1 tablespoon) quince paste
- ☐ 25g (1 tablespoon) Hachiya persimmon pulp
- ☐ 6 ounces Brewed Lao Cang Xiao Shu Tuo Pu-Erh (page 353), hot
- ☐ 1½ ounces Hine H Cognac
- ☐ Satsuma mandarin wheel, for garnish
- ☐ 6 to 8 whole cloves, for garnish

Using a tea strainer and barspoon, extrude the quince paste and persimmon pulp into a prewarmed tempered sharing pitcher. Pour the hot tea through the remaining paste in the strainer into the sharing pitcher, then stir any remaining paste through the strainer with the spoon. Add the Cognac, then pour the mixture into a prewarmed toddy glass. Stud the mandarin wheel with the cloves, and float the garnish in the drink.

Soda & Mineral Water

Beyond the seltzer deployed to lengthen fizzes and collinses, soda didn't become a staple in bars until after Prohibition, when beverage preferences shifted from sophisticated sours and stirred drinks to more saccharine mixtures. By 1946, soda brands like Coca-Cola became fashionable in highballs like the Cuba Libre. Soon after, amid the advent of modern advertising, drinks like the Moscow Mule and the 7 & 7 ushered in an anodyne age that endured until recently, when bartenders like Brian Van Flandern and Eben Freeman introduced house tonic water at Per Se and smoked Coca-Cola at Tailor, respectively. Today, as bartenders' curiosity in house-made sodas continues, the mixer market has evolved to meet the modern palate with "grown-up sodas" that feature lower sugar levels, higher carbonation, and organic ingredients.

Soda's roots go back to our ancestors' fascination with the curative properties of mineral waters that bubbled up naturally from springs. "The effervescing nature of the water was an attractive quality, and was thought to be a natural tonic," writes Darcy O'Neil in *Fix the Pumps*. These restorative waters were bathed in and imbibed at the source, and eventually chemists worked to replicate them, developing recipes for carbonated mineral waters that laid the foundation for an industry to emerge.

Before they were imbibed for pleasure, pharmacists prescribed and dispensed fizzy drinks, tonic syrups, and alcoholic tinctures to treat a variety of ailments. These mixtures were eventually sweetened to make them more palatable, and by 1875, O'Neil reports, "There was a soda fountain—a late-nineteenth-century 'third place' that emerged within pharmacies—in almost every city across America." There, bartender-like "soda jerks" created elaborate concoctions with a pharmacopeia of flavors that were precursors to the modern soda industry.

The soda industry has come a long way since then, but sodas are still made by combining filtered water with a "flavor syrup," which typically includes juice(s), sweetener(s), and food grade acid(s). The mixture is carbonated with carbon dioxide and either kegged, bottled, or served à la minute. In soda fountains, the flavor syrups were combined with carbonated water and stirred together before service. This is how old-school luncheonettes like the Lexington Candy Shop in New York City serve their famous house-made cola.

BUBBLY WATERS

A range of sparkling waters can be used to make a flavored soda if you don't want to add carbonation yourself. They also make good companions for elemental highballs prepared with spirit and bubbly water.

Mineral water Mineral water comes from a natural source and contains a unique makeup of varying levels of sulfur, magnesium, sodium, calcium, potassium, and other trace minerals. Famous mineral waters had their mineral contents analyzed and published in pharmaceutical journals for pharmacists to compound where they couldn't be imported. Mineral water can be still or sparkling. Popular brands include San Pellegrino, Topo Chico, Perrier, and Lurisia.

Seltzer Ironically, mineral-free carbonated waters such as La Croix and Canada Dry are colloquially called seltzer, despite "Seltzer" originally being a brand of naturally carbonated mineral water from Niederselters, Germany. Note: Alcohol-free "seltzer" should not be confused with the growing rash of artificially flavored "hard seltzers," which contain alcohol.

Club soda Club soda is carbonated water with added sodium or potassium, which makes the liquid taste slightly salty. Q and Fever-Tree are commendable examples of this type typically stocked in the mixers aisle.

SODAS

When a flavored syrup or unsweetened flavoring is combined with carbonated water, you have a flavored soda. The possibilities are endless, but here are a few of the most relevant for mixology:

Citrus In *Soda and Fizzy Drinks,* author Judith Levin remarks that "the flavoring of carbonated waters in America developed steadily, but without a lot of documentation." She cites one of the earliest appearances in an 1807 English advertisement for "aerated lemonade." Following the rise of aerated lemonades, citrus emerged as one of the most popular flavorings in the soda realm, owing to the ease with which oils from citrus peels can be extracted and preserved in an oleo saccharum. Most citrus sodas are artificially flavored now, with grapefruit, lemon, lime, and orange sodas being the easiest to find at the grocery store. One of my favorite modern mixers is a lightly carbonated yuzu lemonade from a Japanese company called Kimino.

Ginger ale and ginger beer In *The Oxford Companion to Spirits & Cocktails,* Darcy O'Neil attributes ginger ale's appearance in the early 1800s as "one of the first carbonated mineral waters to add a flavor." Ginger ale and ginger beer were once the same, but have since evolved into two slightly different sodas. Early ginger beers were fermented to a low alcohol content (2 to 3 percent) but today, most ginger beer is not fermented. Instead, "ginger beer" typically refers to a ginger soda (ale) spiked with capsicum or other agents to duplicate the heat of fresh ginger. With both names now typically representing alcohol-free sodas, the key difference is that ginger beer usually tastes more pungent with spice, whereas ginger ale is rhizome focused.

Tonic Author Camper English traces the first known bottling of carbonated water infused with quinine to an 1835 advertisement in *Doctors and Distillers*. At the time, the bark of the *Cinchona* tree was prescribed to prevent malaria and eventually found its ideal delivery vehicle in "tonic" water, which was paired with gin by English soldiers who imbibed this concoction as a "cocktail" with lime juice to ward off scurvy, malaria, and anemia.

The tonic water I poured from soda guns as a young bartender around the turn of the twenty-first century was virtually indistinguishable from the lemon-lime soda dispensed by pressing a different button: cloyingly sweet with none of quinine's characteristic bitterness. A sea change in the soda industry began when Fever-Tree released a drier, bittersweet formulation better suited for more sophisticated palates—and gin—around 2005. Camper English notes that tonic waters like Q and Fever-Tree were faithful to original formulas, "created decades after quinine had already been isolated from the bark."

Safety note: Camper English is a vociferous advocate for food safety behind the bar and wrote a whole book on the gin and tonic, called Tonic Water: AKA G&T WTF. *In the book, he explains how tonic syrups untested for quinine concentration led to cases of cinchonism, whose symptoms include ringing in the ears, abdominal pain, dizziness, dysphoria, and diarrhea.*

Root beer This soda was "first known to have been marketed commercially at the Philadelphia Centennial Exhibition in 1876 by a teetotaling Philadelphia pharmacist named Charles Hires, who is said to have discovered a recipe for a delicious herbal tea on his honeymoon," writes Karen Fick in an article on the soda for *Difford's Guide.*

Like tonic, root beer has historically faced food safety issues. It was originally brewed with sassafras root, banned by the FDA in 1976 because it contains the possibly carcinogenic compound safrole. O'Neil told me, "Sassafras is the classic root beer flavor, but the safrole in it is most likely carcinogenic, and it is also heavily regulated because it is a key ingredient when making ecstasy. As root beer made with sassafras enjoys a bit of a renaissance among foragers and herbalists, it's important to emphasize that it's not recognized as safe by the FDA, so it shouldn't be served in a commercial setting. Darcy adds, "Wintergreen is the modern replacement, which went into effect in the 1960s, so the flavor of root beer is divided in two, though they are similar. Wintergreen in soda is safe, but pure wintergreen oil is not safe to consume due to a compound called methyl salicylate, which is toxic in small or long-term repeated doses."

Cola Coca-Cola was originally formulated by John S. Pemberton of Atlanta, Georgia, in imitation of a French cocaine-spiked wine—you read that correctly—called Vin Mariani. When the city went dry (banning the alcohol, not the cocaine), Pemberton substituted the highly caffeinated West African kola nut for pep. In a subsequent formulation, he added pharmaceutical caffeine and removed some kola nut to mitigate its bitterness. According to Judith Levin, the formulation that went on to become the most famous commercial product of all time was a caramel-colored sugar syrup. (Coca-Cola sells only the syrup and leaves the mixing and bottling to its distributors.) That syrup balanced vanilla extract, elixir of orange, lemon oil, nutmeg, coriander, and neroli and cassia oil with lime juice, citric acid, and phosphoric acid to offset sweetness.

The profitability of cola surged (without a consumer price increase) in the 1970s when the U.S. government began subsidizing corn, which can be processed into high-fructose corn syrup (HFCS). In 1974, American soda companies began substituting HFCS for cane sugar, and by 1984, it replaced cane sugar altogether. This swap is one reason why Coca-Cola products have been stigmatized for their role in the obesity epidemic in America (though the veracity of that impression remains contentious). The tides shifted again around 2010, when Mexican Coca-Cola (formulated with cane sugar) began making its way north of the border. Favored for its more appealing flavor and retro glass-bottle design—plus some international trade drama that is worth reading about if you are so inclined—Coke has staged a comeback in hip restaurants, cafés, and cocktail bars.

SOURCING

Broad distribution for small sodas typically comes after a larger soda corporation takes an equity stake in them, so it might be hard to find craft brands unless they distribute themselves or a local store (without listing fees) stocks them. Judith Levin explains why: "The small companies cannot get their products on the shelves of most big shops. The global companies pay for the shelf space, and the big shops auction the shelf space to the highest bidder." You should be able to find specialty sodas online, in local gourmet shops, or in small, independent grocery stores.

STORAGE

Sodas prepared with fresh citrus that don't have additional acids to preserve them should be stored in the refrigerator and consumed within 24 hours. Sodas prepared with citrus oils and juice stabilized by food-grade acids should be shelf stable as long as they're stored topped up and sealed in the fridge for a week—or longer, if pasteurized.

PREPARATION

To make sodas for use in mixed drinks, you can either carbonate the water yourself (see page 282) or choose from one of the aforementioned commercially available bubbly-water options to mix with a flavor syrup. If you are building from scratch, there are several elements that can be optimized to make flavorful sodas with tight carbonation.

Water source In *On Food and Cooking,* Harold McGee identifies the pH (acidity or alkalinity) of water solutions as "a source of flavor" that has "an important influence on the behavior of the other food molecules." That's why understanding whether your water is "hard," with excess calcium and magnesium, or "soft," with negligible minerality, is a game-changer when making sodas yourself. It allows for more intentional control over the flavor of your ice, soda, cordials, and other house-made ingredients calling for water as the base.

The specialty tea and coffee industries are many years ahead of bartenders in exploring how the chemical makeup of water influences the character of their beverages. Coffee experts in particular are experimenting with mineral additions, subtractions, and adjustments to find the ideal water and specialty-coffee pairings that optimize flavor. In general, chemist Christopher Hendon, who authored *Water for Coffee* with barista champion Maxwell Colonna-Dashwood, prefers soft water because it allows baristas to bring out acidic flavors in coffee and keeps their machines running smoothly. Hard water is a nonstarter for most, as it "turns off the acid" in coffee, he says. All these insights can be applied to the water used to make your own sodas.

McGee writes that "hard water can be softened by precipitating the calcium and magnesium with lime or using an ion-exchange mechanism to replace the calcium and magnesium with sodium." The ion-exchange mechanism is a component of handheld filtration pitchers such as Hendon and Colonna-Dashwood's Peak water pitcher, which contains carbon and both cation and anion exchange resins that strip minerals out of the water. "With soft water, the carbon is doing the work to clean up the taste and smell of water from the tap, whereas with hard water, the ion exchange resins soften the water, enabling the brewer to perceive acidic beverages such as coffee, soda, and cocktails," says Hendon.

Temperature Water chilled to 32°F can dissolve twice as much CO_2 as water at 68°F, yielding a slower release of small bubbles. Warm carbonated water at high pressure yields larger bubbles that pop quickly. For this reason, water should be well chilled before carbonating, and sparkling waters should be stored covered in the fridge, or on ice, well before service.

Flavor syrup A good soda base—known as a flavor syrup—features a mix of sweetener, acid, and juice or flavorings. Originally, soda jerks relied on the natural acid from citrus in fizzy lemonades to balance out the sweetness of flavor syrups. But citrus is expensive and has a limited shelf life, so pharmacists began substituting acid phosphate, which is a mixture of phosphate mineral salts and phosphoric acid. The mineral salts gave phosphates their unique flavor and the phosphoric acid provided a sharp acidic bite. According to Darcy O'Neil, who sells acid phosphate through his website Art of Drink, the sodas were served diluted with water and sugar to improve palatability. Many sodas still use phosphoric acid, which lacks the fruitiness of citric, tartaric, and malic acids.

Homemade flavor syrups should be filtered through a fine-mesh sieve, super bag, or rinsed coffee filter to remove solids. Commercial producers take this a step further by pumping their base through a wood pulp plate and frame filter before pasteurization for safety and shelf stability. For a commercial bar or café, Hendon recommends filtering water with activated carbon to clean up any organic material that may be present, followed by one of two options to address its minerality. The first option calls for using reverse-osmosis water treatment to strip away everything, followed by blending in some unfiltered water to achieve a minor amount of mineralization. The second recommendation is an ion exchange resin, which targets specific ion substitution.

TOOLS

I used to buy a case of mineral water every week, so my soda carbonating kit, which I bought from a brewing supply company, is the single best investment I've made in terms of dollar savings and carbon footprint reduction while researching and writing this book.

To carbonate sodas and water at home, I've found the most economical method is to use a plastic liter bottle attached to a carbonator via a metal carbonator cap that's attached to a five-pound aluminum cylinder of CO_2 hooked up to a regulator that measures the soda pressure and volume of the canister (see page 282). I used a SodaStream for a long time and can attest that the pressure is pitiful and the CO_2 refills are expensive and wasteful. While more aesthetically pleasing and easy to supercharge, soda siphons require expensive, wasteful CO_2 refills, and they're inconsistent and messy in service.

Bars that serve large volumes of soda usually store their sodas refrigerated in Cornelius kegs and sometimes bottle and cap 5- to 12-ounce bottles for retail. This sort of equipment is typically available where brewing supplies are sold or through compressed-gas companies.

When considering carbonation, know that high pressure in a carbonated water system will result in much larger bubbles, while lower pressure produces finer bubbles. While many prefer the brisk effervescence of highly carbonated sodas, Darcy O'Neil likes "smaller bubbles, which pick up more aroma molecules than larger bubbles."

SERVICEWARE

The ideal glass to serve soda in—which also goes for bottles—is clean, dry, and dust and scratch free, because scratches and abrasions in heavily used bottles and glassware form nucleation points where new bubbles can form, causing carbonated water to go flat more quickly. Make sure the water you are using to rinse the glass is clean and there is no lint on your polishing towels.

During my lifetime, the majority of sodas available to me for sale have been overly saccharine, one-dimensional formulas from large multinational companies that use artificial flavorings and high-fructose corn syrup. Thankfully, many of the metrics that mixologists use to select wines, beers, and spirits for their bars are now being applied to choose mixers like tonic water, ginger beer, and grapefruit soda along with mineral waters to prepare highballs and mizuwaris. Brands like Q and Fever-Tree have changed the game with their balanced and complex commercial options.

While the golden age of the soda fountain fizzled out a long time ago, and its renaissance stalled, Darcy O'Neil reminds contemporary bartenders that "this doesn't mean the drinks are lost forever; they just need champions to revive them." In *Fix the Pumps,* he goes on to add: "There are thousands of soda recipes locked up in old publications awaiting rediscovery. These recipes are the last tangible remains of the classic soda fountain and are under siege from companies trying to claim ownership of the American soda."

As O'Neil suggests, early twentieth-century dispenser's formularies—the soda fountain's equivalent of old bar manuals, many of which are available free online— are a great resource to study for inspiration. With alcohol-free offerings gaining popularity, these recipes and techniques represent a timely opportunity for bars and restaurants to grow their beverage sales without incurring the liabilities that accompany increased alcohol consumption. They also make bars more inviting spaces for those inclined to drink in moderation or who abstain entirely.

Transitioning a bar, restaurant, or café from offering bottled beverages to house-filtered still and sparkling water in glass carafes with a creative house-made soda program in place of commercial mixers can make a transformative impact on the business's carbon footprint and influence the interests and practices of its clientele in the process. It's a small step toward reducing glass and plastic pollution, but big changes begin by setting an actionable example for others to follow.

As we've seen with other ingredients in this book, options abound to source from and support small business owners who are making authentic, craft versions of mainstream commercial products. While far from artisanal, inter-national bottlings like Peru's Inca Kola, Scotland's Irn-Bru, and Jamaica's Ting have cult followings among their consumer base who associate national pride with their consumption, just as many Americans once felt about Coca-Cola. Regionally, sodas like North Carolina's Cheerwine, Maine's Moxie, and New York's Dr. Brown's summon similar nostalgia. For bars, cafés, and restaurants that pride themselves on fostering local community with their patrons, these should be considered alongside craft options and formulating sodas of your own when stocking a bar.

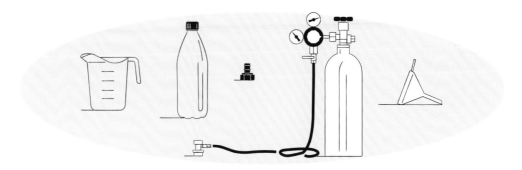

FORCED CARBONATION

from Jim Meehan

I adapted this method for forced carbonation from *The Cocktail Codex* by Alex Day, Nick Fauchald, and David Kaplan. The authors recommend readers "keep three key variables in mind—clarity, temperature, and time"—to achieve maximum carbonation. There's a feature-length video of Dave Arnold explaining forced carbonation on YouTube, called *Setting up a Home On-Tap Carbonation System—Complete and Unabridged,* that goes even further, should you want to dig really deep into the nuances of adding fizzy bubbles to water.

Use this method to carbonate Lemon-Lime Soda (page 290), Grapefruit Soda (page 288), Szechuan Ginger Beer (page 284), and Cola (page 286). YIELDS 28 OUNCES

☐ 28 ounces filtered water, chilled

Pour the chilled filtered water into a 1 liter PET plastic soda bottle.

Cap and chill the bottle in the coldest part of the fridge, removing before any ice chips form.

Remove the cap and pinch the bottle, bringing the fill line just below the bottle neck. Screw on the CarbaCap.

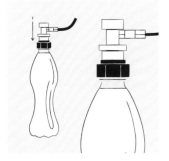

Attach the prepared bottle to the ball lock disconnect.

Turn on the gas, with the primary regulator set to 30 psi.

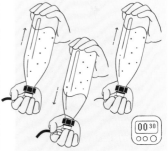

Upturn the bottle and shake vigorously—with one hand on the ball lock disconnect and the other on the bottom of the bottle—for 20 to 30 seconds.

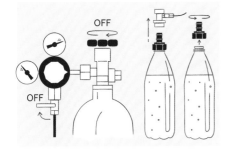

Turn off the gas and detach it from the ball lock disconnect. Slowly unscrew the CarbaCap, and repeat the last five steps.

Reseal the bottle with the original cap.

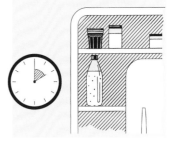

Chill the liquid for at least 2 hours before serving.

SZECHUAN GINGER BEER

by Katie Rose

Katie Rose, who has always loved the numbing effect that Szechuan pepper has on her palate, developed this house ginger beer recipe for her Milwaukee restaurant Goodkind. The addition of Szechuan pepper drives home the scintillating side of the soda: "It's super interesting and provides a sensation that falls outside of my normal senses," she says. "Is it spicy? Is it hot? Is it cool? *What's happening here?*"

Use to make the "Pimm's" Cup (page 168) and the Peeking Duck (page 332) or drink it over ice. YIELDS 32¼ OUNCES

- ☐ 36 ounces filtered water, chilled
- ☐ 162.5g (¾ cup) white cane sugar
- ☐ 162.5g (¾ cup) turbinado sugar
- ☐ 14g (1 tablespoon) green Szechuan peppercorns
- ☐ 2¾ ounces ginger juice (extracted from 225g fresh ginger)
- ☐ 1 ounce lime juice

PREPARE THE FLAVOR SYRUP

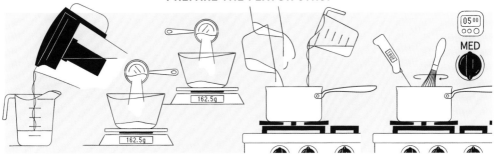

Add 12 ounces of the filtered water, and the cane and turbinado sugars to a medium saucepan and stir over medium heat until the mixture reaches 180°F and the sugar dissolves, around 5 minutes.

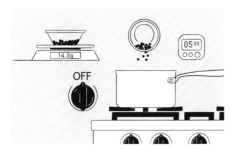

Turn off heat and add the Szechuan peppercorns, then let steep for 5 minutes.

Fine-strain the mixture, let cool, then cover and store in the fridge for up to 1 WEEK. Yields 18 ounces.

PREPARE THE SODA

Prepare the ginger and lime juices.

Pour 5 ounces of the syrup, the remaining filtered water, and the ginger and lime juices into a 1 liter plastic soda bottle. Force-carbonate the mixture (see page 282). Store in the fridge for up to 7 DAYS, re-carbonating as desired.

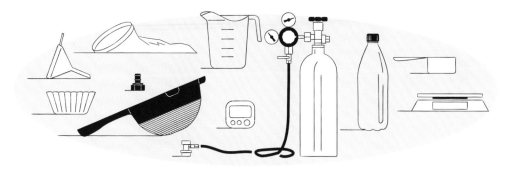

COLA

from Martin Lambert

Martin Lambert, the founder of Adult soda company in the Czech Republic, told me that the basic formula for commercial cola is water, sugar, caramel, acid, and carbon dioxide: "When mixed proportionately, you'll get your basic budget cola taste." The key to making an outstanding cola, he says, is to add emulsified essential oils, but these are hard to source, and the dosages are very finicky. For an at-home version, Martin recommends using spices and kola nuts as a nod to the original Coca-Cola recipe.

Use in Southern Cola (page 296) or drink it over ice. YIELDS 32½ OUNCES

- ☐ 51½ ounces filtered water, chilled
- ☐ 600g (3 cups) demerara sugar
- ☐ 17g (3½ tablespoons) ground ginger
- ☐ 10g (2 tablespoons) green cardamom pods
- ☐ 7g (1 tablespoon) cacao nibs
- ☐ 6.7g (½ tablespoon) citric acid
- ☐ 5g (2 teaspoons) ground kola nuts
- ☐ 5g (1 tablespoon) whole cloves
- ☐ 2.6g (¾ teaspoon) malic acid

PREPARE THE FLAVOR SYRUP

Pour 24 ounces of the filtered water into a medium saucepan and bring to a boil over high heat.

Add the demerara sugar, and turn the heat down to medium, whisking until the sugar dissolves.

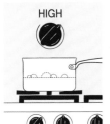

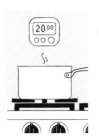

Turn the heat back up to high and bring the mixture to a boil, then turn off the heat again.

Add the ginger, cardamom, cacao, citric acid, kola nuts, cloves, and malic acid.

Infuse for 20 minutes.

While hot, fine-strain the mixture through a fine-mesh strainer.

PREPARE THE SODA

Fine-strain the mixture again through a Super-bag sieve.

Fine-strain a third time through a coffee filter. Store, covered, in the fridge for up to 1 MONTH. Yields 29 ounces.

Pour 5 ounces of the cola syrup into a 1 liter plastic soda bottle. Pour in the remaining filtered water. Force-carbonate (see page 282). Store in the fridge for up to 1 MONTH, re-carbonating as necessary.

GRAPEFRUIT SODA

from Jim Meehan

After previously working to develop the flavor profile of a commercial grapefruit soda, I knew the best flavor syrup would capture the essence of both fresh juice and the peel's aromatic oil. While recipe testing for this book, I serendipitously created this formulation by combining Chad Solomon's acid-adjusted grapefruit juice with Julie Reiner's grapefruit oleo saccharum. The carbonation will never quite match what commercial bottlers can achieve with superior filtration and bottling technology, but it's a compelling alternative if you prefer to make your own.

Use in Grail Ale (page 302), in a classic Paloma (page 170), or drink it over ice.
YIELDS 28 OUNCES

☐ 8 ounces Enhanced Grapefruit Sherbet (page 343)

☐ 20 ounces filtered water, chilled

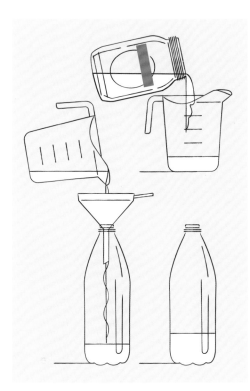

Add the sherbet to a 1 liter plastic soda bottle.

Pour in the filtered water.

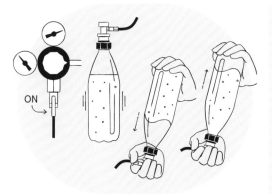

Force-carbonate the mixture (see page 282).

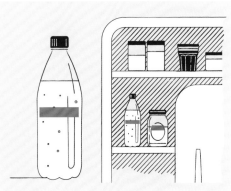

Store in the fridge for up to 4 DAYS, re-carbonating as desired.

LEMON-LIME SODA

from Nick Bennett

Porchlight beverage director Nick Bennett didn't mind using commercial lemon-lime soda in drinks, but he made his own for the restaurant. The house-made soda generates "another level of pride in any cocktail I prepare with it," he says. He adds, "the key to achieve proper carbonation is to keep everything as cold as possible."

Use in the 7 & 7 (page 292) or drink it over ice. YIELDS 25 OUNCES

- ☐ 44 ounces filtered water, chilled
- ☐ 700g (3 cups) white sugar
- ☐ 7g (2 tablespoons) grated lemon zest (from 2 to 4 lemons)
- ☐ 7g (2 tablespoons) grated lime zest (from 2 to 4 limes)
- ☐ 21g (2 tablespoons) peeled fresh ginger
- ☐ Pinch of kosher salt
- ☐ 1 ounce lime juice (from the zested limes)
- ☐ 1 ounce lemon juice (from the zested lemons)
- ☐ 10g (¾ tablespoon) citric acid
- ☐ 5g (1½ teaspoons) malic acid

PREPARE THE FLAVOR SYRUP

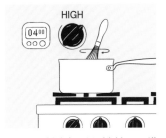

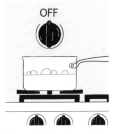

Add 24 ounces of the filtered water and the sugar to a medium saucepan.

Set over high heat, whisking until the sugar is dissolved and the water is boiling, about 4 minutes.

Once boiling, turn off the heat.

Add the lemon and lime zests, ginger, and salt to the saucepan and let infuse for 10 minutes.

Measure out the citrus juices and the citric and malic acids.

PREPARE THE SODA

Fine-strain the mixture into a nonreactive container. Once it cools, add both acids and the citrus juices.

Store covered in the fridge for up to 1 WEEK. Yields 42 ounces.

To prepare the lemon-lime soda, pour 5 ounces of the syrup into a 750 milliliter plastic bottle. Pour in the remaining filtered water. Force-carbonate (see page 282). Store in the fridge for up to 1 WEEK, re-carbonating as necessary.

7 & 7

from Nick Bennett

One approach Nick Bennett learned from Dave Arnold at Booker & Dax was to never assume a recipe is *finished*. For example, Dave continuously rethought the temperature, carbonation, acidity, and bitterness of his magnum opus, the Gin & Tonic. Nick carried this ethos to Porchlight, where he would get the occasional request for a 7 & 7. They didn't carry Seagram's 7 or 7-Up at the bar, so he reimagined the drink, similar to the way Dave did with the Gin & Tonic. "I used what I learned from Dave about carbonation to keg the whole batch and put it on draft," Nick says. "It's been a guest favorite ever since." YIELDS SIX 5-OUNCE SERVINGS

- ☐ 16 ounces Lemon-Lime Soda (page 290)
- ☐ 4 ounces Brewed English Breakfast Tea (page 352), chilled
- ☐ 2 ounces Mellow Corn bonded corn whiskey
- ☐ 2 ounces Dickel No. 12 Tennessee whisky
- ☐ 2 ounces Old Overholt rye whiskey
- ☐ 2 ounces Canadian Club whisky
- ☐ 1 ounce Corsair Triple Smoke whiskey
- ☐ 1 ounce Cointreau liqueur
- ☐ Ice cubes
- ☐ 1 lime, cut into wedges, for garnish

Pour the soda, tea, whiskies, and liqueur through a funnel into a 1 liter plastic soda bottle. Thoroughly chill the mixture in the refrigerator for 3 to 4 hours.

Force-carbonate the mixture (see page 282). Pour into chilled old fashioned glasses filled with ice cubes. Garnish each with a lime wedge. Store 7 & 7 covered, in the fridge for up to 1 month, re-carbonating as necessary.

ANGOSTURA PHOSPHATE

from Darcy S. O'Neil

When I asked Darcy O'Neil, who wrote the definitive contemporary history of soda fountains, *Fix the Pumps,* for a soda recipe, he immediately thought of this one: a classic from the 1913 vest pocket recipe book *Drinks,* by Jacques Straub. "It's an interesting bar/soda fountain cross-over drink," he says. "I've seen it in old bar and soda fountain books, which both consider it a hangover cure." Restorative properties aside, acid phosphate—which Darcy has recreated and sells—was originally used both to acidify a drink when citrus was scarce and to enhance its flavor, much as salt does for a steak. YIELDS 1 SERVING

☐ 3½ ounces seltzer, chilled
☐ 1 ounce Sherbet (page 28), made with lemons

☐ 1 teaspoon Angostura bitters
☐ ½ teaspoon acid phosphate

Add the seltzer, sherbet, bitters, and acid phosphate to a chilled 8-ounce old fashioned glass and stir to integrate.

SOUTHERN COLA

by Greg Best

Greg Best created this low-proof highball for his first cocktail menu at the now-shuttered Restaurant Eugene in Atlanta, in the summer of 2004. "My goal for serving it was to expose guests to the as-then-arcane category of amaro by utilizing a very familiar and beloved ingredient with broad accessibility—Atlanta's own Coca-Cola—as a Trojan Horse of sorts." He came up with the lime ice cubes as a "time release of citrus that allowed a drink that walked dangerously close to being too sweet to finish tart and refreshing." YIELDS 1 SERVING

☐ 4 ounces Cola (page 286), chilled

☐ 1½ ounces Paolucci Amaro Ciociaro

☐ 1 (1¼-inch) Lime Ice Cube (page 357)

☐ 1 lime wheel, for garnish

Add the cola and amaro to a chilled Turkish chimney glass. Add the ice cube and garnish with the lime wheel.

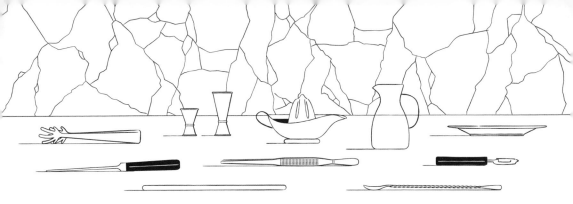

GIN & TONIC (CLASSIC AND MODERN)

from Camper English

The G&T is a pretty straightforward drink, but I love how thoroughly and precisely Camper English, author of *Tonic Water AKA G&T WTF* and *Doctors and Distillers*, approaches the simple highball. For this recipe, he considered four gins, three tonics, nine garnishes, four glassware shapes, and various temperature options and concluded, "the choice of tonic water and ratio of gin to tonic are the most important factors in making a tasty G&T. All the rest is refining from there."

EACH YIELDS 1 SERVING

CLASSIC G&T

☐ Garnish of choice (Camper's preferences, in descending order): coin-sized grapefruit peel, ¼ ounce lime juice, ¼ grapefruit wheel, lime wheel

☐ Large ice cube (2-inch), ice spear, or ice cubes, tempered for 1 to 2 minutes

☐ 2½ ounces Fever Tree or Q tonic water, chilled

☐ 1 ounce London dry gin, such as Beefeater or Tanqueray, chilled

MODERN G&T

☐ Garnish of choice (Camper's preferences in descending order): lime wheel, ¼ ounce lime juice, coin-sized grapefruit peel

☐ Large ice cube (2-inch), ice spear, or ice cubes, tempered for 1 to 2 minutes

☐ 3 ounces Fever Tree or Q tonic water, chilled

☐ 1 ounce New Western–style gin, such as Hendrick's or Aviation, chilled

For each G&T, place the preferred garnish(es) in a chilled old fashioned, wine, or Collins glass. Add a large ice cube, ice spear, or ice cubes to the glass and press down on the ice with the ice tongs to release the juice and oils from the garnish(es). Add the tonic and gin and stir gently to mix.

JAPANESE WHISKY HIGHBALL
from Bobby Heugel

Anvil Bar & Refuge owner Bobby Heugel fell in love with the Kaku Highball at Bar Martha in Tokyo, Japan, which is made with a whisky (Suntory Kakubin) and carbonated water (Wilkinson Tansan) not exported to the United States. When he returned to Houston, he tasted his way through twenty sparkling waters before settling on a substitute—Mountain Valley Spring Water and Suntory Toki whisky. "Is our Highball a Samboa or Rockfish Highball (the two most famous highball bars in Japan)? No, but it's a damn good, 90 percent there, American version of the drink made by people who obviously love it." The key point is this seemingly simple drink has nuanced purpose behind its ingredients selection and preparation methods. YIELDS 1 SERVING

- ☐ 7½ ounces Mountain Valley sparkling spring water, chilled in the fridge
- ☐ 1½ ounces Suntory Toki blended Japanese whisky, chilled in the freezer
- ☐ 1 lemon peel, as garnish (optional)

Add the water and whisky to a chilled highball glass. Serve unadorned or with a lemon twist on the side for the imbiber to garnish themself, if desired.

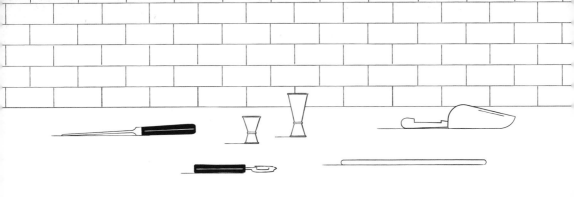

GRAIL ALE

by Jim Meehan

Riffing off Stiegl's popular grapefruit radler—a combination of golden lager and grapefruit soda—I substituted American pale ale, whose resinous hops round out the aroma of the high-toned grapefruit soda, while its tannins balance the sweetness. The grapefruit soda's sulphury astringency pairs well with the bitterness of the pale ale without compromising its hoppy character. YIELDS 1 SERVING

☐ 6 ounces Sierra Nevada pale ale or Athletic Run Wild N/A IPA, chilled

☐ 5 ounces Grapefruit Soda (page 288), chilled

☐ Ice cubes (optional)

☐ 1 half grapefruit wheel, for garnish

Add the ale and soda to a chilled pilsner glass. Add a few ice cubes, if desired. Garnish with the grapefruit half-wheel.

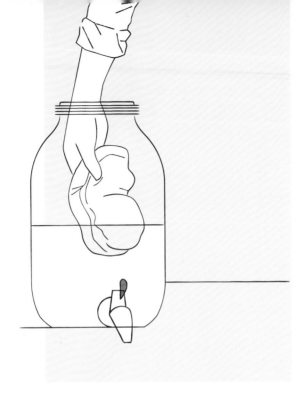

Ferments

The first ferments that likely come to most bartenders' minds are wine, beer, and saké. Less obvious—but no less omnipresent—fermentation is part of the processing of ingredients like spices, coffee, and tea. Some bars stock kombucha or prepare their own tepache, but generally, house-made ferments are not common in bars because their characteristics vary from batch to batch, which makes them difficult to mix with for bartenders who expect factory-like consistency of their ingredients. I'd love to see more house-made ferments in bars and restaurants willing to embrace the wily nature of the process—one of my favorites from Bar Tartine is included on page 313—because the diversity of flavor, scintillating acidity, and singular character of these preparations are unparalleled.

Fermentation is not an ingredient but, rather, "the transformation of food by various bacteria, fungi, and the enzymes they produce," explains the subject's preeminent expert Sandor Katz in *The Art of Fermentation*. This process occurs organically in nature, and "people harness this transformative power in order to produce alcohol, to preserve food, and to make it more digestible, less toxic, and/or more delicious."

Historically, quick ferments of grain into small beers provided calories and sated thirst when clean water was unavailable. Other ferments served a similar purpose: yogurt, cheese, and kefir preserved scarce animal proteins (transforming lactose into lactic acid in the process) for nomadic herdspeople. Lacto-fermented fruits and vegetables brined with salt (think sauerkraut and kimchi) or soured into shrubs with vinegar preserved harvests long before modern refrigeration and global agriculture made "fresh" food a modern convenience.

"People stumbled upon these techniques because it was the thing that kept them alive," says David Zilber, a chef and co-author of *The Noma Guide to Fermentation,* in an interview with *Emergence* magazine. "I don't think it was about creativity: I think it was about inevitability, because these microbes have always been around us. But the fact that we paired up—like wolves becoming man's best friend at some point—it is really a fairy-tale story of two types of species finding the perfect symbiosis in each other."

Still today, cultures all over the world continue to practice unique fermentation traditions. Experts tend to classify ferments in one of two ways: by the substrate (meat, dairy, etc.), or by the microbial process, such as lactic-acid fermentation, acetic-acid fermentation, and alkaline ferments. Because they can be tough to categorize, I've shined the spotlight on the most pertinent processes for beverages in this chapter and include them elsewhere in the book, as they straddle category lines with other ingredient families (such as yogurt in the Dairy chapter and kvass in the Grains & Nuts chapter).

HOW FERMENTATION WORKS

The main characters in any story about fermentation revolve around the proclivities of microorganisms such as yeast and bacteria. The fermentation from microorganisms present in the environment—such as the ambient yeast on the skin of a pineapple used to make tepache—is known as wild or spontaneous fermentation. The fermentation in which selected organisms or "starters"—such as cultivated yeast strains—are added to outcompete native microorganisms is called "inoculation," or "culturing," a human-made approach prized for its ability to create a reliably consistent flavor profile from batch to batch.

Innoculation requires transferring, or "backslopping," a small amount of live ferment into a new batch of the substrate to get a new fermentation started. For ferments like yogurt, kombucha, and sourdough bread, this requires a "mother" culture. As Katz explains, "certain fermentation starters have evolved into distinctive biological forms that reproduce themselves as cohesive communities," like the disk-shaped kombucha mother or kefir grains known as "a symbiotic community of bacteria and yeast" (SCOBY). These organisms are living cultures that grow and evolve over time.

To keep these cultures alive, you must feed them regularly. Yogurt and kefir grains require fresh milk, kombucha requires sweetened tea, and tibicos or water kefir feed on sugar-water alone. The need to sustain live cultures between batches is one reason fermenters build communities to sustain their craft. "Avoiding lab-produced cultures forces you to connect with the community by sharing mother cultures and SCOBYs," Dr. Miin Chan told me. "The microbial circle dance never ends; if you care for your cultures and your community, you will have more cultural bounty than you know what to do with! Instead of scale, look to multiplication; help others to prosper by connecting and giving microbial cultures, both physical and narrative."

Fermented beverages like kombucha, kvass, shrubs, tepache, and ginger bug all share common characteristics. Sandor Katz calls them "sour tonics," offering this insightful description: "They are tasty beverages, somewhat acidic, somewhat sweet, and in some cases lightly alcoholic, teeming with live lactic acid bacteria (among others), and generally regarded as healthful and tonic."

These are the most useful ferments for mixed drinks.

Tibicos and milk kefir These are prepared from a SCOBY of irregularly shaped gelatinous "grains." There are two main varieties: milk kefir grains, which produce a tart, bubbly, low-ABV dairy beverage; and tibicos, which are frequently called water kefir. According to Giancalis Caldwell in *Homemade Yogurt & Kefir,* "milk kefir grains contain microbes that ferment milk sugar, while water kefir grains ferment sucrose (often with fruits, grains, or nuts added). Either can be purchased fresh, dried, or frozen." Tibicos are used in the Ginger Burns (page 313).

Yogurt A creamy, tart, gel-structured milk ferment originally from the Mediterranean region, yogurt is cultured by the actions of bacteria that are most active at elevated temperatures and require a live starter. In *Wild Fermentation,* Sandor Katz recommends consumers look closely for the words "contains live cultures" on the label of their yogurt, as "many commercially available fermented foods are pasteurized, which means heated to the point at which microorganisms die." Mony Bunni's Yogurt (page 98) is a great recipe to start with if you've never made yogurt at home before.

Kombucha and jun *Wild Drinks* author Sharon Flynn characterizes kombucha and jun—both originating from northern China—as "living, naturally sparkling, mildly acidic refreshing drinks with a very small amount of residual alcohol." They are similar ferments, but jun is typically fermented with green tea and honey in a cool environment and kombucha with black tea and cane sugar at room temperature (like Arielle Johnson's Hōjicha Kombucha on page 316). Each requires a SCOBY and a backslop of active ferment to inoculate a new batch.

Kvass An umbrella term for sour fermented beverages from the Baltics, kvass fermentation was first recorded over a thousand years ago in Russia. The central ingredient is bread; usually hearty stale loaves from whole grains, although fresh bread works, too. According to Sarah Owens in *Heirloom,* kvass was specifically prepared "with many variations, including wheat or rye sourdough bread, flour only, sourdough starter only, beets only, sprouted grains, or any combination thereof along with a sugar source to activate carbonation by feeding the wild yeasts and bacteria. Birch sap water or honey was most likely used until granulated sugar became more widely available, and each household is famed to have had its own recipe." The commercial bottlings of kvass I've tried are low proof and as sweet as cola, perhaps adjusted for what the industry perceives as enticing to mainstream palates. Homemade kvass can be quite boozy (try the Borodinsky Rye Kvass from Bonnie Morales, on page 121, for example).

Tepache Tepache is a slightly fizzy beverage from Mexico that is traditionally wild-fermented from yeasts on the skins and cores of pineapple (and sometimes other ingredients like corn, depending on where the drink is made and what grows there). This refreshing, low-ABV beverage is typically sweetened with raw sugar and spiced with canela (Ceylon cinnamon). Rosio Sánchez makes a commendable version (see page 320) with a cultivated yeast strain.

Vinegar From the French *vin aigre,* or "sour wine," vinegar is made from wine, beer, saké, cider, or mead that's been exposed to acetic-acid bacteria long enough for the ethanol to be converted into acetic acid. If the acidity of a vinegar falls below 2 percent, harmful microbes can spoil it, so it must be stored in a glass bottle, in a cool environment, with a narrow neck to reduce the amount of liquid exposed to air. Undiluted spirits can't be made into vinegars because the *Acetobacter* is unable to metabolize anything above 15 percent alcohol by volume.

Shrubs These cordials are prepared with sugar and vinegar for preservation. In *Ferment,* Mark Diacono hypothesizes, "these drinking vinegars are likely to have originated from the necessity to preserve fruit (and some vegetables) in an easily digestible, nutritious form that could be taken on long voyages, and quickly became popular in the nineteenth century and early part of the twentieth. They tend to be both sweet and sharp and may be enriched with herbs and spices. The art and pleasure of a good shrub is in exploring combinations of vinegar, sugar source, fruit and herbs that are both characterful and complex." Distilled white vinegar is used to preserve raspberries in Neal Bodenheimer's Raspberry Shrub (page 318).

Amazaké This is a quick ferment made from cooked rice or barley, plus water and koji—a miraculous mold used for millennia in Asia to make miso, soy sauce, saké, shochu, and many more foods, condiments, and beverages. Westerners typically only encounter amazaké as the base ferment for saké (called nihonshu, in Japan) and other rice-based alcohols, but the beverage "is also a star in its own right" according to Rich Shih and Jeremy Umansky in *Koji Alchemy,* who trace its origins back to early alcohols made from fruits, honey, koji, and rice in regions of what is now China.

Soy sauce *Soy* is derived from the Japanese word *shoyu,* which comes from *sou,* the Chinese name for soybeans. Traditional soy sauces (and tamari, which contains only soybeans and rice and is gluten free) are brewed over a long period of time from a combination of soybeans and wheat grains, with salt, koji, lactic-acid bacteria, yeast, and water. After fermentation, the sauce is pressed from the bean mixture. "Many soy sauces are still brewed this way today, though some larger manufacturers have resorted to less time-intensive processes," writes author Julia Skinner in *Our Fermented Lives*. Check out the Peeking Duck (page 332) to see how this savory sauce can add umami to a cocktail.

SOURCING

Because many ferments require a mother yeast or SCOBY starter, many fermenters cultivate communities of folks who regularly share starters with one another. In the absence of this resourceful, collaborative expertise, you can source starters online from retailers like Cultures for Health or Gem Cultures. For the baker's yeast used in the kvass recipe, I found an acceptable version in the refrigerated aisle of my local grocery store.

STORAGE

To preserve carbonation, transfer your homemade ferments to glass bottles while they're actively bubbling, and seal the bottles. Sandor Katz recommends bottling a portion of your active ferments in plastic soda bottles to monitor the residual carbon dioxide by touch. If the bottle has some give, it's not fully pressurized and can be left alone. If it's taut, it should be refrigerated (along with the rest of the batch) to slow the fermentation before pressure builds and the bottle explodes.

Thick glass bail-top bottles—like the ones Grolsch beer uses—can be purchased from a brewing supply store and are ideal to bottle and serve liquid ferments, as they're resealable and made of thick glass to safely contain carbonation. Many effervescent ferments, which may undergo a secondary fermentation in the bottle if sugar is present, should be burped every couple days to prevent an explosion and to monitor alcohol levels. Once you're satisfied with the ABV and carbonation level, transfer the ferment to the fridge to arrest fermentation.

In professional settings, all preparations are named, dated, and attributed with a Sharpie on carefully cut masking tape placed on the container (and not on the lid) by the cook or bartender who prepared them. This is proper kitchen protocol for all preparations, and is exceptionally useful for live ferments, which have kinetic shelf lives that need to be monitored for service.

PREPARATION

The conditions you set before beginning any fermentation project are important for efficiency, flavor, and safety. "There is a thin line between rot and fermentation, and that line might be best understood as an actual line, like the kind you'd find outside a nightclub," René Redzepi and David Zilber write in *The Noma Guide to Fermentation*. "When you ferment something, you're taking on the role of the bouncer, keeping out unwanted microbes and letting in the ones that are going to make the party pop."

Safety "My motto is cleanliness, not sterility," writes Sandor Katz in *The Art of Fermentation,* adding how "it is certainly important to work with clean hands, utensils, and equipment, but in general, sterile conditions are not necessary for fermentation." The goal is to create a dirt-free environment, not one bleached or scrubbed with antibacterial soap, as fermentation requires the participation of the microorganisms these cleansing agents kill off indiscriminately.

In some cases, there are safety measures baked into procedures for certain ferments. In alcoholic beverages, for example, "alcohol itself is antimicrobial, making it even harder for harmful microbes to take up residence," Julia Skinner explains. Proper percentages of salt and acidity in lacto-ferments like kimchi and sauerkraut are another safeguard that helps maintain the ideal environment for food-safe microorganisms.

At the end of any experiment, experts recommend trusting your gut. "If you taste a small sample and it turns your stomach, remember that your body is designed to reject things that may be harmful to you," write Redzepi and Zilber. "When in doubt, throw it out. . . . The weeks and months of your invested time are not worth risking your health."

Temperature The outcome of a fermentation may be influenced by a variety of factors, including salinity level, acidity level, water quality, oxygen level, time, temperature, substrate quality, and starter type. Avoid fermenting in direct sunlight, and be vigilant with tap water, as chlorine is frequently added to municipal water sources and may slow, change, or prevent your ferments from proceeding.

Temperature—which affects the duration of fermentation—is the easiest element to monitor and adjust. A higher temperature means fermentation will happen more quickly. You can slow a fermentation down by lowering the temperature if there are known agents you don't want to cultivate. For example, lacto-fermentation of fruits and vegetables is kept at a lower temperature to slow yeast growth, according to Arielle Johnson and Lars Williams in *A Field Guide to Fermentation*.

TOOLS AND VESSELS

While commercially oriented fermenters aiming to produce a consistent product recommend pH meters, refractometers, and inoculation chambers to monitor and control ferments, the most basic ferments need only a clean vessel—something as simple as a glass jar. For kombucha, I fermented in a 2-gallon glass jar with cheesecloth affixed to the rim with an elastic band. For tepache, I had no issue fermenting in a 2-gallon plastic bucket with an airlock to keep intrepid fruit flies at bay. In *Wild Fermentation*, Sandor Katz says if you're using plastic, make sure it's food grade. "Do not use plastic buckets that once contained building materials. And do not ferment in metallic containers, which can react with salt as well as the acids produced by fermentation."

The perversely titled Green Revolution, led by agronomists focused on fighting famines and feeding troops in an interminable series of intractable wars all over the planet, industrialized agriculture beginning in the early twentieth century. With our food supply increasingly managed by technologists obsessed with crop yields over all other considerations, society's investment in historic preservation methods like canning, curing, and fermenting largely fell by the wayside.

This situation began to change in the U.S. in the 1960s, when a hippy-led "back to the land" movement, which centered on naturally prepared foods sourced from co-ops and organic markets, gradually led to the commercial revival of live ferments like sauerkraut, kimchi, kombucha, and kefir. After a couple decades of popular dormancy, traditional ferments have regained mainstream appeal and returned to convenience stores, thanks in large part to their adoption by world-famous restaurants such as Noma in Copenhagen and Momofuku in New York City, which have received reams of media coverage for cooking with ferments.

The newfound interest in traditional ferments is certainly something to celebrate, but as their popularity grows at a commercial level, scrutiny is required, as many opportunistic companies are co-opting ferments from their origin cultures and repackaging them as contextless "health foods" that hearken back to the 1960s.

In her righteous article "Lost in the Brine," published on *Eater* in early 2021, fermented foods scholar Dr. Miin Chan explains: "Regardless of whether white interest in these cultural ferments is rooted in social justice or a way to virtue signal white worldliness, BIPOC fermenters are still getting lost in the brine of the industry's overwhelmingly white narrative. Although it's not as if only Japanese people can make Japanese ferments or white people cannot gain expertise or profit from their hard work, there needs to be more recognition of the inequities at play and a collaborative effort to correct them, even when it is uncomfortable for white fermenters."

I must confess that before writing this chapter, I had never (intentionally) fermented anything and I assumed I'd need expensive equipment and frequent access to experts to be successful. After securing direction from folks I looked up to and preparing a few batches of each ferment, the bubbling elixirs began to feel like beloved house plants in my kitchen. I felt a great sense of pride when my ferments became relatively consistent, which Skinner describes in *Our Fermented Lives* as, "the relationship between both the maker and the microbe and between the microbes themselves."

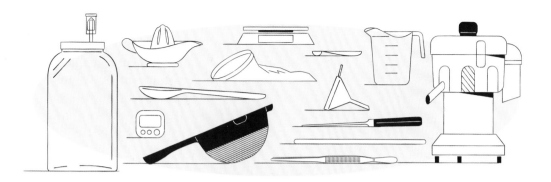

GINGER BURNS

by Cortney Burns

This ginger-lemon tibicos was named by Nicolaus Balla, who managed the back of house with Burns at Bar Tartine, to commemorate both the character of the drink and its namesake's spicy nature. "In 2008, I began seeing a naturopath in Sonoma, who recommended I make water kefir and drink it daily to heal my gut and up my ingested probiotic load," Cortney says of the drink's inspiration. "Bar Tartine was the first restaurant I served it in, and it was on tap from day one to the day we closed her up in 2016."

Use in the Lemon-Ginger Rebujito (page 324) or drink it over ice. YIELDS 28 OUNCES (3½ CUPS)

□ 24 ounces filtered water
□ 50g (¼ cup) sucanat (see page 22)
□ 3g (½ teaspoon) molasses
□ Pinch of Himalayan pink salt
□ 1 lemon, cut into 4 pieces
□ 15g (2 pieces) dried apricots

□ 10g (1-inch piece) fresh ginger, sliced (unpeeled)
□ 45g (¼ cup) water kefir grains (tibicos)
□ 3 ounces lemon juice
□ 1 ounce ginger juice (extracted from roughly 100g fresh ginger)

• CONTINUED •

Add the filtered water and sucanat to a 1-gallon wide-mouth glass jar and stir to dissolve.

Add the molasses, salt, lemon pieces, apricots, fresh ginger, and kefir grains.

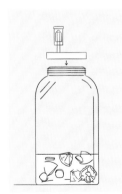

Seal the container with an airlock lid.

Ferment at room temperature for 2 to 3 days, until lightly fizzy.

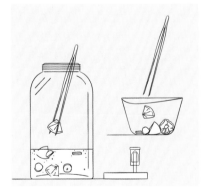

Remove the apricots and lemon pieces with tongs.

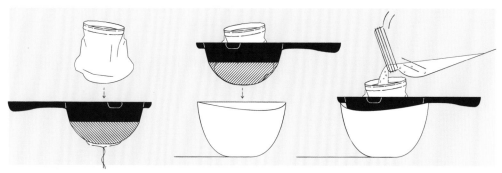

Strain the liquid through a nut milk bag over a fine-mesh strainer. Reserve the grains in a mixture of 50g (¼ cup) sugar and 32 ounces water in an airtight container in the fridge. Replace the syrup weekly.

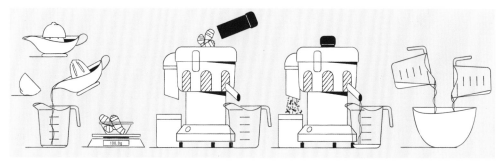

Add the lemon and ginger juices to the ferment.

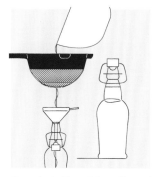  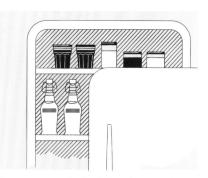

Fine-strain the mixture through a funnel into flip-top bottles with tight-fitting lids, leaving at least 1 inch of headspace.

Store at room temperature until the pressure builds in the containers, for 24 hours.

Store, covered, in the fridge, burping the bottles daily, until fermentation is complete.

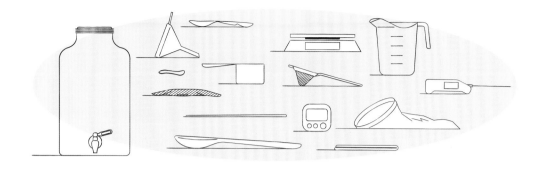

HŌJICHA KOMBUCHA

from Arielle Johnson

World-renowned flavor scientist and author of *Flavorama* Dr. Arielle Johnson says "fermentation is, quite literally, flavor creation on a molecular level, so it can be unexpected and rewarding to see how this process-inherent flavor develops. Hōjicha has a lot of complex character of its own—seaweed, grassy, and umami green tea flavors, as well as malty, toasty, and slightly bitter notes from the roasting process it goes through," she says. "I like how these qualities layer with the acidity and funk that the kombucha fermentation process creates." For first-timers, you can buy the kombucha starter known as a SCOBY (a "symbiotic community of bacteria and yeast") online or from local home brew shops—unless you have a fermenter friend in your circle who can share one with you—and use the liquid it comes in as your "kombucha mother." If more volume is needed, supplement this with a bottled kombucha, then reserve a portion of this fermentation to be the mother of your next batch.

Use in the Gut Punch (page 326) or drink it over ice. YIELDS 96 OUNCES

- ☐ 3 liters filtered water
- ☐ 20g (⅓ cup) Jou Yanagi hōjicha leaves
- ☐ 210g (1 heaping cup) white cane sugar
- ☐ 320 milliliters (11 ounces) kombucha mother
- ☐ 1 SCOBY

Heat the water to 195°F and then add to a 7½ liter (2-gallon) kombucha jar.

Place the tea leaves in a nut milk bag. Plunge the nut milk bag into the hot water and suspend it in place by threading its drawstring through a chopstick placed across the jar's mouth. Infuse for 5 minutes, then remove the bag.

Add the sugar, and stir to dissolve.

Let the tea mixture cool to room temperature, 4 to 5 hours.

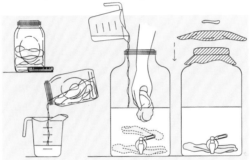

Add the kombucha mother and the SCOBY to the kombucha jar, cover the opening with cheesecloth, and fasten with a rubber band or string (do not seal with a lid).

Ferment at room temperature for 5 to 10 days, tasting each day until it's as tart as you prefer.

Pour off 11 ounces of the kombucha to reserve as a mother for the next batch. Gently remove the SCOBYs from the jar with a clean hand and add them to the reserved kombucha mother.

Decant the remaining kombucha through a fine-mesh strainer into a nonreactive container.

Store, covered, in the fridge, burping the bottles daily, until fermentation is complete.

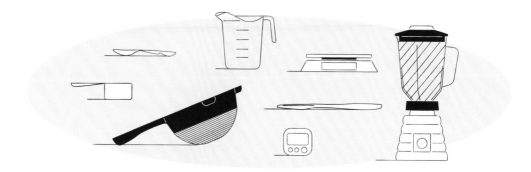

RASPBERRY SHRUB

from Neal Bodenheimer

Neal Bodenheimer combines shrubs with sparkling wine year-round for a low-proof menu offering that's become a proven crowd-pleaser in all his bars in New Orleans. He told me shrubs are "the perfect preparation to show off our produce each season." For this recipe, Neal finds that raspberry seeds enhance the flavor; so he recommends straining the mixture through a medium mesh strainer that lets them pass through. Prepare this with fresh raspberries when they're in season, and use IQF (individually quick frozen) raspberries if you want to mix with it year-round.

Use in the Roffignac (page 322). YIELDS APPROXIMATELY 34 OUNCES

☐ 275g (2 cups) raspberries, fresh or thawed IQF

☐ 275g (1¼ cups) superfine sugar

☐ 10 ounces filtered water

☐ 10 ounces distilled white vinegar

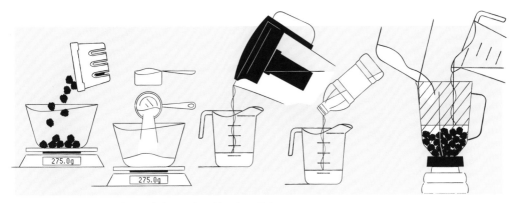

Add the fruit, sugar, water, and vinegar to a blender pitcher.

Purée until smooth, about 1 minute.

Strain the mixture, pressing down with a spatula to extract as much liquid as possible.

Let the mixture settle, and then spoon off and discard any foam from the top.

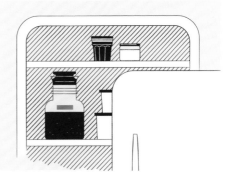

Store, covered, in the fridge for up to 1 MONTH.

TEPACHE

from Rosio Sánchez

Rosio Sánchez honed her skills as a cook at WD-50 in New York and Noma in Copenhagen before opening Hija de Sanchez Taquerias and Sanchez Restaurant in Copenhagen. She confessed that importing her tepache recipe from Mexico to Scandinavia hasn't been easy. "It's actually pretty hard to get great pineapples here," she says. To compensate, she adjusts the amount of sugar in her recipe based on the sweetness of the pineapples and uses a propagated yeast—a tip from fellow Noma alum Arielle Johnson, who suggested it would help with consistency. Sánchez serves the tepache on tap in her restaurants, which adds additional carbonation that accentuates its texture and flavor.

Use in the Slow West (page 328) or drink it over ice. YIELDS 52 OUNCES

- ☐ 1 small (500g) pineapple
- ☐ 42 ounces filtered water
- ☐ 250g (1¼ cups) superfine sugar
- ☐ 87.5g (½ cup) light brown sugar
- ☐ 37.5g (scant ⅓ cup) muscovado sugar
- ☐ 5g (1 teaspoon) White Labs Belgian wit ale yeast (WLP550)
- ☐ 4.5g (one 3-inch quill) Ceylon (canela) cinnamon
- ☐ 3.5g star anise pods (3 pods)
- ☐ 2.5g whole cloves (about 30)

Rinse the pineapple and remove the leaves.

Chop the pineapple into 3-inch triangles with the rind, flesh, and core intact.

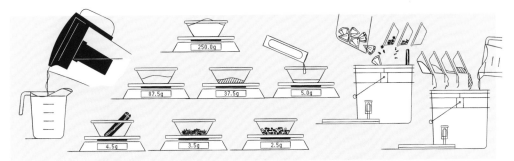

Transfer the pineapple to a clean 2 gallon brewing bucket. Add the water, superfine, brown, and muscovado sugars, yeast, cinnamon, star anise, and cloves.

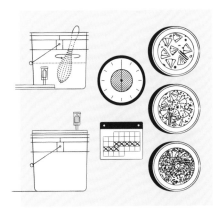

Cover with the air-locked lid and ferment at room temperature. Stir every 12 hours with a whisk and taste each day until it's as dry as you prefer, about 8 days.

Strain the tepache through a funnel into flip-top bottles with tight-fitting lids, leaving at least 1 inch of headspace.

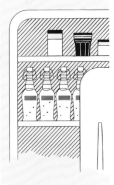

Store, covered, in the fridge, burping the bottles daily, until fermentation is complete.

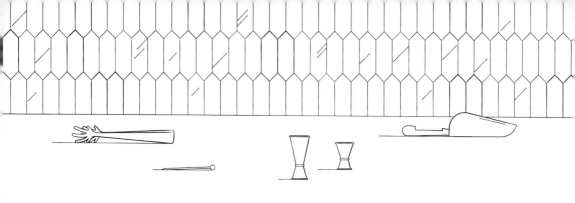

ROFFIGNAC

from Neal Bodenheimer

As a studious New Orleans bar owner, Neal Bodenheimer had heard of the Roffignac from Stanley Clisby Arthur's 1937 book *Famous New Orleans Drinks and How to Mix 'Em,* but he didn't fully appreciate the potential of the drink. Then Paul Gustings, a longtime local bartender, started mixing it with raspberry shrub instead of syrup, which added complexity and refreshing acidity. The original recipe as printed calls for whiskey or Cognac, but Bodenheimer finds "the funky nature of a relatively young Armagnac gives the drink some depth and personality that more refined brandies just can't match." YIELDS 1 SERVING

- ☐ 2 ounces Darroze 8-year-old Armagnac
- ☐ 2 ounces force-carbonated water (see page 282), chilled
- ☐ 1½ ounces Raspberry Shrub (page 318)
- ☐ Ice cubes, or ice spear tempered for 1 to 2 minutes
- ☐ 1 fresh raspberry, for garnish

Add the Armagnac, seltzer, and shrub to a chilled Collins glass. Add a tempered ice spear or a scoop of ice cubes to the glass. Garnish with the raspberry on a pick. Serve with a straw, if desired.

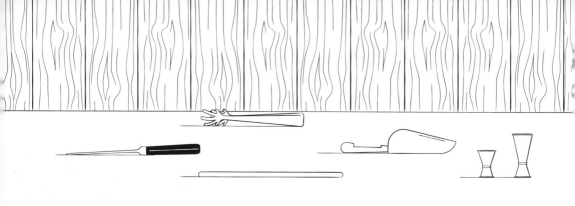

LEMON-GINGER REBUJITO

by Cortney Burns

Cortney Burns was introduced to the Rebujito—a classic Andalusian highball traditionally prepared with fino sherry and lemon-lime soda—in the autumn of 2004, at the Brazen Head in San Francisco. "I used to sit at the end of the bar doing crossword puzzles or reading cookbooks by the light of a Tiffany lamp," she recalls fondly. In this more expressive version of the drink, her Ginger Burns steps in for the lemon-lime soda, which lends incredible complexity and character. Cortney served the drink at Bar Tartine and memorialized the combination in her book *Bar Tartine: Techniques & Recipes,* co-authored by co-chef Nicolaus Balla. YIELDS 1 SERVING

- ☐ 4 ounces Ginger Burns (page 313), chilled
- ☐ 2 ounces Lustau Manzanilla Papirusa sherry, chilled
- ☐ Ice cubes, or 1 large (2-inch) ice cube tempered for 1 to 2 minutes
- ☐ 1 orange wedge, for garnish

Add the Ginger Burns and sherry to a chilled tumbler. Add the large tempered cube or a scoop of ice cubes. Garnish with the orange wedge. Serve with a straw.

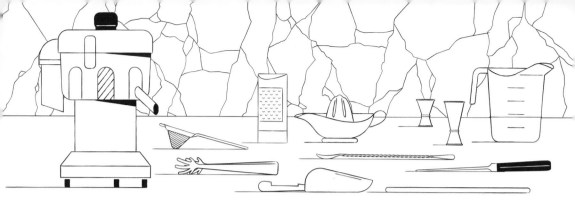

GUT PUNCH

by Jim Meehan

A Bajan saying calls for punch, a word whose etymology may be derived from the Hindi word for "five," to be prepared with "one of sour, two of sweet, three of strong, four of weak." I created this recipe with those classic proportions in mind, with the lemon juice as "one of sour," the 2:1 honey syrup as the "two of sweet," the rum as the "three of strong," the hōjicha kombucha as the "four of weak," and the ginger and nutmeg as the requisite spice element found in historic punches. Bringing in two gut-friendly ingredients—kombucha, which is well regarded for its probiotic qualities, and ginger, which is known as a digestive balm—was the inspiration for the cheeky drink title. YIELDS NINE 4½-OUNCE SERVINGS

☐ 16 ounces Hōjicha Kombucha (page 316)

☐ 12 ounces Banks 7 Golden Blend rum

☐ 4 ounces lemon juice

☐ 4 ounces Honey Syrup (page 338)

☐ ½ ounce ginger juice (extracted from 50g fresh ginger)

☐ 1 large ice block, tempered for 30 minutes, or ice cubes for a pitcher, plus large (2-inch) ice cubes for serving

☐ Nutmeg, freshly grated, for garnish

Add the kombucha, rum, lemon juice, syrup, and ginger juice to a nonreactive container and stir. Cover and chill in the fridge for at least 1 hour.

Add a large tempered block of ice to a punch bowl or large tempered cubes into a pitcher. Fill the bowl or pitcher with the chilled punch. Ladle or pour the punch into chilled punch cups filled with large, tempered ice cubes. Garnish each serving with freshly grated nutmeg.

SLOW WEST

by Claire Sprouse

Claire Sprouse created this for her Crown Heights cocktail bar Hunky Dory in 2019. She used a tepache prepared with turmeric that she fermented with ambient yeast, "making it more herbal, which suits the purposes of the cocktail." As for the name of the drink, she explains: "Slow West is a Western that takes you on a winding lyrical journey through the sun-scorched West. This drink has similar vibes—you could have one, or a few (owing to its relatively low-ABV), on a long afternoon out on the patio." **YIELDS 1 SERVING**

- ☐ 1 lemon wedge, to moisten rim
- ☐ 1 tablespoon kosher salt, for half rim
- ☐ 3 ounces Bordiga extra dry vermouth
- ☐ 2 ounces Tepache (page 320)
- ☐ ½ ounce lemon juice
- ☐ ½ ounce Simple Syrup (page 339)
- ☐ 4 dashes Bitter Truth celery bitters
- ☐ Ice cubes

Moisten half the rim of a chilled pilsner glass with the lemon wedge, then dip the moist half of the rim into the salt. Add the vermouth, tepache, lemon juice, syrup, and bitters into a Boston shaker. Add a scoop of ice cubes and roll the mixture between the 2 tins. Pour the shaker's contents unstrained (including the ice cubes) into the glass and serve.

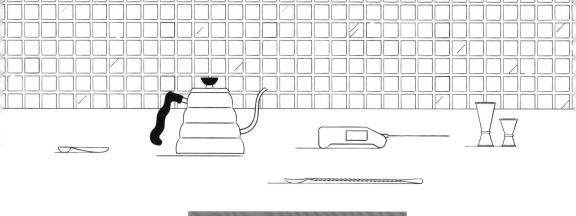

WELCOME MOTHER

by Paul Calvert

Ticonderoga Club co-owner Paul Calvert found the inspiration for this recipe in one of his daily drinks rituals. "Many years ago, I started drinking a plug of Bragg's apple cider vinegar with a glass of water each morning. It's an anti-inflammatory and opens my nose," he says. "There's something aggressive about the way it helps—sort of like when a parent comes to visit and starts in on a 'Are you eating enough?' conversation." The name of the drink has a delightful double entendre: "The 'welcome' in the title refers to the pineapple, an international symbol of hospitality, and the 'mother' refers to the mother in fermentation: a living bacterial womb from which funky, sour, tingly offspring originates," he explains.

YIELDS 1 SERVING

- ☐ 4 ounces filtered water, heated to 195°F
- ☐ 1½ ounces Banks 7 Golden Blend rum
- ☐ ¾ ounce Pineapple Cordial (page 30)
- ☐ ¾ ounce Bragg's apple cider vinegar
- ☐ ½ teaspoon raw orange blossom honey
- ☐ Pinch of cayenne

Add the water, rum, cordial, vinegar, honey, and cayenne to a prewarmed tempered mug, and stir.

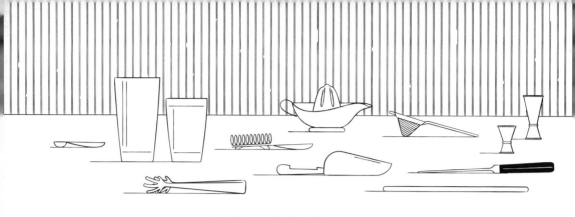

PEEKING DUCK

by Jim Meehan

With the layered flavor profile of Peking duck in mind, I created this Singapore Sling-esque refresher in the fall of 2016 with Aylesbury Duck vodka (now sadly discontinued, so substitute your favorite wheat-based vodka) "peeking" through the other, more flavorful ingredients. While it was originally prepared with PDT Hong Kong's house ginger beer, Katie Rose's Szechuan Ginger Beer works well both conceptually and as an added spice component. YIELDS 1 SERVING

- ☐ ¾ ounce Paul Beau V.S.O.P. Cognac
- ☐ ¾ ounce vodka
- ☐ ½ ounce lemon juice
- ☐ ¼ ounce Amaro Averna
- ☐ ¼ ounce Mandarine Napoléon liqueur

- ☐ ¼ ounce orange juice
- ☐ ¼ teaspoon soy sauce
- ☐ Ice cubes, plus 1 ice spear tempered for 1 to 2 minutes
- ☐ 1½ ounces Szechuan Ginger Beer (page 284), chilled
- ☐ 1 orange half-wheel, for garnish

Add the Cognac, vodka, lemon juice, amaro, liqueur, orange juice, and soy sauce to a Boston shaker. Add a scoop of ice cubes to the shaker. Shake, then add the ginger beer to the shaker. Double-strain through a Hawthorne and a fine-mesh strainer into a chilled Collins glass filled with a tempered ice spear or ice cubes. Garnish with the orange wheel. Serve with a straw.

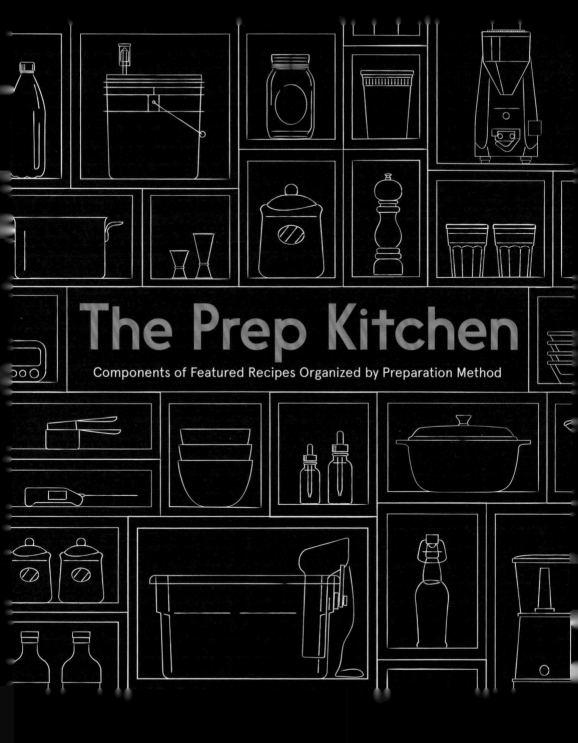

The Prep Kitchen

Components of Featured Recipes Organized by Preparation Method

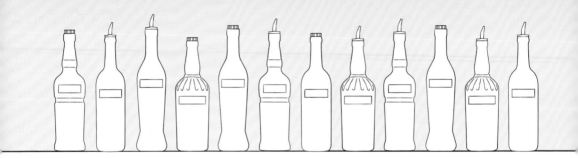

Bar Staples

These recipes are the building blocks bartenders prepare weekly as part of their workstation's mise-en-place to fulfill requests for classic cocktails and menu selections. They are usually stored in labeled 375 to 750 milliliter "cheater" bottles dated and initialed by the bartender who prepared it, capped with pour spouts, arranged in a knee-high bottle caddy affixed to the ice well, or in undercounter bottle "stadiums," or on top of the bar. Depending on the volume and variety of drinks served during a given week, these staples may be made by the quart or in a larger volume. They can be prepared as needed at home and will be stable at room temperature for ten days or up to a month, if stored covered in the fridge.

AGAVE SYRUP

(2:1 by volume)

In *Liquid Intelligence,* Dave Arnold notes that "over 70% of the sugar in agave nectar is fructose, so it doesn't act at all like table sugar." To make an agave syrup with the same brix as 1:1 simple syrup, measure 1 part water to 2 parts agave nectar by volume. Owing to the agave nectar's viscosity, the proportion is closer to 3:1 by weight.

YIELDS 12 OUNCES

- ☐ 8 ounces amber agave nectar
- ☐ 4 ounces filtered water

Add the agave nectar and filtered water to a small saucepan. Heat over medium heat, stirring until the nectar dissolves. Let cool, then store, covered, in the fridge for up to 1 month.

CANE SYRUP

(2:1 by volume and weight)

Leo Robitschek, the author of *The NoMad Cocktail Book,* uses organic evaporated cane sugar, which is crystallized only once in its production process, leaving behind some molasses and trace minerals. He stirs the syrup over heat to dissolve the sugar crystals to yield a 55 brix—or 55 grams of sucrose per 100 grams of solution—syrup. His bartenders use a digital refractometer to check the brix measurement from batch to batch as part of their quality control.

YIELDS 9 OUNCES

- ☐ 220g (1 cup) evaporated cane sugar
- ☐ 110g (4 ounces) filtered water

Add the evaporated cane sugar and filtered water to a medium saucepan. Heat over medium heat, stirring until the sugar dissolves. Let cool, and then store, covered, in the fridge for up to 1 month.

DEMERARA SYRUP

(2:1 by volume and weight)

Demerara is a type of sugar that comes from the first crystallization stage of light cane juice and takes the form of large moist, amber crystals. Unlike superfine sugar, demerara crystals do not readily dissolve in room-temperature water, so they must be heated and stirred frequently to prepare into a syrup.

YIELDS 14 OUNCES

- ☐ 350g (1½ cups) demerara sugar
- ☐ 175g (6 ounces) filtered water

Add the demerara sugar and filtered water to a medium saucepan. Heat over medium heat, stirring persistently until the sugar dissolves. Let cool, and then store, covered, in the fridge for up to 1 month.

HONEY SYRUP

(2:1 by volume)

The flavor of honey depends on which flowers the bees were pollinating before their honey was collected. To make honey syrup, Chad Solomon starts with 2½ parts honey to 1 part water by weight for orange blossom, acacia, and clover honey, and he ups the proportion to 3:1 by weight for more intense single-flower honeys such as leatherwood. A ratio of 2:1 by volume typically equates to 3:1 by weight, as honey is much denser than water.

YIELDS 10 OUNCES

- ☐ 275g (6 ounces) raw honey
- ☐ 3 ounces filtered water

If your honey is solid, place the container of raw honey in a saucepan partly filled with hot water for 5 minutes to loosen it.

Add the runny honey and filtered water to a medium saucepan. Place over low heat and stir until the honey is dissolved, about 1 minute. Let cool, then store, covered, in the fridge for up to 2 months.

MOLASSES SYRUP

(2:1 by volume)

Former Privateer Rum head distiller Maggie Campbell used Grade A molasses to make the rum at the distillery because the sulfur content is lower and it's less refined. She describes the flavor as "nutty and fruity with a hint of singed cane."

YIELDS 12 OUNCES

- ☐ 325g (8 ounces) Crosby's Fancy Molasses
- ☐ 4 ounces filtered water

Add the molasses and filtered water to a medium saucepan. Heat over medium heat, stirring until the molasses dissolves. Let cool, and then store, covered, in the fridge for up to 2 months.

SIMPLE SYRUP

(1:1 by volume and weight)

While granulated white cane sugar crystals are approximately the same weight and volume as water in a 1:1 mixture, weighing each ingredient is preferable, as sugar and water have different densities. Unlike syrups prepared from sugars with larger crystals, white sugar can be shaken or stirred into the solution without heat. If you heat the water to dissolve the sugar, avoid boiling it to minimize evaporation and maintain equal proportion.

YIELDS 12 OUNCES

- ☐ 200g (1 cup) white cane sugar
- ☐ 240g (8 ounces) filtered water

Add the sugar and filtered water to a medium saucepan. Heat over medium heat, stirring until the sugar dissolves. Let cool, and then store, covered, in the fridge for up to 1 month.

RICH SIMPLE SYRUP

(2:1 by volume and weight)

The Commissary PDX co-founder Sean Hoard insists that rich simple syrup—with a 2:1 ratio of sugar to water—is more stable and texturally superior to traditional simple syrup, with its 1:1 ratio. "The added viscosity carries more flavor through the mid-palate of a cocktail," he says, adding how "on a practical level, rich simple syrup contains less water, which allows the bartender more leeway to dilute a drink through shaking and stirring." Alternatively, it's less forgiving of imprecise measurement, so careful jiggering is recommended when mixing with it.

YIELDS 16½ OUNCES

- ☐ 400g (2 cups) white cane sugar
- ☐ 240g (8 ounces) filtered water

Add the sugar and filtered water to a medium saucepan. Heat over medium heat, stirring until the sugar dissolves. Let cool, and then store, covered, in the fridge for up to 1 month.

SORGHUM SYRUP

(3:1 by volume)

According to Paul Calvert, "Sorghum was once called 'mountain gold' because the stalks—which look a bit like wheat and young corn—grow in the mountains like wild, flowering grass." The sorghum grown by the Hughes family is his favorite because "it's bright and tangy, without the burnt notes other bottlings have, and has wonderful green citrus notes; making it an excellent sweetener for cocktails." I also thought the Hughes sorghum was delicious and loved the old-school checkout process. I called the farm and they shipped me two jugs directly, which I paid for through the honor system by mailing a handwritten check.

YIELDS 11 OUNCES

☐ 350g (8 ounces) sorghum syrup
☐ 2⅔ ounces (⅓ cup) filtered water

Add the sorghum syrup and filtered water to a medium saucepan. Heat over medium heat, stirring until it dissolves. Let cool, and then store, covered, in the fridge for up to 2 months.

MINERAL SALINE

(10 percent by weight)
from Chad Solomon

After reading about mineral salts in Darcy O'Neil's *Fix the Pumps,* Chad Solomon experimented with syrups and saline using Crazy Water No. 4, a mineral water bottled in Mineral Wells, Texas. "Naturally mineralized water comes from its unique mineral signature. Minerality can enhance flavor and texture when utilized to brew coffee and used in cocktails too," Solomon says. "The key is to be mindful that saline—mineralized or not—has a threshold. The right amount enhances a cocktail's complexity, but too much can flatten it."

YIELDS 9 OUNCES

☐ 25g (1⅙ tablespoons) kosher salt
☐ 9 ounces Crazy Water No. 4 or other high-content mineral water

Add the salt and mineral water to a nonreactive container. Stir until the salt dissolves. Store, covered, in the fridge indefinitely.

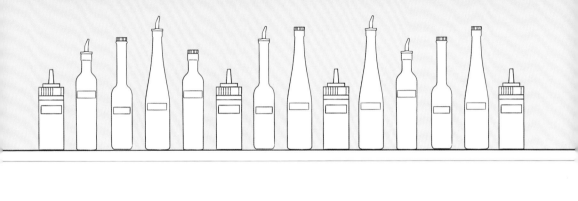

Specialty Cordials

These flavorful syrups—artfully called cordials in the UK—are infusions that incorporate roots, spices, herbs, vegetables, and juices to dissolve a sweetener. This section includes preparations that mirror techniques illustrated elsewhere in the book but feature different components. I've grouped them as "specialty cordials," to distinguish them from the more utilitarian Bar Staples.

GENMAICHA SYRUP

from Jillian Vose

Jillian Vose initially prepared a toasted brown rice syrup for the Riot Act (page 140) and was pleased with the taste but was disappointed with the murky brown color the syrup cast in the cocktail. Her colleague Long Thai suggested substituting genmaicha, a green tea blended with toasted and puffed brown rice. It corrected the syrup's color and improved the cocktail's complexity.

YIELDS 12 OUNCES

- ☐ 8 ounces filtered water
- ☐ 10g (2½ tablespoons) genmaicha
- ☐ 200g (1 cup) white cane sugar

Heat the water to 185°F in a heatproof saucepan. Add the tea leaves, remove from the heat, and let infuse for 2 minutes. Fine-strain the mixture into a heatproof vessel.

While the tea is still hot, add the sugar and stir until it dissolves. Once the syrup has cooled, store, covered, in the fridge for up to 1 week.

GINGER-AGAVE SYRUP

from Danielle Tatarin

Danielle Tatarin uses raw agave nectar as a sweetener in her mezcal-based drinks because it has a rounder mouthfeel on the finish. "Usually, I cut it 50-50 with water, tea or another flavorful ingredient such as ginger juice to reduce its sweetness," she says. To distribute the ginger-juice sediment throughout the syrup, Danielle stirs continuously while mixing and shakes it for service. Use this in the Gota de Sandía (page 38).

YIELDS 6 OUNCES

- ☐ 100g (3 ounces) raw organic agave nectar
- ☐ 3 ounces ginger juice (extracted from 300g fresh ginger)

Add the agave nectar and ginger juice to a nonreactive container and stir vigorously to blend. Store, covered, in the fridge for up to 2 weeks. Shake the mixture before each service.

GRAPEFRUIT-LIME SHERBET

from Julie Reiner

Julie Reiner concedes that grapefruit juice isn't tart enough to balance the sweetness of an oleo saccharum made with its peel, "but I felt that the grapefruit oils really complemented the jasmine tea" in Dragon Pearl Punch (page 262), she says. For the required acidity, Julie and Clover Club partner Tom Macy tested the oleo saccharum with lemon and lime juice, and the latter won the taste test.

YIELDS 13 OUNCES

- ☐ 3 Ruby Red grapefruits
- ☐ 200g (1 cup) superfine sugar
- ☐ 8½ ounces lime juice (from 6 to 8 limes)

With a swivel peeler, pare the peels from the grapefruits, each in one long spiral. Place the peels in a pint mason jar. Add the sugar and screw on the cap. Shake the jar to evenly coat the peels with the sugar. Infuse for 4 to 6 hours or overnight to extract the oil from the peels.

Add the lime juice to the mason jar and re-seal the jar. Shake vigorously to dissolve any remaining sugar. Remove the peels with tongs and compost them. Store, covered, in the fridge for up to 1 day.

Shake the jar to evenly coat the peels with the sugar. Infuse for 4 to 6 hours or overnight to extract the oil from the peels.

Add 8 ounces of the "Enhanced" Ruby Red Grapefruit Juice to the mason jar and re-seal the jar. Shake vigorously to dissolve any remaining sugar. Remove the peels with tongs and compost them.

Combine the contents of the mason jar with the remaining enhanced grapefruit juice in a quart container. Store, covered, in the fridge for up to 1 week.

ENHANCED

GRAPEFRUIT SHERBET

from Jim Meehan

The phosphoric and citric acid in Chad Solomon's "enhanced" grapefruit juice provide acidity to both balance the sweetness of the grapefruit juice and extend its shelf life. It's too sweet to use in a punch, but perfect as the juice base for a soda's flavor syrup. Use in the Grapefruit Soda (page 288).

YIELDS 24 OUNCES

- ☐ 3 Ruby Red grapefruits
- ☐ 200g (1 cup) superfine sugar
- ☐ 20 ounces "Enhanced" Ruby Red Grapefruit Juice (page 162)

With a swivel peeler, pare the peels from the grapefruits, each in one long spiral. Place the peels in a pint mason jar. Add the sugar and screw on the cap.

CELERY SYRUP

from Don Lee

Don Lee's celery syrup was inspired by a cocktail of Phil Ward's mixed with Scrappy's celery bitters. When Don tested the bitters in his Celery and Nori (page 204), he didn't taste enough celery. According to Lee, "straight celery juice was overwhelming in the recipe, so I ended up incorporating the juice into a lighter celery syrup."

YIELDS 8 OUNCES

- ☐ 30g chopped celery (from 1 trimmed 12-inch rib)
- ☐ 275g (8 ounces) Simple Syrup (page 339)

Add the celery and syrup to a blender and blend until smooth, about 1 minute. Let sit for 30 minutes, then fine-strain the syrup. Store, covered, in the fridge for up to 1 week.

MALABAR HONEY SYRUP

by Jim Meehan

Clover honey pairs perfectly with Spirit Tea's Malabar tonic, a blend of piney Malabar black peppercorns, earthy Chinese ginger, Thai turmeric, lemongrass, and American licorice root. Spirit Tea's co-founders Jordan Scherer and Taylor Cowan fell in love with this blend—the company's first herbal—because its sourcing and processing aligned with their tea-sourcing ethics. Use in the Malabar Silver Corn Fizz (page 74)

YIELDS 12 OUNCES

- ☐ 4½ ounces Malabar Infusion (page 62)
- ☐ 550g (12 ounces) raw clover honey

Strain the infusion into a nonreactive container. While still hot, add the honey and stir to dissolve. Store the syrup, covered, in the fridge for up to 1 month.

PANDAN SYRUP

from Nico de Soto

"Ideally," Nico de Soto says, "you get your pandan fresh from a market in Indonesia," but for his bar Mace in New York City, Nico sources it frozen from purveyors in Chinatown and thaws it before preparing this syrup. If he wants to accentuate the pandan flavor, he supplements the recipe with 6 drops of Butterfly pandan extract to boost its nutty aromatics. Use in the L'Alligator C'est Vert (page 208).

YIELDS 13 OUNCES

- ☐ 10g pandan leaves (about 9)
- ☐ 550g (16¾ ounces) Simple Syrup (page 339)
- ☐ 2g (1 tablespoon) kosher salt

Add the pandan leaves, syrup, and salt to a blender and blend until smooth, about 1 minute. Fine-strain the syrup through a fine-mesh strainer, then strain a second time through a nut-milk or Super Bag sieve. Store, covered, in the fridge for up to 1 week.

OOLONG TEA SYRUP

from Jim Meehan

In addition to balancing tea's tannins with its sweetness, sugar helps preserve its aroma and flavor. A flash-brewed oolong tea would also work here if there isn't enough time to cold-brew the tea. Use in the Longball (page 260).

YIELDS 24 OUNCES

- ☐ 450g (2 cups) white cane sugar
- ☐ 16 ounces Mizudashi Cold-Brewed Oolong Tea (page 258)

Add the sugar and tea to a nonreactive container and stir until the sugar dissolves. Store covered in the fridge for up to 1 week.

Spirit Infusions

Cocktails are traditionally constructed using alcoholic or nonalcoholic mixers—or both—to buttress the character of the base spirit. Occasionally, bartenders use the base spirit as a canvas upon which to infuse flavor too. A subtly flavored spirit like vodka allows infused ingredients to be present without distraction, while more flavorful media such as mezcal require bolder ingredients to stand out. The variables include the flavor of the spirit (solvent) and ingredient (substrate), the spirit's alcoholic strength, the time allotted for extraction, the surface area of substrate, and the ambient temperature and pressure under which the infusion occurs. It's a little like brewing tea, with the strength of the spirit functioning similarly to the heat of the water.

BLUEBERRY-INFUSED GIN

by Jim Meehan

For this infusion, I used freeze-dried wild blueberries from Maine that Rodrick Markus sells at Rare Tea Cellar in Chicago. The freeze-drying process captures the berries' flavor at their peak ripeness, which is extracted and preserved for perpetuity in the gin infusion. Use in the Kind of Blueberry (page 176).

YIELDS 8 OUNCES (1 CUP)

- ☐ 8 ounces Tanqueray gin
- ☐ 6g (2 tablespoons) freeze-dried blueberries

Add the gin and blueberries to a nonreactive container, cover, and infuse at room temperature for 1 hour.

Fine-strain the mixture and eat, repurpose, or compost the blueberries. Store, covered, out of direct sunlight indefinitely.

CHILE-AND-GRAPEFRUIT-PEEL–INFUSED MEZCAL

by Danielle Tatarin

Danielle Tatarin's original recipe for this infusion was prepared with the small Tuxtla chile from southern Mexico, but she says "any chile would work; it will just add a different spice and smoke element." Use this infusion to make the Gota de Sandía (page 38).

YIELDS 23½ OUNCES

- ☐ 1 Ruby Red grapefruit
- ☐ 25 ounces Gota Gorda Espadín mezcal
- ☐ 4.5g chiles de árbol (3 medium-sized chiles)

With a swivel peeler, pare the peel from the grapefruit in one long spiral. In a nonreactive container, combine the mezcal, peel, and chiles, and let sit at room temperature for 1 hour. Remove the peel and compost it. Let chile infusion sit for another hour, then fine-strain the mezcal into a nonreactive container and compost the chiles. Store, covered, out of direct sunlight indefinitely.

COCONUT-BANANA-INFUSED BOURBON

by Kevin Diedrich

While in Japan, Kevin Diedrich tasted a Nikka whisky banana-chip infusion by his host Naoki Tomoyoshi, which inspired him to make a cocktail with a similar profile when he returned home. After a few attempts to infuse both ingredients, he found either "the banana was too much, or the coconut wasn't enough," he says. To accommodate each ingredient, he split the infusion into two parts, extracting each ingredient's desired flavor profile. When straining the bourbon and coconut, I split the batch into two and used multiple coffee filters suspended over multiple fine-mesh strainers to expedite the process. Use in the Banana Stand (page 178).

- ☐ 225g (1½ cups) freeze-dried banana chips
- ☐ 25 ounces Elijah Craig Barrel Proof bourbon
- ☐ 200g (8 ounces) raw unrefined coconut oil

Add the banana chips and bourbon to a nonreactive container, cover, and infuse at room temperature for 24 hours.

Strain the bourbon through a fine-mesh strainer into another nonreactive container. Compost (or eat!) the banana chips. Add the coconut oil, cover, and let infuse at room temperature for 12 hours.

Place the infusion into the freezer to solidify the coconut oil, at least a few hours or overnight. Strain the bourbon through a coffee filter suspended within a fine-mesh strainer. Compost the coconut solids. Store, covered, out of direct sunlight indefinitely.

EARL GREY TEA–INFUSED GIN

by Audrey Saunders

According to Audrey Saunders, the tannins from the Earl Grey provide a tactile sensation beyond the bergamot flavors. "I want those tannins to act as another layer in the structural foundation of the infusion—it holds up better in the shaker," she says. "Short infusions are often wimpy. Of course, you get some flavor, but they often lack the overall structure and depth I'm looking for." Use in the Earl Grey MarTEAni (page 264).

YIELDS 8 OUNCES

- ☐ 4g (1 tablespoon) Earl Grey tea leaves
- ☐ 8 ounces Tanqueray gin

Add the tea and gin to a nonreactive container, cover, and infuse at room temperature for 2 hours.

Fine-strain the gin into another nonreactive container. Store, covered, in the fridge for up to 2 weeks.

BUTTER-WASHED GIN

by Monica Berg

The butter Monica Berg uses in her infusion comes from a nineteenth-century farm in Norway, called Fannremsgården. "The butter from this region is cultured, so it has amazing tang and acidity that work wonders in a Martini-style drink, as the fat softens the alcohol ever so slightly, whilst the lactic acid provides acidity." Use in the Buttered Martini (page 104).

YIELDS 12 OUNCES

- ☐ 12 ounces Hepple gin
- ☐ 75g (5 tablespoons) cultured butter, cut into 1-inch squares

Add the gin and butter to a nonreactive container, cover, and infuse at room temperature for 48 hours.

Place the container in the fridge and infuse for an additional 24 hours.

Strain the gin through a coffee filter within a fine-mesh strainer. Store, covered, in the fridge for up to 1 month.

GRILLED-PINEAPPLE-INFUSED GENEVER

by Gregory Buda

During cocktail development for a drink called the Bandit's Roost (that features yellow Chartreuse, Amere Nouvelle, bay leaf, and green peppercorns), Gregory Buda found fresh pineapple was too bright and fruity. It didn't integrate well with the other flavors, so he grilled it "in order to 'darken' the flavor a bit and bring in smoky, caramelized sugar notes," he explained. "It worked really well, and it paired perfectly with the herbal, malty, slightly oaky character of the Bols barrel-aged genever." The barrel-aged bottling is difficult to source, so Jillian Vose uses the unaged formula in the Riot Act (page 140).

YIELDS 17 OUNCES

- ☐ 300g slices Grilled Pineapple (page 158)
- ☐ 17 ounces Bols Genever

Add the pineapple and genever to a nonreactive container, cover, and infuse at room temperature for 8 hours.

Fine-strain the mixture into a nonreactive container and compost the pineapple.

Store, covered, in the fridge for up to 1 week.

NORI-INFUSED APPLE BRANDY

by Don Lee

Don Lee observes bartenders frequently trying to balance big flavors—such as nori—with too many other bold flavors. For better results, Don suggests choosing "a big flavor" and supporting it with lighter flavors to let it shine; or mixing it with other equally flavorful ingredients, so they all share the spotlight, as do the apple, nori, and celery in his Celery and Nori (page 204). Note how short the infusion time is: the 100-proof apple brandy quickly and thoroughly extracts the big flavor of the nori, so only 90 seconds is needed.

YIELDS 8½ OUNCES

- ☐ 8½ ounces Laird's Straight Apple Brandy Bottled in Bond
- ☐ 1 (2g) nori sheet

Add the brandy and nori to a nonreactive container and infuse for 90 seconds. Fine-strain the brandy into a nonreactive container and compost the nori. Store, covered, at room temperature for up to 1 month.

KRAMBAMBULYA

from Israel Morales

This infusion—called Krupnik in Poland and Lithuania—is called Krambambulya in Belarus. Kachka co-owner Israel Morales says it's classified as a *nastoika* (infusion). "Honey is the base flavor supported by various spices/herbs/citrus zest depending on whose family is making it." Use in the Castle on a Cloud (page 130).

YIELDS 38 OUNCES

- ☐ 4.5g (one 3-inch quill) Ceylon cinnamon
- ☐ 2 whole cloves
- ☐ 1 whole (5g) nutmeg, cracked
- ☐ 0.5g allspice berries (about 5)
- ☐ 1 star anise pod
- ☐ 6g (2 teaspoons) black peppercorns
- ☐ 1 whole (4.5g) vanilla bean
- ☐ 15g fresh orange peel (from ½ orange)
- ☐ 10g fresh lemon peel (from ½ lemon)
- ☐ 15 ounces Everclear grain alcohol
- ☐ 6 ounces Taaka vodka
- ☐ 16 ounces filtered water
- ☐ 180g (4.25 ounces) raw honey

Preheat the oven to 350°F. Spread the cinnamon, cloves, nutmeg, allspice, star anise pod, and peppercorns on a baking sheet and toast in the oven until fragrant and browned, about 5 minutes. Let cool.

Place the toasted spices, the vanilla bean, citrus peels, grain alcohol, and vodka in a nonreactive container. Cover and infuse at room temp for 2 days.

Fine-strain the infusion and compost the solids.

Bring the water to a boil in a medium saucepan. Remove from the heat and stir in the honey until dissolved. Let cool.

Add the honey syrup to the infusion. Store, covered, out of direct sunlight indefinitely.

Note: Rack off the sediment after a few days if you prefer a precipitate-free infusion.

P.C.H. ORANGE BITTERS

from Kevin Diedrich

Kevin Diedrich blends three commercial bottlings for the orange bitters blend used at Pacific Cocktail Haven in San Francisco, as he's found many ingredients prepared in-house are not always better than ones made by "the pros," he says. "We found that blending allows for taking the best characteristics from specific spirits/bitters and gearing them toward a specific profile or introducing another flavor into the mix." Use in the Banana Stand (page 178).

YIELDS 2¼ OUNCES

- ☐ ¾ ounce Fee Brothers West Indian Orange Bitters
- ☐ ¾ ounce Regan's Orange Bitters No. 6
- ☐ ¾ ounce Angostura Orange Bitters

Funnel the bitters into a bitters decanter. Cover the decanter with a dasher top. Store, covered, when not in service indefinitely.

PINK PEPPERCORN TINCTURE

from Jessica Gonzalez and Lynnette Marrero

Pink peppercorns are dried fruits from the Peruvian peppertree, which is a member of the cashew family. The peppercorns are faintly citrusy with rose notes and are much softer than dried black peppercorns. Jessica Gonzalez says they add "a dryness and complexity, similar to how skin contact affects white wines." Use in the Llama del Rey (page 132).

YIELDS 2 OUNCES

- ☐ 2 ounces Devil's Springs 151 Proof vodka
- ☐ 1g (1 teaspoon) pink peppercorns

Add the pink peppercorns and vodka to a nonreactive container, cover, and infuse at room temperature for 2 hours.

Fine-strain the tincture into a nonreactive container and compost the peppercorns. Funnel the tincture into a bitters decanter, then cover the decanter with a dasher top. Store, covered, when not in service indefinitely.

SOBACHA-INFUSED APPLE BRANDY

by Masahiro Urushido

Masahiro Urushido chose an unaged apple brandy for this infusion because he wanted the full flavor of aromatic grain to shine through in the drink and not be distracted by wood flavors from an aged bottling. "I was really trying to capture the unique toastiness of Dattan soba: a different type of buckwheat than the variety used for soba noodles." Use in the Thunderbird (page 138).

YIELDS 8 OUNCES

- ☐ 8 ounces Neversink apple brandy
- ☐ 7.5g (1 tablespoon) Kettl Nagano sobacha

Add the apple brandy and sobacha to a nonreactive container, cover, and infuse at room temperature for 45 minutes.

Fine-strain the brandy into a nonreactive container and compost the sobacha. Store, covered, at room temperature for up to 1 month.

Sugar-Free Solutions

These preparations are the outliers that use previously illustrated techniques featuring idiosyncratic preparations. While ingredients such as the licorice root water and radicchio "juice" are rare sightings on a cocktail menu, they each contribute complexity and depth to a recipe when in the hands of a skilled mixologist, and many of them—like the tea and tisane recipes ahead—are delicious unmixed. And there's Greg Best's lime ice cubes: the only solid-state solution in the book.

BORICHA COLD BREW

from A-K Hada

Boricha, "barley tea" in Korean, is a popular toasted barley tisane prepared and served either hot or cold. Whole roasted kernels require a longer infusion than finely-ground grain in bags, which are better suited for cold infusion owing to the larger surface area for water extraction. Use in the Pomme and Circumstance (page 36) or drink it over ice.

YIELDS 14 OUNCES

- ☐ 15 ounces filtered water, at room temperature
- ☐ 15g (scant ¼ cup) boricha

Add the boricha and filtered water to a nonreactive container, cover, and infuse in the fridge for 2 hours.

Fine-strain the infusion into a nonreactive container and compost the barley. Store, covered, in the fridge for up to 1 day.

BREWED ENGLISH BREAKFAST TEA

from Nick Bennett

Rare Tea Co. founder Henrietta Lovell traces the term *English Breakfast* back to New York City in 1901, when it was used to describe how the English served their tea at breakfast. The tea—traditionally served with milk and sugar or a lemon—was a blend of black teas from Assam, Ceylon, and Kenya, which was novel for the time of its invention, as teas were previously sourced and sold from a single origin. Use in the 7 & 7 (page 292) or drink it unmixed.

YIELDS 5 OUNCES

- ☐ 2.5g (1 teaspoon) English Breakfast tea
- ☐ 5 ounces filtered water, heated to 195°F

Add the tea leaves to a prewarmed brewing apparatus. Add the hot water to the brewing apparatus, cover, and steep the tea for 2 minutes. Fine-strain the liquid into a prewarmed teacup and compost the leaves.

BREWED HŌJICHA

from Julia Momosé

The dark color and rich, savory character of hōjicha misleads many to characterize it as a black tea, but it is technically a roasted green tea. It is produced by drum-roasting the stems and late-harvest leaves to bring out its toasted, nutty flavors. *Kuki* means "stalks," and such blends (with fewer leaves) have less caffeine, making this type of tea ideal to sip throughout the day and serve with meals. Use in the Comfort's Toddy (page 266). The first infusion is ideal for cocktails because it is the most flavorful, but additional infusions are enjoyable as well.

YIELDS 5¼ OUNCES

- ☐ 5g (1½ tablespoons) Hoshinomura kuki-hōjicha
- ☐ 5½ ounces filtered water, heated to 195°F

Add the tea leaves to a prewarmed brewing apparatus. Add the hot water, cover, and steep the tea for 2 minutes. Fine-strain the liquid into a prewarmed teacup. Retain the leaves for further infusions and compost them when finished.

BREWED LAO CANG XIAO
SHU TUO PU-ERH

from Jim Meehan

A quality pu-erh will be delicious over multiple infusions, each time coaxing out different flavors from the tea. For consistency from toddy to toddy, use only the first infusion after "washing" the leaves. After pouring out the tea to prepare the toddy, the bartender may present the leaves to the guest for further infusions. Use in the Q.P. Warmer (page 270).

YIELDS 6 OUNCES

- ☐ 6 ounces filtered water, at 212°F (for each infusion)
- ☐ 1 mini tuóchá (6g) Lao Cang tuocha pu-erh

In a brewing apparatus, combine the boiling water and tuóchá to "wash" the leaves and hydrate the cake. After 5 seconds, fine-strain the infusion into the teacups to warm them before discarding the liquid. Gently break apart the tuóchá with a pick or your (clean) hands. Measure another portion of hot water over the leaves, cover, and let sit for 3 minutes. Fine-strain the liquid into a prewarmed teacup. Retain the leaves for further infusions and compost them when finished.

CASCARA INFUSION

from Tyler Kleinow

Cascara, meaning "husk" in Spanish, refers to the pulpy "cherry" surrounding the coffee seed. This husk is typically discarded or repurposed as compost by processors, but if it's cultivated carefully, it can be dried and brewed like a tea. Tyler Kleinow's London Bridge (page 232) became so popular at Marvel Bar that he formed a company dedicated to importing quality cascara to secure a steady supply for the Twin Cities.

YIELDS 14 OUNCES

- ☐ 16 ounces filtered water, at room temperature
- ☐ 20g (4½ tablespoons) cascara

Add the filtered water to a medium saucepan. Over high heat, bring the water to a boil, and then turn off the heat. Add the cascara to the saucepan and steep for 30 minutes. Fine-strain the infusion into a nonreactive container and compost the cascara. Store, covered, in the fridge for up to 3 days.

COQUITO "TEA" INFUSION

from Pablo Moix

During his time in the Caribbean, Pablo Moix was struck by the frequency which baking spice blends appeared in spirits like Bajan Falernum and Jamaican Pimento Dram, in ferments such as mavi (known as mauby on other islands), and in infusions such as St. Lucian sorrel and this spice "tea" from Puerto Rico. "The spices turn up in most traditional drinks—with or without alcohol—and the majority of desserts on the island, which pair well with preparations like Coquito." Use this to make his Coquito (page 108).

YIELDS 2½ OUNCES

- ☐ 8 ounces filtered water, at room temperature
- ☐ 31.5g (seven 3-inch quills) Ceylon cinnamon
- ☐ 2g whole cloves (about 30)

Add the filtered water to a medium saucepan. Over high heat, bring the water to a boil, then add the cinnamon and cloves and reduce the heat to medium-low. Simmer for 20 minutes. Fine-strain the infusion (while still hot) into a nonreactive container and let cool. Compost the solids. Store, covered, in the fridge for up to 3 days.

FLASH-BREWED JASMINE TEA

from Ravi Kroesen

Ravi Kroesen recommends the flash-brew method for all iced-tea applications because "you don't have to plan 6 to 10 hours ahead, as you do with cold infusions." Kroesen sources jasmine tea in both "delicate pearls with characteristic silver buds, and consistent unbroken loose leaf with some buds." The key is to source with quality in mind. "There should be an aromatic balance between the tea and clean jasmine notes." Use in the Dragon Pearl Punch (page 262) or drink it over ice.

YIELDS 25½ OUNCES

- ☐ 16g (2 heaping tablespoons) jasmine pearls
- ☐ 10 ounces filtered water, brought to 185°F
- ☐ 138g (1 cup) ice cubes

Measure the jasmine pearls into a pre-warmed brewing apparatus. Measure the hot water into the brewing apparatus, cover, and steep the tea for 4 minutes. Fine-strain the infusion into a nonreactive container. Add the ice cubes and stir the mixture until the ice dissolves. Store, covered, in the fridge for up to 3 days.

HIBISCUS INFUSION

from Danielle Tatarin

Hibiscus grows everywhere in Mexico and is sold dried in most markets for preparing agua frescas. Danielle Tatarin infuses hibiscus into her mezcal, candies it for garnishes, steeps it into infusions for color and acidity, and blends it with salt to rim glasses. "Once the hibiscus is hydrated and the infusion is strained, I add the flowers to salads or cook them with butter and garlic in my quesadillas." Use in the Gota de Sandía (page 38) or drink it over ice.

YIELDS 11 OUNCES

- ☐ 60g dried hibiscus flowers
- ☐ 14 ounces filtered water, at room temperature

Add the hibiscus and filtered water to a nonreactive container. Cover and infuse for 1 hour at room temperature. Fine-strain the infusion into a nonreactive container and reserve the flowers for other uses or compost them. Store, covered, in the fridge for up to 1 day.

LEMON-INFUSED OLIVE OIL

from Kristina Magro

For Kristina Magro, the lemon-infused olive oil integrates well with her Salad Bar (page 210) by "adding an aromatic citrus element that floats on the surface of the drink like bitters on a Pisco Sour. The olive oil adds weight and fat and holds the essence of the lemon perfectly in the crown of the cocktail."

YIELDS 3 OUNCES

- ☐ 75g (3 ounces) extra-virgin olive oil
- ☐ 40g fresh lemon peel (from 2 lemons)

Add the olive oil and lemon peels to a nonreactive container. Infuse for 8 hours at room temperature.

Remove the peels with tongs and compost them. Funnel the olive oil into a dropper bottle. Store, covered, for up to 1 month at room temperature.

LICORICE-ROOT WATER

from Tyler Kleinow

At Marvel Bar, where Tyler Kleinow created and served this recipe, the bartenders "used a lot of water-based tisanes and infusions, as roughly 75 percent of us—including myself—came from the specialty coffee world." He recalls, "We would make spirit-free versions quite frequently, so the infusion was a better option than a spirit-based tincture." Use in the London Bridge (page 232).

YIELDS 3½ OUNCES

- ☐ 4 ounces filtered water
- ☐ 10g (2 tablespoons) chopped/sifted organic licorice root

Add the filtered water to a small saucepan. Over high heat, bring the water to a boil. Turn off the heat. Add the licorice and steep for 30 minutes. Fine-strain the infusion into a nonreactive container and compost the licorice root. Store, covered, in the fridge for up to 1 week.

RADICCHIO "JUICE"
from Kristina Magro

Radicchio, a chicory common in Italian cuisine, needs to be washed and soaked in water to soften its naturally bitter properties. "The more it soaks, the less bitter it becomes," says Magro, who notes, "unrinsed radicchio has a muddy texture and taste." This preparation is best used fresh, before it starts to oxidize and lose its vibrancy (up to 6 hours). Use this in the Salad Bar (page 210).

YIELDS 9 OUNCES

- ☐ 1 small head (525g) radicchio
- ☐ 64 ounces filtered water, chilled

Peel off and compost any damaged leaves and rinse the radicchio under tap water. In a large bowl, submerge the radicchio in cold filtered water and let soak for 30 minutes. Discard the water and place the head on a cutting board. Core the radicchio and spin the leaves in a salad spinner. Run the leaves through an extractor. Store the extracted "juice," covered, in the fridge for up to 6 hours.

LIME ICE CUBES
from Greg Best

Greg Best uses ice melt as a time-release mechanism to gradually dispense citrus into the Southern Cola (page 296). The recipe was so well-received at Restaurant Eugene in Atlanta, that he re-introduced it for the opening menu of Holeman and Finch Public House in 2008. At this time, he began pairing different varieties of citrus ice with his ever-expanding amaro selection.

YIELDS 7 CUBES

- ☐ 6 ounces lime juice
- ☐ 2 ounces filtered water

Add the lime juice and filtered water to a mixing glass. Pour the mixture into 7 1¼-inch ice cube molds of a silicone ice tray. Place the tray in the freezer. Once frozen solid, store covered in a freezer bag for up to 1 month.

Afterword

Over the five-year journey of writing this book, my perspective on each ingredient—and how mixology itself fits into the ecosystem of our foodways—has evolved. Gleaning insights from so many brilliant experts in their respective fields gave me a taste for and a newfound interest in beverage matters beyond the glass.

If you've landed there with me, I imagine you'll likely enjoy deeper, philosophical books about food and cooking like *The Omnivore's Dilemma*, *The Third Plate*, *The Secret Life of Groceries*, *The Jemima Code*, *Taste Makers*, *Eating to Extinction*, and *The Way We Eat Now*. These books led me to works by other food writers like Sydney Mintz, Rachel Carson, Euell Gibbons, Wendell Berry, Robin Wall Kimmerer, and others whose writing examines how our food and identity are intertwined, warts and all.

After ingesting as much wisdom as I could from my research and attempting to synthesize and highlight what was most pertinent for bartenders—because that's my culinary area of expertise—I come back to the cliché that we are what we eat.

In the scope of this work, though, I'd argue that the idiom misses the mark. I believe what we eat and drink is actually a reflection of both who we are and how we want others to perceive us. In other words, I'd suggest that what we eat and drink may be seen as a relatable reflection of our personal favorites, our cultural traditions, and our regional specialties, but they can also be used to refract—accurately or deceptively—what we want others to believe about ourselves and our customs, both individually and collectively. Drinks are an extension of food, and in this case they serve more like trick mirrors—borrowing writer Jia Tolentino's conceit—than as representative reflections of our true selves.

I researched, tested, and wrote this book during the COVID-19 pandemic, as a racial reckoning in the United States—precipitated by the murder of George Floyd—unfolded. This happened simultaneously with call-outs of systemic inequities in the hospitality and food-media worlds. These events helped solidify my belief that when we survey what we eat and drink as writers today, we need to grapple with our subjects' connection to systems of capitalism, white supremacy, and patriarchy. As a white, American, cisgender male from an upper-middle-class Midwestern upbringing, I have unjustly benefited from these pernicious systems and welcome accountability and owe reparations as a result of it.

As food and drink makers learn more about where our ingredients come from, the demands upon the land and workers who farm and transport them to us, and the origin stories of the cuisines we cook with—which are shaped largely by women of color and have disproportionately profited white men in this country— we, men in particular, need to reckon with and reconcile these inequities. As a society, we must all individually and collectively decide who and what we're choosing to venerate, as well as why—and consider what implications this has now and for future generations.

My hope is that recipes like the ones featured in this book will be rightfully recognized as culinary arts alongside gastronomical indulgences like pastry and meat, which should be served and enjoyed in moderation. No longer saddled with the harmful cultural baggage intemperate booze consumption travels with, I believe this book, including its recipes, ingredients, ideas, and the value systems from which they originated—a figurative bartender's pantry, represents an example of an optimistic universal conception for what a twenty-first-century bar program can become. I hope it shakes and stirs its readers in the process.

Acknowledgments

From Jim

FAMILY

I'd like to thank my wife, Valerie (who has the final approval on all recipes); my daughter, Olivia (who may be the next published author in our household); and my son, Arlo (who already has an affinity for mixing drinks). For the last five years they've afforded me time away from our orbit to daydream as I researched, recipe-tested, and wrote this book. They cleared out of the house for the photo shoots without complaint, and even left a spot for me on the couch to return to movie nights when I finished. I'd also like to thank my mom and dad, who cooked from scratch for us whenever they could and inspired a deep appreciation for good food and company. Much love to our extended Meehan, Esposito, Simi, Quandt, Clark, Wong, and Columbo relatives as well.

BART SASSO

Shout out to my old pal Greg Best, who reintroduced me to his partner Bart Sasso via an event post he designed for a *Meehan's Bartender Manual* book party at the Ticonderoga Club in 2017. When I asked him if I could have it—an intricate, tattoo-like decoration on all the blank space on the book cover—he told me he designed it with Adobe. At the event, he surprised me with a copy of my book with the exact same art hand-drawn on the cover with a Sharpie. At that moment, I promised myself to find a project for us to work on together.

Since then, we've spent countless hours on hundreds of calls, making this book. In the time we've known each other, we've gone through a (I hope) once-in-a-lifetime pandemic; he's moved from Atlanta to Boston, and had three children with his wife, Sarah. In addition to being the most talented, creative, hardworking designer I've ever worked with, Bart is kind, generous, and rock-solidly dependable. We began this project as partners and will conclude it as lifelong friends.

AJ MEEKER

After seeing the work he did on my friend Joshua McFadden's books and a few other clients, I knew AJ would be the perfect photographer for this project. I wanted the book's photos to have a timeless, organic look and feel, so I asked him if he'd ever consider shooting a book on film, not knowing what he'd think. As an art school grad who came up as a film photographer, he was thrilled and chose a 1950s medium-format Hasselblad camera to bring my aspirations to life.

We shot the book masked together in my house, with the windows open before vaccinations were available and anyone had much understanding of how Covid spreads. Over a dozen shoots across a calendar year to capture produce in season, we shot every drink twice—once on film and once with a digital camera in case the film shot didn't work. I made the drinks in my kitchen and handed them off to AJ to place in locations I helped scout. Every drink was shot in a different location in my house, primarily with natural light, in a unique vessel. Despite the difficulty level of the job, AJ was a joy to work with and the photos reflect it.

EMMA JANZEN

After four years working on this project with Bart and AJ, with all the recipes sourced and tested, photographed and illustrated, I was absolutely petrified at the prospect of synthesizing everything I'd read, interviews I'd conducted, insights I'd gotten from the recipes, and ideas that had been swirling around in my head into the chapters of a cohesive narrative. With two books under my belt, I knew I needed help, but I wasn't sure who could salvage my progress and what I really needed.

Around that time, I just so happened to have been in touch with author Emma Janzen, a writer and photographer I'd met in Chicago, who asked me to blurb her two most recent books with Julia Momosé and Toby Maloney. Suddenly, the light went on. Toby and Julia are among the best bartenders in the world, but they weren't previously published and their books were ingeniously written in their voices. The common denominator between both their books was Emma, and right then, I knew she could help me if I could convince her of the value of the project.

The narrative you see here came together after dozens of long calls between Oregon and Michigan, thanks to her expert hands as a peerless journalist. I was so blocked when we started; our first few months consisted of long rambling calls during which she'd take notes and ask questions. A year later I was writing again, and every aspect of what you read here is more compelling than the tangle of ideas it emerged from, because it crossed Emma's desk before we turned it in.

INKWELL

Bart and I spent over a year working on our proposal for Kim Witherspoon & Jessica Mileo, who wouldn't shop it for us until they were satisfied with it. Their instincts about all aspects of this project have been spot on, and I am so grateful for their support.

TEN SPEED

Thanks to the best culinary imprint on the planet. To Aaron Wehner, for championing this project and suggesting its title; Kelly Snowden, for acquiring it and navigating us through the toughest part of the pandemic; Betsy Stromberg, for taking on this book after perfecting my last one; Jane Chinn, for helping us create the perfect package; and last and most important, to Molly Birnbaum, who took this book on as her first project as editor-in-chief of the imprint and brought us home.

CONTRIBUTORS

I collected many of these recipes during the most harrowing moments of the pandemic. Looking back on the emails, texts, and calls checking in with folks, with multiple follow-up questions and other matters, brought me back to a frightful time. The quotes you see in each recipe annotation and subject primer are only the tip of a mountain of transcripts I compiled from many colleagues new and old, who were exceedingly generous with their time, insights, and resources.

Most of my calls, texts, emails, and interviews ended up as recipes or were quoted in the chapter text, but a few did not, yet still influenced this book greatly. Special thanks to Dave Arnold, Mandy Aftel, Christine Anderson, Chris Hannah, Wayne Curtis, Jessica Koslow, Ben Jones, Micah Melton, Jean Nihoul, Quinn Fucile, St. John Frizzell, Tracy Ging, Garret Richard, Darrell Corti, Davide Segat, Dale DeGroff, and Ivano Tonutti for sharing their expertise.

ADVANCED READERS

Special thanks to H. James Lucas for your meticulous recipe edits and illustration feedback on a tight timeline and to Ravi Kroesen, Michael Yung, Arielle Johnson, Darcy O'Neil, Glenn Roberts, Maggie Campbell, and Lior Sercarz for graciously fact-checking each chapter prologue of your respective expertise. I remain permanently indebted to Harold McGee for fact-checking and providing valuable feedback on the whole manuscript.

PANTRY PURVEYORS

Thanks to Kristen Perrakis of Williams Sonoma; Ally Barajas, Jeanette Fischer, and Matthew Davis of Breville; Tess Denton Rex of M. Tucker; Rodrick Markus of Rare Tea Cellar; Greg Boehm and Shawn Kelley of Cocktail Kingdom; Yoko Kumano and Kayoko Akabori of Umami Mart; and Tung Chiang of Heath Ceramics. It takes a village to fill a pantry, and mine is exceedingly well stocked, thanks in part to you all.

From Bart

In October of 2012, my wife, Sarah, and I took a trip to New York City to visit her newly relocated brother and sister-in-law, and we were able to secure entry to PDT with the help of friend and colleague Greg Best. It was one of those rare experiences that exceed all expectation. After being shown to a perfect table in the city's (world's?) hottest cocktail bar, and enjoying our first round, Jim Meehan himself delivered the second round, warmly thanked us for coming in, and sent a bevy of Crif Dogs snacks to the table. My wife's family sat there bewildered as to how I was so well connected in their new home . . . and I vibrated with the excitement of possibility for months after. At Christmas, I received a leather-bound edition of *The PDT Cocktail Book* as a gift, with a personalized inscription from Jim, arranged by my wife and Greg. It now seems completely surreal to be writing my own acknowledgments for a book Jim and I created together.

First and foremost, thank you, Jim, for this incredible opportunity. Never in my wildest dreams could I have imagined this is where our paths would have led while shaking your hand at PDT almost twelve years ago. You warned me very early on that making a book together would not be an easy endeavor, and while I have to say that was not an adequate enough disclaimer, I'm so incredibly proud of what we created. I sincerely hope this book inspires all who pick it up to get a little, or a lot, outside of their comfort zone. The juice is worth the squeeze.

CONTRIBUTORS

Thank you to all those who contributed to this book and were named alongside their methods and recipes. I learned so much from your instruction—not only technique but also passion and generosity. Much of this education has changed the way I think about and make things in my own home for my family and our guests.

TEAM

This book wouldn't have been possible without a team of truly talented and patient people: AJ Meeker, an amazing photographer who delivered images of often complex compositions that capture the heart and soul of their contributors while maintaining the spirit of their within-reach recipes. Emma Janzen, who jumped into Jim's narrative, lockstep, and delivered a highly approachable handbook with deceptively deep substance. Kim Witherspoon, Betsy Stromberg, Molly Birnbaum, and the entire Ten Speed Press team, who allowed us the space and time to navigate too many ideas and an extremely unpredictable few years— thank you for that and your guidance throughout the process.

FRIENDS AND FAMILY

To my partners at Ticonderoga Club in Atlanta: Regan Smith, Greg Best, David Bies, and Paul Calvert. I am forever grateful for your friendship, guidance, and support. Especially to Regan and Greg, who brought me into this world of food, beverage, and hospitality so many years ago and have created so many opportunities for me.

To my parents and sister, Jan, Don, and Rebecca Sasso. We had a Tervis tumbler in our house growing up, with a patch in it that said "Try It, You'll Like It." I still think about that to this day—it feels apropos to mention with regard to the effort, and rewards, this book offers. And when things get tough, we've always said to each other, "Just keep going. One foot in front of the other"—a mantra I'm grateful for.

Finally, and most important, to my wife, Sarah, and my three kids, Remy, Margot, and Estelle, for all of their love, support, and patience with me over the course of making this book. The first conversation I ever had with Jim about this book took place on the same day we brought Remy, our eldest, home from the hospital. A lot of life happened during the making of this book, and I'll forever, fondly, remember these years.

From Emma

Jim, thank you so much for the invitation to be part of this remarkable project. Bearing witness to the way you researched, synthesized, and carefully considered every detail of this text was nothing short of awesome. I'm thankful to call you a colleague and a friend.

Bart, your delightful illustrations served as a lighthouse for the tone and pace of this text whenever I found myself trying to figure out which way to turn. Molly, your sharp edits likewise improved this text at every juncture; it's been an honor working with you. And to the rest of the brilliant behind-the-scenes team at Ten Speed, you are the gold standard! I'm so proud to be a tiny cog in this complex bookmaking machine alongside you all. Thank you, thank you!

To my parents, you've long helped me cultivate a deep curiosity and respect for the provenance of the things I eat and drink. Thank you for inspiring that worldview and for helping me be a better steward of the earth in the process. To the rest of my family, thanks for the love and support, and for the time away as I disappeared into this work. And Zach, the way you gracefully allow me the space to chase big projects, help me navigate through them, then join me in celebrating the victories both large and small that follow is a gift I don't take for granted.

Finally, to all the bartenders, chefs, and savvy journalists whose expertise and insights we have showcased in these pages, we stand on your shoulders; and I hope by doing so we bring a new audience to your doorsteps. The work you do makes the world a richer and more delicious place, and that is no small thing.

Bibliography

GENERAL

Arnold, Dave. *Liquid Intelligence*. New York: W.W. Norton, 2014.

Arthur, Stanley Clisby. *Famous New Orleans Drinks And How To Mix 'Em.* New Orleans: American Printing, 1937.

Beebe, Lucius. *The Stork Club Bar Book*. New York: Rinehart, 1946.

Day, Alex, Nick Fauchald, David Kaplan, and Devon Tarby. *Cocktail Codex.* Berkeley, CA: Ten Speed, 2018.

Hoffman, Peter. *What's Good?* New York: Abrams, 2021.

Lorr, Benjamin. *The Secret Life of Groceries*. New York: Avery, 2020.

McGee, Harold. *Keys to Good Cooking*. New York: Penguin, 2010.

McGee, Harold. *On Food and Cooking*. New York: Scribner, 2004.

Mogannam, Sam, and Dabney Gough. *Bi-Rite Market's Eat Good Food.* Berkeley, CA: Ten Speed, 2011.

Mlynarczyk, Gabriella. *Clean + Dirty Drinking*. San Francisco: Chronicle, 2018.

Nestle, Marion. *What to Eat*. New York: North Point, 2007.

Owens, Sarah. *Heirloom*. Boulder, CO: Roost, 2019.

Robitschek, Leo. *The NoMad Cocktail Book*. Berkeley, CA: Ten Speed, 2019.

Saladino, Dan. *Eating to Extinction*. New York: Farrar, Straus & Giroux, 2022.

Sharma, Nik. *The Flavor Equation*. San Francisco: Chronicle, 2020.

Thunberg, Greta. *The Climate Book*. New York: Penguin Press, 2023.

Waters, Alice. *We Are What We Eat*. New York: Penguin, 2021.

Wilson, Bee. *The Way We Eat Now*. New York: Basic, 2019.

Wondrich, David, and Noah Rothbaum, eds. *The Oxford Companion to Spirits & Cocktails*. Oxford, UK: Oxford University Press, 2022.

SUGARS

Campos, Adriane. "The Ultimate Guide to Unrefined and Raw Sugars." *What Sugar,* 2020. whatsugar.com/post/unrefined-vs-raw-vs-refined-cane-sugar

Goldstein, Darra, ed. *The Oxford Companion to Sugar and Sweets*. Oxford, UK: Oxford University Press, 2015.

Simmons, Marie. *Taste of Honey*. Kansas City, MO: Andrews McMeel, 2013.

SPICES

Bitterman, Mark. *Salted: A Manifesto on the World's Most Essential Mineral, with Recipes.* Berkeley, CA: Ten Speed, 2010.

Duguid, Naomi. *The Miracle of Salt.* New York: Artisan, 2022.

Ford, Eleanor. *The Nutmeg Trail.* New York: Apollo, 2022.

Hemberger, Allen, Nick Kokonas, and Grant Achatz. *The Aviary Holiday Cocktails Book.* Chicago: Alinea Group, 2019.

Hemphill, Ian. *Spice Notes and Recipes.* Sydney, Australia: Macmillan, 2006.

Lawson, Jane. *The Spice Bible.* New York: Abrams, 2008.

Nosrat, Samin. *Salt, Fat, Acid, Heat.* Simon & Schuster, 2017.

Sercarz, Lior Lev. *The Spice Companion.* New York: Clarkson Potter, 2016.

Sharma, Nik. *Season.* San Francisco: Chronicle, 2018.

DAIRY

Cree, Dana. *Hello, My Name Is Ice Cream.* New York: Clarkson Potter, 2017.

Mendelson, Anne. *Milk: The Surprising Story of Milk Through the Ages.* New York: Knopf, 2008.

Mendelson, Anne. *Spoiled.* New York: Columbia University Press, 2023.

Thakrar, Shamil, Kavi Thakrar, and Naved Nasir. *Dishoom.* London: Bloomsbury, 2019.

GRAINS & NUTS

Berens, Abra. *Grist.* San Francisco: Chronicle, 2021.

Hanson, Thor. *The Triumph of Seeds.* New York: Basic, 2015.

Jullapat, Roxana. *Mother Grains.* New York: W.W. Norton, 2021.

Loomis, Susan Herrmann. *Nuts in the Kitchen.* New York: HarperCollins, 2010.

McFadden, Joshua. *Grains for Every Season.* New York: Artisan, 2021.

McGarry, Jack, Sean Muldoon, and Jillian Vose. *The Dead Rabbit Mixology & Mayhem.* New York: Harvest, 2018.

Olvera, Enrique, and Daniela Soto-Innes. *Tu Casa Mi Casa.* New York: Phaidon, 2019.

FRUITS

Ackert, Robert. *Fruits in Cooking.* New York: Macmillan, 1973.

Ballister, Barry. *The Fruit & Vegetable Stand.* Woodstock, NY: Overlook, 2001.

Berens, Abra. *Pulp.* San Francisco: Chronicle, 2023.

Davidson, Alan. *Fruit.* London: Mitchell Beazley, 1991.

Herbst, Sharon, and Ron Tyler. *The New Food Lover's Companion,* 5th ed. Hauppauge, NY: Barron's Educational Series, 2013.

Vestinos, Peter. "Keep Mint Fresh on the Bar Top." *USBG,* 2017. usbg.org/connect/browse/blogs/blogviewer?BlogKey=c9aa0985-17df-450c-b0dc-a1b9a676a8c4/

Waters, Alice. *Chez Panisse Fruit.* New York: HarperCollins, 2002.

VEGETABLES, FLOWERS & HERBS

Ahmed, Selena, Ashley Duval, and Rachel Meyer. *Botany at the Bar: The Art and Science of Making Bitters.* White Lion Publishing: Roost, 2019.

Diacono, Mark. *Herb: A Cook's Companion.* London: Quadrille, 2021.

Gunders, Dana. *The Waste-Free Kitchen Handbook.* San Francisco: Chronicle, 2015.

Jones, Farmer Lee. *The Chef's Garden.* New York: Avery, 2021.

Madison, Deborah. *Vegetable Literacy.* Berkeley, CA: Ten Speed, 2013.

Newman, Mary, and Constance L. Kirker. *Edible Flowers.* London: Reaktion, 2016.

Stewart, Amy. *The Drunken Botanist.* Chapel Hill, NC: Algonquin, 2013.

Zaslavsky, Alice. *In Praise of Veg.* Sydney, Australia: Murdoch, 2020.

COFFEE

Coffee Collective. *The Fundamentals of Excellent Coffee.* Copenhagen: Self-Published, 2021.

Hoffman, James. *The World Atlas of Coffee.* Buffalo, NY: Firefly, 2015.

Moldvaer, Anette. *The Coffee Book.* New York: DK Books, 2021.

Pauwels, Katrien. *Specialty Coffee.* Tielt, Belgium: Lannoo, 2019.

Rodriguez, Ashley. "The Invisible Labor of Coffee." *Boss Barista* (website), 2022. bossbarista.substack.com/p/the-invisible-labor-of-co

Smith, K. Annabelle. "The History of the Chicory Coffee Mix That New Orleans Made Its Own." *Smithsonian Magazine,* 2014. smithsonianmag.com/arts-culture/chicory-coffee-mix-new-orleans-made-own-comes-180949950

Wendelboe, Tim. *Coffee with Tim Wendelboe.* Oslo, Norway: Schibsted Forlag, 2010.

TEA

Akbar, Ahmed Ali. "What America Gets Wrong About Tea." *Thrillist,* January 23, 2023. thrillist.com/drink/nation/tea-culture-in-america

Beckwith, Sebastian, and Caroline Paul. *A Little Tea Book.* New York: Bloomsbury, 2018.

Earls, Averill. "A Spot of Tea: Empire, Commodities, and the Opportunities in Britain's Tea Trade." *Dig* (A History Podcast), January 23, 2023. digpodcast.org/2022/11/06/tea-empire

Gebely, Tony. *Tea: A User's Guide.* Weaverville, NC: Eggs and Toast Media, 2016.

Keating, Brian, and Kim Long. *How to Make Tea.* New York: Abrams Image, 2015.

Lovell, Henrietta. *Infused.* London: Faber & Faber, 2019.

Mangan, Zach. *Stories of Japanese Tea*. New York: Princeton Architectural Press, 2022.

Rappaport, Erika. *A Thirst for Empire*. Princeton, NJ: Princeton University Press, 2017.

Trivedi-Grenier, Leena. "There's a Lot More to Masala Chai Than Spiced Milk Tea." *Epicurious,* April 25, 2021. epicurious.com/expert-advice/masala-chai-history-recipe-article

SODA & MINERAL WATER

Arnold, Dave. "Setting Up a Home On-Tap Carbonation System." *YouTube,* 2020. youtube.com/watch?v=q2ZsYUPkXQ8

Hendon, Christopher, and Maxwell Colonna-Dashwood. *Water for Coffee*. Bath, UK: Self-published, 2015.

English, Camper. *Doctors and Distillers*. New York: Penguin, 2022.

English, Camper. *Tonic Water AKA G&T WTF*. San Francisco: Alcademics, 2016.

Frick, Karen. "Root Beer." *Difford's Guide for Discerning Drinkers*. diffordsguide.com/beer-wine-spirits/category/270/root-beer

O'Neil, Darcy. *Fix the Pumps*. Ontario, Canada: Art of Drink, 2010.

Levin, Judith. *Soda and Fizzy Drinks*. London: Reaktion, 2021.

Miller, Ian. *Water*. London: Reaktion, 2015.

Morgenthaler, Jeffrey. "How to Build Your Own Carbonation Rig," 2014. jeffreymorgenthaler.com/how-to-build-your-own-carbonation-rig/

Straub, Jacques. *Drinks*. Chicago: Hotel Monthly Press, 1914.

FERMENTS

Burns, Cortney, and Nicolaus Balla. *Bar Tartine*. New York: Chronicle, 2014.

Caldwell, Gianaclis. *Homemade Yogurt & Kefir*. North Adams, MA: Storey, 2020.

Chan, Miin. "Lost in the Brine." *Eater,* January 25, 2023. eater.com/2021/3/1/22214044/fermented-foods-industry-whiteness-kimchi-miso-kombucha

Diacono, Mark. *Ferment From Scratch*. London: Quadrille, 2022.

Flynn, Sharon. *Wild Drinks*. Melbourne, Australia: Hardie Grant, 2023.

Johnson, Arielle, and Lars Williams. *A Field Guide to Fermentation*. Copenhagen, Denmark: Self-published, 2016.

Katz, Sandor. *The Art of Fermentation*. White River Junction, VT: Chelsea Green, 2012.

Katz, Sandor. *Wild Fermentation*. White River Junction, VT: Chelsea Green, 2003.

Morales, Bonnie, and Deena Prichep. *Kachka*. New York: Flatiron, 2017.

Redzepi, René, and David Zilber. *The Noma Guide to Fermentation*. New York: Artisan, 2018.

Shih, Rich, and Jeremy Umansky. *Koji Alchemy*. White River Junction, VT: Chelsea Green, 2020.

Skinner, Julia. *Our Fermented Lives*. North Adams, MA: Storey, 2022.

Index

Note: Page references in *italics* indicate photographs.

A

Abou-Ganim, Tony, 142
absinthe
   L'Alligator C'est Vert, 208, *209*
   Windowsill Spritz, 172, *173*
Adams, Chanel, 150, 236
agave nectar, 24–25, 27
   Agave Syrup, 337
   Ginger-Agave Syrup, 342
Ahmed, Selena, 181
Akbar, Ahmed Ali, 250
allspice, 50
almonds
   blanching, 119
   Orgeat, 118–20
   toasting, 119
aloe liqueur
   Lava Lamp, 174, *175*
Amaro Averna
   Peeking Duck, 332, *333*
Amaro Ciociaro
   Southern Cola, 296, *297*
Amaro Nonino
   Riot Act, 140, *141*
amazaké, 308
Anderson, Ray, 111
Anderson, Sam, 174, 245
Angostura Phosphate, 294, *295*
aniseed, 48
Ankrah, Douglas, 154
Anthony, Fortuna, 192, 200
apple brandy
   Celery and Nori, 204, *205*
   Nori-Infused Apple Brandy, 348
   Sobacha-Infused Apple Brandy, 350
   Thunderbird, 138, *139*

apples, 144
   Chicha Morada, 128–29
   Pomme and Circumstance, 36, *37*
   Thunderbird, 138, *139*
apricots, 145
   Ginger Burns, 313–15
aquavit
   Bloody Marion, 70, *71*
Armagnac
   Roffignac, 322, *323*
Arnold, Dave, 282, 292, 337
Arroz con Rum, 134, *135*
Arthur, Stanley Clisby, 322

B

Back to the Roots, 238, *239*
Baja Grenadine, 32–33
Balla, Nicolaus, 313, 324
bananas, 150
   Banana Stand, 178, *179*
   Coconut-Banana-Infused Bourbon, 346–47
Bandera, 68, *69*
barley, 112–13. *See also* boricha
Bartender's Ice Cream, 94–97
basil, 182
   Gin Basil Smash, 206, *207*
Bayless, Rick, 58
Beckwith, Sebastian, 1–2, 251, 254
beer
   Grail Ale, 302, *303*
beets, 185
   Back to the Roots, 238, *239*
   Beet-Raspberry Syrup, 194–95
Bennett, Nick, 245, 290, 292, 352
Berens, Abra, 6, 114, 117, 188
Berg, Monica, 85, 104, 347

Bermejo, Julio, 27
Best, Greg, 296, 351, 357
Bitters, P.C.H. Orange, 349
Bjerkan, Heidi, 104
blackberries, 146
   Blackberry Consommé, 166
   "Pimm's" Cup, 168, *169*
Bloody Marion, 70, *71*
blueberries, 146
   Blueberry-Infused Gin, 346
   Kind of Blueberry, 176, *177*
B-Marion Spice Blend, 60–61
Bodenheimer, Neal, 146, 318, 322
boricha, 112
   Boricha Cold Brew, 352
   Pomme and Circumstance, 36, *37*
Borodinsky Rye Kvass, 121–23
   Castle on a Cloud, 130, *131*
bourbon
   Banana Stand, 178, *179*
   Coconut-Banana-Infused Bourbon, 346–47
   Penny, 236, *237*
   Pomme and Circumstance, 36, *37*
Bradsell, Dick, 238
brandy
   Riot Act, 140, *141*
   See also apple brandy; Armagnac; Cognac; plum brandy
brown sugar, 23
buckwheat, 113
   Sobacha-Infused Apple Brandy, 350
   Thunderbird, 138, *139*
Buda, Gregory, 140, 158, 348
Bunni, Mony, 34, 98, 100
Burns, Cortney, 22, 313, 324

butter
  Buttered Martini, 104, *105*
  Butter-Washed Gin, 347
  sourcing, 85
  storing, 85
  types of, 85
Butz, Earl, 89

C

cacao beans, 48
cachaça
  Arroz con Rum, 134, *135*
Caldwell, Giancalis, 307
Calvert, Paul, 26, 30, 44, 151, 330, 340
Campbell, Maggie, 24, 26, 40, 338
cane sugar, 21–24
  Cane Syrup, 24, 337
caraway seeds, 48
carbonated water
  Forced Carbonation, 282–83
  in mixed drinks, 272
  types of, 273–74
  See also sodas
cardamom, 48
cascara, 218
  Cascara Infusion, 354
  London Bridge, 232, *233*
cashews
  Arroz con Rum, 134, *135*
  Cashew Horchata, 126–27
Castle on a Cloud, 130, *131*
cayenne pepper, 49
celery, 186
  Celery and Nori, 204, *205*
  Celery Syrup, 343
  Dragonfly, 136, *137*
  seeds, 49
Chai, Kadak Spicy, 91–93
Champurrado, 58–59
  Children of the Corn, 72, *73*
Chan, Miin, 306, 312
cherries, 145
  Preserved Cherries, 155–57
Chicha Morada, 128–29
  Llama del Rey, 132, *133*
chicory, 51
Children of the Corn, 72, *73*

chiles. *See* peppers
chocolate
  Champurrado, 58–59
  Children of the Corn, 72, *73*
Choked Up, 76, *77*
cider
  Pomme and Circumstance, 36, *37*
  Thunderbird, 138, *139*
  What Cheer, 44, *45*
cinnamon, 51
Clark, Melissa, 28
Clark, Michael, 89
cloves, 50
club soda, 274
Cochi Americano
  Light as a Feather, 202, *203*
coconut, 151–52
  Banana Stand, 178, *179*
  Coconut-Banana-Infused Bourbon, 346–47
  Coquito, 108, *109*
  Cream of Coconut, 160–61
  Dragon Pearl Punch, 262, *263*
  L'Alligator C'est Vert, 208, *209*
coffee
  alternatives to, 218
  Back to the Roots, 238, *239*
  brewing methods for, 219–21
  commercial production of, 222–23
  Espresso, 228–31
  Falling Water, 240, *241*
  Flash-Brewed Iced Coffee, 224–25
  flavored, 218
  harvesting and processing, 215
  history of, 213
  Kahvesi Corretto, 234, *235*
  in mixed drinks, 212
  Penny, 236, *237*
  preparing, 218–19
  roasting, 216
  serving, 221
  single-origin vs. blends, 216–17

  sourcing, 216–17, 222–23
  species and varieties, 213–14
  storing, 217
  tea vs., 250
  troubleshooting, 221
  Türk Kahvesi, 226–27
  See also cascara
Cognac
  Masala Milky Tea Punch, 102, *103*
  Peeking Duck, 332, *333*
  Q. P. Warmer, 270, *271*
Cointreau
  7 & 7, 292, *293*
cola
  history of, 276
  making, 286–87
  Southern Cola, 296, *297*
Colliau, Jen, 152, 160
Colonna-Dashwood, Maxwell, 219, 277, 278
Comfort's Toddy, 266, *267*
confectioners' sugar, 23–24
Coquito, 108, *109*
  Coquito "Tea" Infusion, 354
coriander, 49
corn, 112
  Champurrado, 58–59
  Chicha Morada, 128–29
  Children of the Corn, 72, *73*
  Corn Water, 196–97
  Llama del Rey, 132, *133*
  Malabar Silver Corn Fizz, 74, *75*
Corti, Darrell, 9
Cowan, Taylor, 62, 344
Craddock, Harry, 221
cream, 82–83
Cree, Dana, 82, 84, 94
crème de cacao
  Comfort's Toddy, 266, *267*
  Dragonfly, 136, *137*
cubeb berries, 50
cucumbers, 186
  Cucumber-Mint Cordial, 34–35
  Cultural Consumption, 100, *101*
cynar
  Choked Up, 76, *77*

D

dairy
  commercial production of, 89–90
  environmental costs of, 89
  history of, 79
  in mixed drinks, 78
  storing, 82
  See also individual dairy products
dates, 152
  Oat Milk, 124–25
Davidoff, Maria, 130
Davidson, Alan, 144
Davis, Matthew, 216
Day, Alex, 282
DeGroff, Dale, 142, 206
demerara, 23
  Demerara Syrup, 337
Derby, Francis, 204
de Soto, Nico, 152, 208, 344
Diacono, Mark, 308
Diedrich, Kevin, 150, 151, 178, 346, 349
Dragonfly, 136, *137*
Dragon Pearl Punch, 262, *263*
Dufresne, Wylie, 74, 196
Duguid, Naomi, 54
Duval, Ashley, 181

E

Earl Grey tea, 244–45
  Earl Grey MarTEAni, 264, *265*
  Earl Grey Tea–Infused Gin, 347
Earls, Averill, 250
English, Camper, 184, 275, 298
Enhanced Grapefruit Sherbet, 343
"Enhanced" Ruby Red Grapefruit Juice, 162–63
Ensslin, Hugo, 176
espresso. *See* coffee

F

Falling Water, 240, *241*
Fauchald, Nick, 282
fennel seeds, 49

fermentation
  definition of, 305
  process of, 305–6
ferments
  commercial production of, 311–12
  history of, 305, 311–12
  list of, 306–9
  in mixed drinks, 304
  preparing, 310–11
  sourcing, 309
  storing, 309–10
  See also individual ferments
Fernet Vallet liqueur
  Arroz con Rum, 134, *135*
Fick, Karen, 275
Field, Colin, 184
flowers
  commercial production of, 188
  list of, 184
  in mixed drinks, 180, 184
  preparing, 185, 189
  sourcing, 185, 188
  storing, 185
  See also individual flowers
Flynn, Sharon, 307
Forced Carbonation, 282–83
Ford, Eleanor, 47
Fort, Audrey, 206
Freeman, Eben, 272
Fripp, Patricia, 8
fruits
  climacteric vs. non-climacteric, 143
  commercial production of, 153
  as garnishes, 153
  juicing, 153
  list of, 144–52
  in mixed drinks, 142
  preparing, 153
  ripening, 143
  sourcing, 152, 153–54
  storing, 152
  See also individual fruits

G

Gebely, Tony, 247, 248
gelato, 83–84

genever
  Grilled-Pineapple-Infused Genever, 348
  Riot Act, 140, *141*
Genmaicha Syrup, 342
gin
  Blueberry-Infused Gin, 346
  Buttered Martini, 104, *105*
  Butter-Washed Gin, 347
  Choked Up, 76, *77*
  Dragonfly, 136, *137*
  Earl Grey MarTEAni, 264, *265*
  Earl Grey Tea–Infused Gin, 347
  Gin and Tonic, 298, *299*
  Gin Basil Smash, 206, *207*
  Kind of Blueberry, 176, *177*
  Light as a Feather, 202, *203*
  London Bridge, 232, *233*
  "Pimm's" Cup, 168, *169*
  Wondermint Malted, 106, *107*
ginger, 51, 186
  Ginger-Agave Syrup, 342
  Ginger Burns, 313–15
  Gut Punch, 326, *327*
  Lemon-Ginger Rebujito, 324, *325*
  Penicillin, 42, *43*
ginger ale, 274
ginger beer, 274
  Peeking Duck, 332, *333*
  "Pimm's" Cup, 168, *169*
  Szechuan Ginger Beer, 284–85
Glaser, John, 42
Gokan, Shingo, 148, 268
Goldstein, Darra, 21
Gomez, Ricky, 190
Gong Fu Shu Pu-Erh, 254–55
Gonzalez, Jessica, 132, 151, 350
Gota de Sandía, 38, *39*
Gough, Dabney, 18, 188
Grail Ale, 302, *303*
grains
  allergies to, 114
  commercial production of, 117
  definition of, 112
  history of, 111
  list of, 112–13
  in mixed drinks, 110, 111

preparing, 114
sourcing, 113, 117
storing, 113–14
whole vs. refined, 112
See also individual grains
grapefruit, 148–49
  Chile-and-Grapefruit-Peel–
    Infused Mezcal, 346
  Enhanced Grapefruit
    Sherbet, 343
  "Enhanced" Ruby Red
    Grapefruit Juice, 162–63
  Grail Ale, 302, *303*
  Grapefruit-Lime Sherbet,
    342–43
  Grapefruit Soda, 288–89
  Paloma, 170, *171*
  Pomme and Circumstance,
    36, *37*
  Sangrita Verde, 66–67
grapes, 146–47
  Llama del Rey, 132, *133*
  See also raisins
Grenadine, Baja, 32–33
Gunders, Dana, 152, 187
gur, 22
Gustings, Paul, 322
Gut Punch, 326, *327*

H

Hada, A-K, 36, 352
half-and-half, 82
Hanson, Thor, 111
hazelnut liqueur
  Wondermint Malted,
    106, *107*
heirloom varieties, 8
Hemphill, Ian, 47
Hendon, Christopher, 219,
  277, 278
herbs
  commercial production
    of, 188
  list of, 182
  in mixed drinks, 180, 181
  preparing, 184, 189
  sourcing, 183, 188
  storing, 183
  See also individual herbs
Heugel, Bobby, 300

hibiscus, 184
  Baja Grenadine, 32–33
  Gota de Sandía, 38, *39*
  Hibiscus Infusion, 355
  Sorrel, 192–93
Hires, Charles, 275
Ho, Tien, 204
Hoard, Sean, 115, 118, 164,
  172, 339
Hoffman, James, 213, 216, 222
hōjicha
  Brewed Hōjicha, 353
  Comfort's Toddy, 266, *267*
  Gut Punch, 326, *327*
  Hōjicha Kombucha, 316–17
honey, 17–19
  Honey Syrup, 338
  Malabar Honey Syrup, 344
honeydew melon, 147
  Lava Lamp, 174, *175*
horchata
  Arroz con Rum, 134, *135*
  Cashew Horchata, 126–27
horseradish, 186
  Bloody Marion, 70, *71*
Hudák, Martin, 146, 194, 220,
  228, 238

I

ice cream
  Bartender's Ice Cream,
    94–97
  composition of, 83
  sourcing, 84
  storing, 84
  types of, 83–84
  Wondermint Malted,
    106, *107*
Ice Cubes, Lime, 357
Ipswich Old Fashioned, 40, *41*

J

jaggery, 22
Japanese Whisky Highball,
  300, *301*
Johnson, Arielle, 245, 307, 311,
  316, 320
Jones, Farmer Lee, 185, 187
Jullapat, Roxana, 112, 113
jun, 307

K

Kadak Spicy Chai, 91–93
  Masala Milky Tea Punch,
    102, *103*
Kadri, Sana Javeri, 56, 57,
  91, 102
Kahlúa
  Banana Stand, 178, *179*
Kahvesi Corretto, 234, *235*
Kaplan, David, 282
Kastner, Martin, 221
Katz, Sandor, 4, 305, 306, 307,
  309, 310, 311
Keating, Brian, 243
Kind of Blueberry, 176, *177*
Kirker, Constance L., 185
Kleinow, Tyler, 232, 354, 356
kombucha, 307
  Gut Punch, 326, *327*
  Hōjicha Kombucha, 316–17
Krambambulya, 349
  Castle on a Cloud, 130, *131*
Kratena, Alex, 104
Kroesen, Ravi, 243, 245, 248,
  249, 256, 355
kumquats, 150
  Choked Up, 76, *77*
kvass, 307
  Borodinsky Rye Kvass,
    121–23
  Castle on a Cloud, 130, *131*

L

L'Alligator C'est Vert, 208, *209*
Lambert, Martin, 48, 286
Lava Lamp, 174, *175*
lavender, 182
Lawson, Jane, 48, 49
Lee, Don, 204, 343, 348
lemons, 149–50
  Dragonfly, 136, *137*
  Earl Grey MarTEAni, 264, *265*
  Gin Basil Smash, 206, *207*
  Ginger Burns, 313–15
  Gut Punch, 326, *327*
  Kind of Blueberry, 176, *177*
  Lemon-Ginger Rebujito,
    324, *325*
  Lemon-Infused Olive Oil, 356
  Lemon-Lime Soda, 290–91

lemons, *continued*
London Bridge, 232, *233*
Longball, 260, *261*
Oleo Saccharum, 28–29
Peeking Duck, 332, *333*
Salad Bar, 210, *211*
7 & 7, 292, *293*
Sherbet, 28–29
Slow West, 328, *329*
Levin, Judith, 274, 276–77
licorice root, 52
Licorice-Root Water, 356
Light as a Feather, 202, *203*
limes, 149
Cultural Consumption,
100, *101*
Grapefruit-Lime Sherbet,
342–43
Lemon-Lime Soda, 290–91
Light as a Feather, 202, *203*
Lime Ice Cubes, 357
Llama del Rey, 132, *133*
Paloma, 170, *171*
Sangrita Roja, 64–65
Sangrita Verde, 66–67
7 & 7, 292, *293*
Sorrel Rum Punch, 200, *201*
Southern Cola, 296, *297*
Llama del Rey, 132, *133*
London Bridge, 232, *233*
Long, Kim, 243
Longball, 260, *261*
Loomis, Susan Herrmann,
114, 115
Lorr, Benjamin, 188
Lovell, Henrietta, 248, 352

M
Macquarrie, Miles, 145, 155
Macy, Tom, 342
Madison, Deborah, 181, 185
Magro, Kristina, 187, 210,
356, 357
Malabar Infusion, 62–63
Malabar Honey Syrup, 344
Malabar Silver Corn Fizz,
74, *75*
Mangan, Zach, 245, 248,
249, 252
maple syrup, 19–20

maraschino liqueur
Kind of Blueberry, 176, *177*
Penny, 236, *237*
Markus, Rodrick, 249, 258, 346
Marrero, Lynnette, 132, 151, 350
Martini, Buttered, 104, *105*
Marty, Christopher, 106, 182
Masala Milky Tea Punch, 102, *103*
McCoy, Bob, 40
McFadden, Joshua, 56
McGee, Harold, 4, 17, 48, 49,
50, 83, 111, 114, 115, 116,
143, 145, 147, 153, 277, 278
McLuen, Lydia, 190
melons, 147
Gota de Sandía, 38, *39*
Lava Lamp, 174, *175*
Mendelson, Anne, 4, 79, 80, 81,
86, 87, 89, 90
Meyer, Joerg, 182, 206
Meyer, Rachel, 181
mezcal
Children of the Corn, 72, *73*
Chile-and-Grapefruit-Peel-
Infused Mezcal, 346
Gota de Sandía, 38, *39*
milk
commercial production
of, 87
evaporated, 87, 88
history of, 79–80
homogenized, 80–81
kefir, 306–7
pasteurized, 80
powdered, 87, 88
raw, 89–90
sourcing, 81–82
storing, 82
sweetened condensed,
87, 88
Mineral Saline, 340
mineral water, 273
mint, 182
Choked Up, 76, *77*
Cucumber-Mint Cordial,
34–35
Light as a Feather, 202, *203*
Mint Conditioning, 190–91
Mint Spruce Syrup, 198–99
Wondermint Malted, 106, *107*

Mlynarczyk, Gabriella, 146,
166, 168
Mogannam, Sam, 18, 19, 188
Moix, Pablo, 108, 354
molasses, 21–22
Molasses Syrup, 338
Moldvaer, Anette, 213
Momosé, Julia, 245, 266, 353
Morales, Bonnie, 121, 147
Morales, Israel, 49, 349
Morgenthaler, Jeffrey, 28
muscovado, 22

N
Nam, Pang "Penny" Yik, 236
nasturtium, 184
Neri, Ria, 48, 226, 240
Nestle, Marion, 8
Newman, Mary, 185
Nguyen, Sahra, 214
nori
Celery and Nori, 204, *205*
Nori-Infused Apple Brandy,
348
Nosrat, Samin, 54, 55
nutmeg, 49
nuts
allergies to, 116
definition of, 114
fat content of, 114–15
history of, 111
list of, 115
milks, 116
in mixed drinks, 110, 111
preparing, 116
sourcing, 115–16
storing, 116
See also individual nuts

O
oats, 112
Dragonfly, 136, *137*
Oat Milk, 124–25
Old Fashioned, Ipswich, 40, *41*
Oleo Saccharum, 28–29
Olive Oil, Lemon-Infused, 356
Olvera, Enrique, 126
O'Neil, Darcy, 273, 274,
275–76, 278, 279, 280,
294, 340

oolong tea
  Longball, 260, *261*
  Mizudashi Cold-Brewed
    Oolong Tea, 258–59
  Oolong Tea Syrup, 344
oranges, 147–48
  P.C.H. Orange Bitters, 349
  Peeking Duck, 332, *333*
  Sangrita Roja, 64–65
orchids, 184
  Longball, 260, *261*
organic ingredients, 8
Orgeat, 118–20
Owens, Sarah, 307

P
packaging, 7
Paloma, 170, *171*
pandan leaves
  L'Alligator C'est Vert, 208, *209*
  Pandan Syrup, 344
panela, 22
paprika, 49
Parsley, Lydia, 49, 112, 124, 152
passion fruit, 150
  Penny, 236, *237*
Pasteur, Louis, 80
Pauwels, Katrien, 217
P.C.H. Orange Bitters, 349
peaches, 145
  Peach Purée, 164–65
  Windowsill Spritz, 172, *173*
Peeking Duck, 332, *333*
Pemberton, John S., 276
Penicillin, 42, *43*
Penny, 236, *237*
peppercorns, 51
  Pink Peppercorn
    Tincture, 350
peppers, 186–87
  Chile-and-Grapefruit-Peel-
    Infused Mezcal, 346
  Sangrita Verde, 66–67
persimmons
  Q. P. Warmer, 270, *271*
piloncillo, 22
"Pimm's" Cup, 168, *169*
pineapple, 151
  Chicha Morada, 128–29
  Grilled Pineapple, 158–59

Grilled-Pineapple–Infused
  Genever, 348
Llama del Rey, 132, *133*
Pineapple Cordial, 30–31
Riot Act, 140, *141*
Sangrita Verde, 66–67
Tepache, 320–21
Welcome Mother, 330, *331*
What Cheer, 44, *45*
Pink Peppercorn Tincture, 350
pisco
  Llama del Rey, 132, *133*
plum brandy
  Falling Water, 240, *241*
Pomme and Circumstance,
  36, *37*
port
  What Cheer, 44, *45*
powdered sugar, 23–24
prickly pear
  Baja Grenadine, 32–33
Prueitt, Elizabeth, 2

Q
quinces, 144
  Q. P. Warmer, 270, *271*

R
radicchio, 187
  Radicchio "Juice," 357
  Salad Bar, 210, *211*
raisins, 147
  Borodinsky Rye Kvass,
    121–23
Ramirez, Erik, 128, 132, 151
raspberries, 146
  Back to the Roots, 238, *239*
  Beet-Raspberry Syrup,
    194–95
  Raspberry Shrub, 318–19
  Roffignac, 322, *323*
Rebujito, Lemon-Ginger,
  324, *325*
Redzepi, René, 310
Reiner, Julie, 23, 151, 245, 262,
  288, 342
rice, 113
  Arroz con Rum, 134, *135*
  Cashew Horchata, 126–27
Rich Simple Syrup, 339

Riot Act, 140, *141*
Roberts, Glenn, 117
Robertson, Chad, 2
Robitschek, Leo, 76, 150,
  182, 337
Rodriguez, Ashley, 222
Roffignac, 322, *323*
root beer, 275–76
Rose, Katie, 22, 168, 198, 202,
  284, 332
rosemary, 182
Ross, Sam, 42
rum
  Arroz con Rum, 134, *135*
  Coquito, 108, *109*
  Cultural Consumption,
    100, *101*
  Dragon Pearl Punch, 262, *263*
  Gut Punch, 326, *327*
  Ipswich Old Fashioned,
    40, *41*
  Llama del Rey, 132, *133*
  Masala Milky Tea Punch,
    102, *103*
  Sorrel Rum Punch, 200, *201*
  Speak Low, 268, *269*
  Welcome Mother, 330, *331*
Rye Kvass, Borodinsky, 121–23

S
Salad Bar, 210, *211*
Saladino, Dan, 7
salt, 54–56
  Mineral Saline, 340
Sanchez, Judy, 23
Sánchez, Rosio, 23, 151,
  308, 320
sangrita
  Bandera, 68, *69*
  Sangrita Roja, 64–65
  Sangrita Verde, 66–67
Saunders, Audrey, 242, 245,
  264, 347
Scherer, Jordan, 344
Schilling, Abby, 6
Schmidt, Adam, 102
Scotch
  Penicillin, 42, *43*
seeds, 111–12. *See also* grains;
  nuts; *individual seeds*

seltzer, 274
Sercarz, Lior Lev, 47, 52, 53, 60, 70
7 & 7, 292, *293*
Sharma, Nik, 47, 51
Sherbet, 28–29
    Angostura Phosphate, 294, *295*
    Dragon Pearl Punch, 262, *263*
    Enhanced Grapefruit Sherbet, 343
    Grapefruit-Lime Sherbet, 342–43
sherry
    Banana Stand, 178, *179*
    Lemon-Ginger Rebujito, 324, *325*
    Salad Bar, 210, *211*
    Speak Low, 268, *269*
Shih, Rich, 308
shiso, 182
shochu
    Comfort's Toddy, 266, *267*
Shoemaker, Daniel, 115, 118, 164
shrubs, 308
    Raspberry Shrub, 318–19
Simple Syrup, 339
    Rich Simple Syrup, 339
Skinner, Julia, 309, 310, 312
Slape, David, 118
sloe gin
    Light as a Feather, 202, *203*
Slow West, 328, *329*
Small, Noah, 22, 58, 72
sobacha
    Sobacha-Infused Apple Brandy, 350
    Thunderbird, 138, *139*
sodas
    Cola, 276, 286–87
    commercial production of, 280–81
    Grapefruit Soda, 288–89
    history of, 273
    Lemon-Lime Soda, 290–91
    list of, 274–76
    in mixed drinks, 272
    preparing, 277–79
    serving, 279
    sourcing, 276–77, 280–81

storing, 277
Szechuan Ginger Beer, 284–85
Solomon, Chad, 162, 170, 288, 338, 340, 343
Sorghum Syrup, 26, 340
Sorrel, 192–93
    Sorrel Rum Punch, 200, *201*
sourcing suggestions, 6–9
Southern Cola, 296, *297*
soy sauce, 308–9
    Peeking Duck, 332, *333*
sparkling wine
    Lava Lamp, 174, *175*
    Longball, 260, *261*
    Malabar Silver Corn Fizz, 74, *75*
    Windowsill Spritz, 172, *173*
Speak Low, 268, *269*
spices
    blends, 52–53, 60–61
    commercial production of, 56–57
    dry-roasting, 54
    etymology of, 47
    harvesting and processing, 47–48
    list of, 48–52
    in mixed drinks, 46, 47
    sourcing, 52–53
    storing, 53
    toasting, 53–54
    whole vs. ground, 52
    See also individual spices
Sprouse, Claire, 116, 328
Spruce Syrup, Mint, 198–99
star anise, 49–50
Stewart, Amy, 181, 182
Straub, Jacques, 294
sucanat, 22
sugars
    choosing, 16
    commercial production of, 26–27
    in mixed drinks, 16
    types of, 17
    See also cane sugar; *individual sugars*
sunflower seeds
    Oat Milk, 124–25

syrups
    Agave Syrup, 337
    Beet-Raspberry Syrup, 194–95
    Cane Syrup, 24, 337
    Celery Syrup, 343
    Demerara Syrup, 337
    Genmaicha Syrup, 342
    Ginger-Agave Syrup, 342
    Honey Syrup, 338
    Malabar Honey Syrup, 344
    Mint Spruce Syrup, 198–99
    Molasses Syrup, 338
    Oolong Tea Syrup, 344
    Orgeat, 118–20
    Pandan Syrup, 344
    Rich Simple Syrup, 339
    Simple Syrup, 339
    Sorghum Syrup, 26, 340
Szechuan Ginger Beer, 284–85
    Peeking Duck, 332, *333*
    "Pimm's" Cup, 168, *169*

T
Tatarin, Danielle, 38, 342, 346, 355
tea
    annual consumption of, 250
    Brewed English Breakfast Tea, 352
    Brewed Hōjicha, 353
    Brewed Lao Cang Xiao Shu Tuo Pu-Erh, 353
    coffee vs., 250
    Comfort's Toddy, 266, *267*
    definition of, 243
    Dragonfly, 136, *137*
    Dragon Pearl Punch, 262, *263*
    Earl Grey MarTEAni, 264, *265*
    Earl Grey Tea-Infused Gin, 347
    Flash-Brewed Jasmine Tea, 355
    Genmaicha Syrup, 342
    Gong Fu Shu Pu-Erh, 254–55
    history of, 243, 250
    Hōjicha Kombucha, 316–17

Kadak Spicy Chai, 91–93
Lava Lamp, 174, *175*
Longball, 260, *261*
Masala Milky Tea Punch,
    102, *103*
in mixed drinks, 242
Mizudashi Cold-Brewed
    Oolong Tea, 258–59
Oolong Tea Syrup, 344
preparing, 246–49
processing, 243–45
Q. P. Warmer, 270, *271*
Riot Act, 140, *141*
serving, 249–50
7 & 7, 292, *293*
sourcing, 245–46
Speak Low, 268, *269*
storing, 246
Teapot-Brewed Jasmine
    Tea, 256–57
types of, 244–45, 251
Usucha Matcha, 252–53
See also jun; kombucha
Tepache, 308, 320–21
    Slow West, 328, *329*
tequila
    Bandera, 68, *69*
    Cultural Consumption,
        100, *101*
    Paloma, 170, *171*
Thai, Long, 342
Thunberg, Greta, 89
Thunderbird, 138, *139*
thyme, 182
tibicos, 306–7
    Ginger Burns, 313–15
tomato juice
    Bloody Marion, 70, *71*
Tomoyoshi, Naoki, 346
tonic water, 272, 275
    Gin and Tonic, 298, *299*
turbinado, 22
Türk Kahvesi, 226–27
    Kahvesi Corretto, 234, *235*

U

Umansky, Jeremy, 308
Urushido, Masahiro, 138, 350
Usucha Matcha, 252–53
    Dragonfly, 136, *137*

V

Van Flandern, Brian, 272
vanilla, 50
Vázquez, Osvaldo, 32, 38, 64,
    66, 68, 151, 186
vegetables
    commercial production
        of, 188
    list of, 185–87
    in mixed drinks, 180, 185
    preparing, 187, 189
    sourcing, 187, 188
    storing, 187
    See also individual
        vegetables
vermouth
    Buttered Martini, 104, *105*
    "Pimm's" Cup, 168, *169*
    Salad Bar, 210, *211*
    Slow West, 328, *329*
Vestinos, Peter, 190
Vexenat, Charles, 208
vinegar, 308. *See also* shrubs
vino amaro
    Falling Water, 240, *241*
vodka
    Back to the Roots, 238, *239*
    Krambambulya, 349
    Longball, 260, *261*
    Peeking Duck, 332, *333*
    Pink Peppercorn
        Tincture, 350
    Windowsill Spritz, 172, *173*
Volfson, Yana, 115, 126, 134
Voltaggio, Michael, 166
Vose, Jillian, 140, 151, 342

W

Ward, Phil, 343
watermelon, 147
    Gota de Sandía, 38, *39*
Waters, Alice, 4
Weill, Kurt, 268
Welcome Mother, 330, *331*
Wendelboe, Tim, 221
What Cheer, 44, *45*
whiskey
    Comfort's Toddy, 266, *267*
    Japanese Whisky Highball,
        300, *301*

Malabar Silver Corn Fizz,
    74, *75*
7 & 7, 292, *293*
    See also bourbon; Scotch
Williams, Lars, 311
Wilson, Bee, 8–9
Windowsill Spritz, 172, *173*
wine
    Llama del Rey, 132, *133*
    Penny, 236, *237*
    See also port; sherry;
        sparkling wine
Wondermint Malted, 106, *107*
Wondrich, David, 28

Y

yogurt, 307
    Cultural Consumption,
        100, *101*
    history of, 86
    making, 98–99
    sourcing, 86
    storing, 86
    styles of, 86
Young, Naren, 148
Yung, Michael, 217, 219, 220,
    224, 236
yuzus, 148
    Speak Low, 268, *269*

Z

Zaslavsky, Alice, 183
Zilber, David, 305, 310
Zohar, Ori, 52

Published in the United States by Ten Speed Press, an imprint of the Crown Publishing Group,
a division of Penguin Random House LLC, New York.
TenSpeed.com

Ten Speed Press and the Ten Speed Press colophon are registered trademarks of Penguin
Random House LLC.

Typefaces: Colophon Foundry's Apercu and ITC's Clearface

Library of Congress Cataloging-in-Publication Data
Names: Meehan, Jim. | Sasso, Bart. | Janzen, Emma.
Title: The bartender's pantry: a beverage handbook for the universal bar
Identifiers: LCCN 2023021526 (print) | LCCN 2023021527 (ebook) | ISBN 9781984858672 (trade
    paperback) | ISBN 9781984858689 (ebook)
Subjects: LCSH: Bartending—Handbooks, manuals, etc. | Cocktails. | LCGFT: Cookbooks.
Classification: LCC TX951 .M3548 2024 (print) | LCC TX951 (ebook) | DDC 641.87/4—dc23/
    eng/20230508
LC record: lccn.loc.gov/2023021526
LC ebook record: lccn.loc.gov/2023021527

ISBN 978-1-9848-5867-2
Ebook ISBN 978-1-9848-5868-9

Printed in China

Editor: Molly Birnbaum | Editorial assistant: Gabby Urena
Production editors: Mark McCauslin and Natalie Blachere
Designer: Betsy Stromberg | Production designers: Mari Gill and Faith Hague
Production manager: Jane Chinn
Copyeditor: Carole Berglie | Indexer: Ken DellaPenta
Proofreaders: Jacob Sammon and Marlene Tungseth
Publicist: Kristin Casemore | Marketer: Chloe Aryeh

10 9 8 7 6 5 4 3 2 1

First Edition